THE HUMMINGBIRD
AND THE HAWK

Conquest and Sovereignty
in the Valley of Mexico, 1503–1541

by R. C. Padden

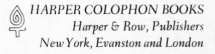 HARPER COLOPHON BOOKS
Harper & Row, Publishers
New York, Evanston and London

THE HUMMINGBIRD
AND THE HAWK

FOR PHILIP W. POWELL

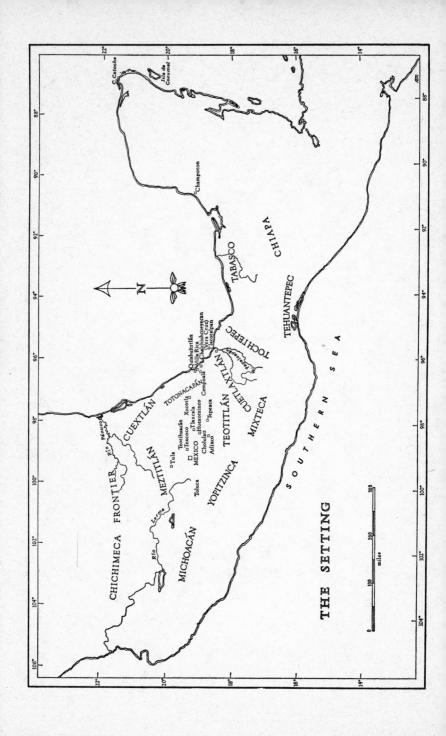

For the past dozen or so years I have been preparing a volume that examines the main currents of life and religion in Mexico in the sixteenth century. Such a work necessarily presumes intensive investigation of the phenomena of culture change. After spending considerable time in this area of research, I came to realize that during the first half of the sixteenth century there were two distinct processes of change functioning simultaneously: one governed by revolutionary force, that is, the Spanish exercise of sovereignty, and another governed by evolutionary forces that existed before the conquest and continued well into the post-conquest period. Central to this problem was the fact that in both Spanish and Indian minds sovereignty was inextricably associated with religion. And sovereignty, by virtue of its awesome power of enablement, was one of the most dynamic of cultural determinants. It thus became apparent to me that my research would have to include some investigation of preconquest society, that I would have to determine, as far as the sources would permit, the nature and exercise of Aztec sovereignty and its relationship to cultural change during the course of its evolution. With this much behind me it would then be necessary to re-examine the conquest itself with particular reference to the prolonged contest between Cortés and Montezuma II for control of that power of enablement and all that it implied. Finally, I hoped to delineate, if possible, the significance and influence of these contending forces in the formation of society during the twenty years immediately following Spanish victory. Such lines of research have eventuated in the present study.

Although nearly one-third of this book is concerned with preconquest Mexico, it does not pretend to be a definitive or exhaustive treatment of Aztec society. It merely attempts to follow the sometimes elusive evolution of Aztec sovereignty from its origins to its demise and examines only those cultural traits and social phenomena that were related to it.

I am indebted to the Doherty Foundation for support of those portions of my researches in Mexican archives that were undertaken in 1956. I have also received considerable material support from the Latin American Center of the Institute for International Studies and the History Department of the University of California, for which I am most grateful. John Barr Tompkins and the staff of the Bancroft Library have my thanks for unstinted contributions of time and service. Most of all do I owe my wife a debt of gratitude for her patient understanding of the historian's plight.

R. C. P.

West De Pere
November 7, 1965

A NOTE ON SOURCES AND METHOD

When the historian turns from the more familiar documentation of the conquest period and takes up the codices, annals, and other Nahuatl writings that purport to relate the Indian past, he encounters formidable problems, the central one of which lies in the nature of the sources themselves. To get at the essence of the problem, it would be well to begin by sketching the circumstances under which these written sources came into being.

The ancient Nahuatl tradition was oral, not written. History, literature, philosophy, mythology, astrology, all were oral disciplines; their practitioners used pictographic manuscripts as ideological catalogues. Without popular reading and written works to be read, the overwhelming mass of Aztec society, both plebeian and noble, was entirely dependent upon the mental skills of persons so trained in the oral arts. Without them the Aztecs were rootless in a moving and complex world. Those who possessed the tradition held the past, the present, and the future in their hands and on their lips. But between 1507 and 1521 most of the individuals possessed of the tradition would die, first in purges initiated and sustained by Montezuma II, and then as a consequence of the Spanish conquest and its aftermath of cultural dislocation and pestilence. Nearly all of the pictographic manuscripts perished with those who could interpret them. From that time to this the problem has been constant: how to recover the ancient Aztec mind?

The first step was taken by Pedro de Gante (Peter Van den Moere), one of three Franciscans from the Spanish Netherlands who arrived in New Spain early in 1524. Gante was an intellectual neighbor of Erasmus and was steeped in the atmosphere of the northern Renaissance and Christian humanism; he carried a perspective that was needed in the kingdom of New Spain. It was in Texcoco that Gante began his ministrations to the Indians. Even as he labored among them from dawn to dusk, performing mass baptism, he began to question not only the propriety of his endeavor—baptism without understanding on the part of the recipient—but its logic as well. How, he queried, could the Indian accept and comprehend Christianity without a prior acquaintance with Latinity? Could the Indians actually master Latin? He founded a school for Indian youths in the ancient palace of the Texcocan kings to find out. Like several Franciscans who would follow him, Gante was simultaneously acquiring a knowledge of Nahuatl, to which he now attempted to fit the Roman alphabet. His experiments in the palace school indicated that the Indians could go as far intellectually as their tutor cared to lead. Gante moved to the capital where he repeated the experiment in a larger school, with the same result. The next step was foundation of a college for superior studies, taken in 1536 with opening of the Franciscan college for Indians, Santa Cruz de Tlatelolco, located in what had by then become the Indian quarter of the capital.

Gante's work with the Nahuatl language was soon taken up by other Franciscans who had subsequently arrived in New Spain, among whom were counted Andrés de Olmos, Toribio de Motolinía, and Bernardino de Sahagún. It was they who perfected Nahuatl as a written language and collected large numbers of pictographic manuscripts that concerned the Indian past, even as other members of their Order seized and burned as many as could be found because they were considered inimical to the success of the Christian evangel that was now in full flood. The manuscripts that survived provided the basis for Sahagún's magnificent linguistic and ethnological works and Olmos' great work that has since been lost to posterity. In all, the Franciscan scholars preserved the mass of documentation that supports Angel María Garibay Kintana's monumental two-volume study of the history of Nahuatl literature, which is by far the best of contemporary studies.

With founding of the College of Santa Cruz, formal study of Nahuatl was assured, and it was conducted at a professional level in the modern sense. There emerged a coterie of Indian students who excelled and became research assistants to their Mendicant mentors. Trained first in Spanish and Latin, they graduated to Nahuatl as it had been created by their professors in written form. It was these same Indian scholars and others who followed in their tradition who wrote most, perhaps all, of the codices and commentaries that we use today as source materials. These works are, for the most part, interpretations or descriptions of pictographic manuscripts, maps, and genealogical records that survived the conquest and its aftermath.

When we approach these materials in contemporary research, there are certain reservations that must be taken into account. In the first place, neither the Franciscan scholars nor their research assistants knew everything that was to be known about the manuscripts—nor, for that matter, do we today. Very few of the manuscripts have survived to the present, and so we must depend upon colonial commentaries, however much they may leave to be desired. A second and more immediate concern is the problem of written Nahuatl itself. Garibay K. seems to think that the oral Nahuatl of the ancient tradition lost something when it was subjected to the limitations of the Roman alphabet. Might not the imposition of canons of syntax and grammar, as conceived by the friars, have achieved even greater limitation and distortion? Furthermore, the Indians who used this essentially Franciscan version of Nahuatl were both Christianized and Latinized, and could not have escaped a profound intellectual refraction. Every time one of them draws a moral distinction, it is a question of whether it is Christian or Aztec in origin. We commonly tend to attach greater significance to a document that is written in Nahuatl, presumably because it lies closer to the ancient Indian mind. But had he chosen to do so, its author could in all probability have written it in either Spanish or Latin. It seems to me, therefore, that such documents might as precisely reflect the Franciscan mind of the time in which they were written.

When we advance in the sixteenth and seventeenth centuries to the works of Durán, Ixtlilxochitl, Alvarado Tezozomoc, and kindred writers of their times, we encounter another complication in the fact that they availed themselves of both known and unknown codices and other sources, many of which have since been lost. We are grateful that they did so, but we must bear in mind that their own intellectual refractions are superimposed over those of the authors they utilized. The many *Historias* and *Relaciones* of the Mendicant scholars are somewhat easier to use, simply because we understand more of their attitudes and can more directly determine the refractive power of the monastic lens.

How valid are the quotations in these sources? This is a question that every researcher must ask, and one that is not readily answered. Some Mexicanists dismiss them outright; most entertain serious reservations. Mistrust stems from the suspicion that they have been distorted, if not actually invented, by the authors and compilers of the codices. This suspicion is demonstrably well founded in a few instances, but is not valid as a generalization. Sahagún's work, meticulously researched, stands every test of criticism that modern research can apply. The *Florentine Codex* frequently quotes Montezuma directly or otherwise reveals his innermost thoughts and reflections. As far as we know, the Aztec glyphs did not permit such sophisticated reporting. But somehow the learned *sabios,* possessors of the old oral tradition who worked with Sahagún, managed to reconstitute his very words. Every time that such quotations can be compared with Spanish sources, they prove to be startlingly accurate. The *Florentine Codex* thus stands as our closest verbatim connection with the preconquest past, intellectual refractions of its authors notwithstanding. It is also an invaluable aid in evaluating the other codices and sources that surround it. Nahuatl poetry, of course, is another kind of connection with the past and shares the strength and weakness of other Nahuatl materials.

There are still more points of a positive nature that should be made in regard to the quotations. The imperial Aztecs were meticulous keepers of records, a fact more remarkable when one considers that beyond the glyph they were entirely dependent upon the sense of hearing and the power of memory. The extent to which a person trained to use these senses, a "hearer," could maintain control over a body of miscellaneous data and report it with precision is incredible. From the moment Cortés and his men landed on the beach at Vera Cruz, Montezuma received detailed and accurate reports of every translated word, every act, every facial expression. This is all verified, for the Aztecs were now confronted by men who could write the materials needed for verification. It seems probable that the Aztecs grew accustomed to remembering what they heard with greater precision than we do that which we read for the simple reason that we can always go back to the source while they could not. Sound is always transient. The entire realm of Aztec intellect was one primarily associated with vocal sounds rather than written words; there must have been profound psychological implications in this that we do not yet understand. Granted that they needed their pictographs to serve as ideological depositories and to provide historical depth, they nevertheless dwelt in a world of otological and verbal perception that all but escapes our comprehension. The quotations in the codices may have greater validity than we oftentimes think.

The way in which a historian reacts to sources such as these is in large part determined by the school of historical faith to which he belongs. Those who are steeped in the methodological ideals of the nineteenth century and the scientism of the early twentieth find it difficult and uncomfortable to work with uncertain evidence, essentially because their professional fulfilment requires attainment of final certainty. The kind of sources we are examining cannot produce it. On the other hand, an ethnohistorian imbibes the scientism of the present, and although he takes certainty where he can find it, he finds himself challenged rather than intimidated by uncertain evidence. He is accustomed to working within a theory of probability. Since the splitting of the atom, science has seized upon probability as avidly as it had predictability in an earlier century; and although predictability remains as an element of scientific method, calculated probability has arisen as an empirical alternative to certainty. It is precisely this that has freed social scientists from their former bondage. The man working in ethnohistory can accept ascertainment of probability as professional fulfilment, and this, I suppose, was what our teachers were getting at when they told us that every generation writes its own history.

It seems quite obvious that conclusions derived from uncertain evidence must remain tentative, for the historian can hardly claim proof beyond the ability of his sources to provide it. If such conclusions are negated to some extent by this qualification, they nevertheless retain positive heuristic value. And that is what ethnohistorical research is all about.

Although the sources I have used in reconstructing certain aspects of Aztec life are for the most part the same ones that others have used before me, my rendition of the Aztec past will in some instances be found to stand in contradiction to theirs. This difference of interpretation has origin in methodology. Anthropologically oriented reconstructions of Aztec society are almost invariably achieved within a synchronic framework. That is, the researcher extracts from the sources the elements of culture that interest him without reference to their chronological associations. These extracted elements are then placed side by side in order to present a comprehensive view of the culture under examination. Such a reconstruction has its uses, but since cultural traits taken from widely separated historical periods and rejoined in a timeless mosaic lose their chronological identities, the entire resulting structure must perforce lack historical reality and validity. It is inescapable that any view of the past must lose its historicity in direct proportion to its departure from chronological sequence. The way in which methodological approach affects interpretation is well demonstrated in the problem of explaining human sacrifice as it was institutionalized by the Aztecs. Within a fundamentally synchronic framework, the anthropologist reconstructs both the physical practice of human immolation and its philosophical justification. Having done so, he assumes a priori that such sacrifice was the consequence of philosophical principle and explains it as such. In my own researches on the problem I felt constrained to establish the practice and its philosophical justification in actual chronological sequence. I found human sacrifice fully developed as a calculated instrument of Aztec statecraft quite in advance of its subsequent philosophico-religious justification and elaboration. The significance of such a distinction is manifest.

Anyone who attempts to reconstruct the Aztec past, whatever his orientation, is obliged to depend heavily upon the works of Durán and Ixtlilxochitl for continuity and breadth, especially if his finished work is to be narrative in character. There are large areas where other sources are either silent or deficient. The works of Sahagún and Motolinía tend to be vertical rather than horizontal in nature, oftentimes sacrificing latitude for depth. But they do provide a critical basis upon which contradictions and weaknesses in the others may in part be resolved. The best that one can do in attempting to depict the evolution of cultural traits under these circumstances is to evolve a tentative structure through critical analysis and comparative techniques, using Sahagún as the primary control. As the structure develops and assumes character, approaching the moment of Spanish arrival, definite patterns of culture appear, as do the personalities of the men who directed the course of Mexican empire through what were to be its final years. Thus far the researcher has largely been working between hypothesis and intuition. On a tentative basis he has identified cultural traits and tensions, personalities and motivations. The moment of truth arrives when the jagged edge of the completed structure is placed against the equally irregular edge of the written documentation provided by the conquerors. If they dovetail, if the Montezuma who emerged from Sahagún's and Durán's sources is consistent with the Montezuma that was known to Cortés and Bernal Díaz, if the cultural traits and patterns and tensions abstracted from uncertain sources are verified by written sources and are shown to have had influence upon the course of conquest and continuing significance in the formation of post-conquest society, then the tentative structure has in retrospect achieved a high degree of probability, if not certainty. I cite the Law of Continuity: the principle that all change, sequence, or series in nature is continuous, and does not go *per saltum*.

A few words remain to be said about documentation. From the beginning it was my intention to address this book to both specialists in the field and the reading public. For the sake of narrative I have kept the footnotes minimal in number and content, but without depriving the scholar of an adequate knowledge of my sources. In order to achieve this balance, I clustered the references: each footnote contains the principal sources from which preceding narrative was derived. Only in such a manner was it possible to reconstruct dialogues and insert appropriate quotations without impeding movement of the eye with interminable citations of source. If the specialist desires to seek me out on any given point, he needs but read on to the next citation.

CONTENTS

ILLUSTRATIONS

THE HUMMINGBIRD
AND THE HAWK

Chapter I

Huitzilopochtli

When the ancient Aztecs first loom on the historical horizon—in the early years of the eleventh century of Our Lord—we vaguely make them out to be a poor and barbarous people, refugees from the seeming malevolence and caprice of nature. They seek shelter in natural caves or build rude huts; they live on wild growing things and all manner of insects and small animals, oftentimes consumed raw because they do not have full control over fire. They have no formal religion, no gods, save the sun that lights their days and gives them precious warmth against the winter's cold. No benevolent deity, this, for in season it gives thirst and scourges them with burning rays. Moving from place to place, the Aztecs wander aimlessly; but ever so gradually they drift to the south, possibly because the living seems to grow easier, the face of nature less grimly fixed. Legend tells us that they call themselves Aztec after their mythical ancestral home of Aztlán. Later, as they wandered, they called themselves Mexica * in honor of a great tribal leader named Mecitli.

* May-shee-ka.

2

This was not a unique pattern of migration that they followed; it had been set for centuries. Earliest man in Mesoamerica had drifted in the same southerly course, ever seeking respite from an unrelenting struggle with nature in which preservation of life itself was counted as triumph.[1] In the more hospitable climes of the southern plateau he tarried, eventually to take part in civilization's greatest drama, the taming of the seed. As he bent the growth of plants to his will, he apprehended a host of beings, both within and without the world of nature, who had much to do with the success or failure of his endeavors. These inscrutable forces had their way and eluded his grasp until certain of his fellows made them their particular concern. Thereafter, it was only with Their Aid that he could fathom, and in some measure control, the mysteries of life and growing things. But even to him planting and harvest made plain the chronology of seasons within which one could learn to calculate the passage of time. It took generations to comprehend and relate the whole, to conceptualize the fundamental rhythm of nature.

We do not know as much as we should like about the early seed-planters and the peoples who came after them in endless procession down through the centuries of time.[2] Clay figurines, potsherds, and earthen mounds give tangible evidence of increasing sophistication of culture and thought. Even so, we are constantly forced to assume more than we actually know. Influences from the Mixteca and the far south are traced, only to disappear in what seem to be blending processes of an unknown nature. Part of our problem stems from the simple fact that we are dealing with the ebb and flow of centuries. Out of it there emerged a brilliant civilization at the beginning of the Christian era. We believe its locus to have been Teotihuacán, although further explorations may well change our minds. But we do know that it was a vast ceremonial center, boasting colossal pyramids and religious structures that indicate extraordinary architectural refinement and artistic taste. The oldest annals refer to it as a mythical

3

place, and its very name means "Home of the Gods." At the height of their later power, the Mexica visited the ruins of Teotihuacán, poking around just as tourists do today, standing in awe and speculating on the nature of its builders and the temper of their times. They had every reason to do so, for it appears that Teotihuacán was one of the great sources for most of the Mesoamerican civilizations that followed it. The Mexica doubtless knew far more about the place than we do, but it is useless to speculate on this because we shall never know their minds. From our vantage point we see some of what preceded Teotihuacán and most of what followed it. What lies between is fragmentary. Just one of the fragments, however, is sufficiently inclusive to enable us to get a rather good idea of the quality of thought that was sustained by the builders of Teotihuacán:

"When we die, it is not true that we die; for still we live, we are resurrected. We still live; we awaken. Do thou likewise."

In this manner they spoke to the dead when one had died; if [it were] a man they spoke to him—they addressed him—as the god Cuecuextzin. And if [it were] a woman, her they addressed as Chamotzin: "Awaken! It hath reddened: the dawn hath set in. Already singeth the flame-colored cock, the flame-colored swallow; already flieth the flame-colored butterfly." [3]

The seed-planters' primordial quest for life ended in Teotihuacán with man's most sublime concept: the immortality of his own soul.

For reasons that remain unknown to us, the splendor of Teotihuacán began to fade in the seventh century. Northern barbarians pressed against its frontiers, crude searchers who had not yet discovered the secret of the seed. They attacked blindly, without reason or regard; their function was but to destroy, particularly that which they did not understand. Teotihuacán was eventually abandoned to the winds and sands, her people in futile flight before the barbarian wave. The only order to come out of the ensuing chaos was provided by one of the greater invading chieftains, Mixcoatl, who fashioned an empire of sorts out of the wreckage of the central plateau. Ranging as far south as what are today the states of Guerrero and Morelos, he set up a capital at Culhuacán around 900 A.D., although it is idle to suppose that his rule extended very far beyond the reach of his fist. The invaders, who were known as Chichimeca * ("Sons-of-dogs"), proceeded to absorb the culture that was possessed by the refugees of Teotihuacán. Blood and culture commingled, and out of the union there issued a variant of old Teotihuacán, which, by 968, came to be centered in Tula. This civilization precisely followed the course and fortunes of its predecessor, reaching heights of power and sophistication, only to weaken and be overrun by uncivilized tribes out of the north. The Tolteca, as they called themselves, could not protect what they had fashioned. Tula fell to the barbarians in 1168.

Crushing defeat of the capital initiated a great Toltec diaspora that lasted upwards of a century. As in the past, cultured Tolteca came to terms with Chichimeca invaders. By the end of the thirteenth century, they had formed a number of city-states, Xicco, Atzcapotzalco, Xaltocan, Texcoco, and Culhuacán, among others. The latter, since it had been founded by Mixcoatl, claimed direct descent from the Toltec kings. This was absurd, but it did lend an air of legitimacy that the other successor states conspicuously lacked. The heights of Toltec creative achievement were nowhere approached, even though each of the states considered itself the cultural and political successor of Tula. It was, as matter of fact, this preoccupation with succession that caused the vigor of the city-states to be spent in continuous feuding and warfare. Xaltocan controlled the northern reaches of the lake system of the valley of Mexico; Texcoco held the eastern shore. Atzcapotzalco was the dominant power of the west, while the south was intimidated by Culhuacán. Annals of the time indicate that

* Chee-chee-may-ka.

transient alliance alternated with intrigue and betrayal to nurture an endless chain of hatred and violence.

The Mexica entered this Merovingian world in 1253. During their long migration from the north, they had learned the rudiments of agriculture, accepting as matter of course the rites and deities that made it possible. They also paid homage to a tribal deity whom they called Huitzilopochtli,* or Southern Hummingbird. We do not know precisely how or when this god was acquired by the wandering Mexica, although it seems likely that he was adopted simultaneously with the science of agriculture from more highly civilized heirs of Teotihuacán with whom the Mexica came into prolonged contact. Brilliant plumage of exotic birds served as symbol and motif of deity everywhere in Mesoamerica—and still does—which would make our problem all but insoluble were it not for the fact that the Tarascans of Michoacán, among whom the Mexica lived for a time, were religiously enamored of a tiny green hummingbird that flourished in the vicinity of Tzintzuntzan, their capital city. The very name Tzintzuntzan is derived from *tzintzuni*, the Tarascan word for hummingbird. It is my guess that Tzintzuntzan's later position as market place for the entire Tarascan empire was prefigured by widespread traffic in the sacred plumage of this diminutive bird from very early times. At any rate, the Tarascan *tzintzuni* yields the Nahuatl *huitzilin*, to which was added *opochtli*, meaning literally "on the left." And so it is that the most common rendering of Huitzilopochtli is "Hummingbird-on-the-left." But this raises the question, "On the left of what?" Since time immemorial in Mexico, the directions right and left have also meant north and south respectively in relation to the setting sun. Since the Mexica approached Michoacán from the north, they would consider themselves to have arrived in the south, so that Huitzilopochtli would be a "Southern Hummingbird." Perhaps most

---

* Weet-zeel-ō-pōch-tly.

6

significant is the fact that through their entire course of empire the Mexica adorned Huitzilopochtli with green hummingbird crests that were invariably procured and fashioned in Michoacán.[4]

It seems most probable that it was the aura of divinity that the Mexica borrowed from the Tarascans, rather than a finished godhead. Bernardino de Sahagún's researches convinced him that Huitzilopochtli was a great warrior or chieftain who was deified after death.[5] This may well have been the case, for such was anciently established custom in Mesoamerica. After his death in 936, the conqueror Mixcoatl was deified, eventually to become a focal deity of the Tolteca-Chichimeca. Among primitive peoples chieftain worship is not far removed from ancestor veneration and may be taken as an important step toward a more sophisticated tribal polity. Under duress of competition with more advanced peoples, such a change is more readily made; for the Mexica, it may well have happened in Michoacán, with the result that Huitzilopochtli, first as a man and later as a god, became their prime totemic symbol.

In spite of their measured accomplishments, the Mexica were patently barbarous when they approached the valley of Mexico, or so they seemed to the people of the successor states, who proved to be unwilling tutors:

> And when the Mexica came (for it is true they wandered a long time), they were the last. As they came, as they followed their course, nowhere were they welcomed; they were cursed everywhere; they were no longer recognized. Everywhere they were told: "Who are these uncouth people? Whence do you come?" Thus they could settle nowhere; in no other place was repose accorded them; they were pursued everywhere.[6]

Having neither lands of their own nor the cultural requisites that sovereignty in the lake community demanded, the Mexica were forced to make the most of their meager talents if they were to survive in the

7

rabid world they had entered. The one thing they could do best was fight, not, as it turned out, for themselves, but for others. They approached the ruling lords of Atzcapotzalco and were accepted in military service as mercenaries. Residence was granted them in Chapultepec, some say in the very place where the park now stands. The wars in which they subsequently became engaged had their inevitable fortunes, most of them turning out well for the Mexica. But in 1298 the lords of Culhuacán, perhaps disturbed by the growing Tepanec strength at Atzcapotzalco, directed an assault against the Mexica that was entirely successful; the Mexica were carried off en masse to Culhuacán, there to begin life anew as slaves.

The captivity was a painful episode, yet it was not without compensation. Even under oppression the Mexica could observe and emulate the civilized arts of their captors; later events were to prove how much they learned. In 1322, a quarter-century after their disastrous defeat at Chapultepec, the Mexica broke away from Culhuacán and fled to uninhabited wetlands that extended into the lake. It seems probable that the flight resulted from meticulous planning; the swampy refuge, with its watery barriers, impenetrable thickets and cyprus groves, afforded excellent natural protection. Waterfowl, fish, and animal life were of sufficient abundance to offer a commercial potential beyond the needs of subsistence. Small patches of arable soil were to be found on scattered hillocks, which could be augmented by construction of *chinampas,* or "floating gardens," a technique that may have been perfected by the Culhuaque. Such was the place the Mexica determined to call their own. These wetlands lay between Texcoco and Atzcapotzalco; although uninhabited by either, each laid claim to them as its frontier. Atzcapotzalco, having conquered Xaltocan, was now the major power on the lake, and so the Mexica made obeisance and paid the tribute that was required. The Mexica named their new home Tenochtitlán, the derivation of which remains in dispute.

* * *

The sovereignty implicit in the founding of Tenochtitlán in 1325 was not actually realized until 1375, when the Mexica enthroned their first king and assumed the trappings of state. Governmental sophistication was but symptomatic of a more general cultural refinement. Over the years, skilled construction of chinampas and dikes had given their home a more pronounced insular character, leaving no doubt as to its future shape and form. Technically, they mastered the problems of flood control and military defense. The city itself was built on fill, materials being obtained through trade with mainland communities surrounding the lagoon. For the sake of accuracy one should refer to Tenochtitlán as a dual city, since in 1337 a dissident faction, in argument over land control and distribution and political leadership, separated and founded their own city of Tlatelolco in the northernmost reaches of the wetlands. Although the two cities rapidly filled out their boundaries and found themselves fused as one, the Tlatelolca refused to recognize the sovereignty or lordship of the Tenochcan kings. Even so, they managed to agree in matters that affected their mutual security, so that they were able to present the lake community with a semblance of unity: they were all Mexica.

During these fruitful years, the Mexica isolated themselves whenever possible from the intrigue and warfare that were so much a part of life on the lake. As vassals of the Tepaneca of Atzcapotzalco, they were drawn into its struggle with Texcoco from time to time, although the only real enemy the Mexica had was Atzcapotzalco itself. In the first place, the ruling Tepanec lords were incensed when the Mexica went to the king of Culhuacán and asked him for his grandson to be their legitimate lord and sovereign. He granted their request and Acamapichtli became the first king of the Mexica. In addition to thus declaring themselves sovereign, they now boasted a king in whose veins flowed the blood of the ancient Toltec dynasty, or at least, so they could claim. From now on they chose to be known as Culhua-Mexica and posed as legitimate claimants to the succession of ancient

9

Tula. Although they continued to receive Mexican tribute under what was now but a shadowy claim of suzerainty, the Tepanec lords could not forgive such presumption and temerity. A second issue that festered beneath the surface of placid diplomacy was one of more immediate concern to the dwellers of Tenochtitlán. The island city suffered from a chronic lack of potable water; its native springs could not supply the demands of growth. Strategically, the shortage of water rendered the city vulnerable; materially, it limited its ambitions. Great natural springs at Chapultepec constituted the most accessible source, but they were held tightly in the grasp of Atzcapotzalco. As long as the Tepaneca were willing, the Mexica could draw water from that source, so that control of the springs was like a throttle, with the lords of Atzcapotzalco holding the cord. However it might be rationalized, the entire future of Tenochtitlán rested on control of that water supply, and both the Mexica and Tepaneca understood it. The Mexica dissimulated and continued to strengthen themselves while the lords of Atzcapotzalco increased their tribute demands and grew haughtier still.

In 1428 Itzcoatl * ascended the Mexican throne, bringing in his wake a new regime that harbored plans of a most ambitious nature. Itzcoatl's nephew sat on the throne of Texcoco; intimate friends wielded influence in the court of Tlacopan (Tacuba), a small state that bordered Atzcapotzalco and provided a potentially soft underbelly to the Tepanec state and empire. Negotiations provided secret agreements that united the armies of Texcoco and Tenochtitlan and neutralized Tlacopan. In a given hour the allies struck a devastating blow that finished Atzcapotzalco; the city and its environs were put to ferocious slaughter; many of those who managed to survive were enslaved. Victory was followed by formation of a Triple Alliance: the Mexica, Texcoco, and Tlacopan bound themselves in an imperial

---

* Eetz-cō-watl.

partnership of sorts, although distribution of the spoils of war was indicative of the weighting of the alliance. The Mexica incorporated the throne of Atzcapotzalco, took a large portion of land, including Chapultepec, and a generous share of tribute. From the beginning, Tlacopan was clearly a junior partner, and soon Texcoco was to find itself intimidated by the ambitious lords of Tenochtitlán. The Mexica knew precisely where they were going. Almost overnight they had put themselves on the highroad to empire.

As the fortunes of the Mexica rose in dramatic scale, Huitzilopochtli too gained new and unforeseen eminence. In his former role as an obscure tribal deity, he had been functional only in so far as he lent identity to a maturing Mexican polity. In practical affairs, like the everyday work of growing food, Tlaloc, the god of rain and fertility, the earth goddess Coatlicue, and Chicomecóatl, the Mesoamerican Ceres, were infinitely more prominent and venerated than he. Unlike these gods, Huitzilopochtli was neither omnipresent nor indispensable. In his original role he was but one of many deities who could not compete in men's minds with the ancient but eternal trinity of seed, earth, and water, for in these lay the marrow of life itself. I am suggesting that left to his own limitations, Huitzilopochtli should have withered and died, as do all primitive totemic symbols, victims of the cultural transition from becoming to being. The trail of Mesoamerican history is strewn with such remains.

However this may be, we find Huitzilopochtli reborn and transformed with creation of the Mexican empire. In reading various texts, one hesitates to decide which came first, the empire or Huitzilopochtli's role as its symbol, so intimately are the two associated. Perhaps the most arresting facet of the problem is the character that he assumes: the Hummingbird savors human blood and feasts on the hearts of men; he presides over calculated brutality and human slaughter; he inspires terror and despair; he justifies Mexican rule and rule of others by the Mexica; rising above all other deities, he is the Lord of Creation. One sees in him embodiment of the imperial idea as the Mexica conceived it. Now honored tradition insists that Huitzilopochtli *was* the Lord of Creation, that the Mexica were his chosen people, that it was he who "ordered them to leave their own land [of Aztlán], promising to make them princes and lords of all the provinces which had been founded by the other six [Chichimec] tribes before them, rich lands abounding in gold, silver, precious stones, feathers, and rich robes, and all manner of precious things." [7] This is how the conquering Mexica told the story of their success, and it has stood the test of time, if not of criticism, to the present day.

None but the hardiest *indigenistas* continue to accept this traditional myth. Yet, there lingers a persistent temptation to assume that such a promise was actually made, perhaps by an elder or priest in the name of Huitzilopochtli, and that the Mexica believed in it to the extent that it led them to seek its fulfilment. [8] This requires us to accept the proposition that Huitzilopochtli, whatever his form, was a sentient and moving force in the lives of the Mexica from the earliest times. Leaving aside the strong probability that Huitzilopochtli did not exist before the Mexica came into contact with the Tarascans of Michoacán—and this was not long before their arrival in the valley of Mexico—paleolithic barbarians such as the Mexica could not possibly have been lured into migration by the relatively sophisticated rewards that were offered. Nor could they have had a clear conception of the distant future, without which the promise could have neither sense nor meaning. Until the Mexica entered the central valley and rubbed elbows with more cultured neighbors, they had no system of writing and no calendar, no comprehension of the depth of time or the measured recording of its passage. They did, of course, have a collective memory by means of which they maintained tribal traditions and limited chronological associations, but this is not the same thing as a conceptualized historical sense upon which all projections of a distant future must inevitably rest. I am saying that their concept of time was not sufficiently linear: they could not have had a future because they did not have a past.

How long they were able to maintain oral traditions is open to question. As far as we know, they departed from their northern haunts sometime early in the eleventh century.[9] It appears unlikely that they had acquired the ability to write in any form until the middle of the thirteenth century, which would require that oral traditions of departure from Aztlán be over 200 years old before they could be recorded in glyphs. While compiling the information to be contained in his famous *Relación,* Alonso de Zorita was plagued by the historical contradictions that were supplied by his Indian informants. In exasperation he complained that it was virtually impossible to generalize on the pre-Columbian past because most of the codices had disappeared, with the result that the Indians could no longer remember their own history.[10] In less than fifty years after the conquest, the Mexica were having difficulty in recalling their distant past without the aid of glyphs. How, then, could they have done so as barbarians for over two centuries before the art of writing in glyphs was acquired?

The Mexica had no such promise dangling before them during their long wandering; they did not gain their ends by means of a carrot and stick held in the hand—or claw—of Huitzilopochtli. If the latter was not the guiding genius behind the rise of the Mexican state and empire, there is no alternative but to assume that the role was assigned to him *after* the Mexica had risen to a position of imperial prominence. Clearly, then, we stand in the presence of myth as interpretation of history. This fact, and not the myth itself, is of the greatest significance because it tells us to look more closely into the affairs of the men who created Huitzilopochtli, rather than to seek in traditional fashion the influence of Huitzilopochtli upon the lives and fortunes of the Mexica.[11]

Chapter II

The Pipiltin

Sometime during their long period of wandering, the Mexica organized their tribe around the *calpulli* (pl. *calpultin*), or "clan," kinship being a simple means of cementing a plain but viable polity that could with time and motive be transformed into a more intricate form of communal association. Even before the introduction of agriculture, the calpulli was probably the organ of civil and military management, exercising the discipline and restraints upon its members that survival demanded. After the Mexica became dependent upon agriculture, the calpulli acquired greater significance through its control of land. It does not appear likely that land management in itself posed a serious problem for tribal leaders until the captivity in Culhuacán; before that time they were on the move more often than not, and, as mercenaries, they were more concerned with military problems than with agriculture. But in Culhuacán the calpulli became an effective governing agency: it held all of the lands apportioned by the Culhuaque in common, each member of the calpulli receiving a plot sufficient for support of his family that could be inherited but not alienated. In effect, each householder owned his own land and retained control over it as long as he worked it and did not otherwise break the laws of the community. The calpulli also governed matrimony, administered justice, maintained civil discipline and religious cult. Each calpulli had a council of elders, a headman, and an "elected" speaker who represented its interests in council. If not a precisely democratic scheme, it did provide for a measure of equity. When the Mexica fled to the wetlands in the lake and began to construct their city, arable land was held at a premium; calpulli control was the perfect instrument for its administration, and it doubtless achieved its highest development during the first fifty years in Tenochtitlán.[1]

But the very act of settlement in the lake created formidable obstacles to continuation of the calpulli mode of political administration. In order to compete successfully with other lake dwellers, the Mexica needed to centralize administrative authority. Soon after its founding, Tenochtitlán was thus divided into four quarters, or *barrios,* as the Spaniards later called them. Each barrio contained four or five calpultin. While the officials of each calpulli continued to maintain their own religious temples, send out warriors under their own banners and officers, and control lands worked by their members, it was the barrio that emerged as the most significant political unit. When Acamapichtli became king in 1375, centralization was complete; any vestige of calpulli political authority was inimical to the function of royal administration. The calpulli retained its emotional strength as a symbol of identity for its members and continued to wield economic power through its control of land. Likewise, the supreme council of speakers enjoyed weighty authority in military and administrative affairs and might be said to have acted as a cabinet to the early kings.

There was, however, a growing gulf between the speakers and the commoners for whom they spoke. The old system was being outgrown: the speakers had evolved into an elite, by lake world standards a nobility that maintained office through restriction of candidacy to certain families. A ruling oligarchy had matured while the political

15

authority of the calpulli was expiring. At the accession of Acamapichtli, there were ten great families who monopolized the office of speaker and all other administrative and religious posts of consequence.[2]

When these same nobles went to Culhuacán for a king in 1375, it marked a major turning point in Mexican history. For untold generations they had measured excellence and status by genealogical means; the foremost family, the Tenoch, traced its origins all the way back to the lineage of Iztacmixcohuatl, the legendary progenitor of the entire tribe. Among the successor states of the lake district, however, the only lineage that commanded respect was that which led directly back to the Toltec kings, and so the Mexica now turned their backs on their ancestors and sought a foreigner for a king. Acamapichtli was a son of a Mexican lord and Culhua princess. Culturally, he was the product of the finest tradition of Culhuacán, having been reared and educated in the court of his grandfather, the king of the Culhuaque. While they were at it, the Mexica also requisitioned a Culhua bride so that there should be no doubt about the legitimacy of their royal house. Unfortunately, historical accident marred the plot: the new queen proved barren. Now the ruling families decided to give the king their own daughters "so that from them might issue the lineage of the ruling lords of the land." Acamapichtli approached his assignment with vigor, fathering a multitude of children in just a few years. The queen's sterility was kept a state secret, since the Mexica were desperately anxious to maintain the fiction of a Culhua blood line. The queen feigned many of the births as her own, so that even the lesser gentry, as well as the commons, was prone to accept the myth.[3]

Even as Acamapichtli set himself to the task, so did the lords, who took multiple wives from the offspring of their social peers and the king. There was a great deal of mating of old men and young girls, just as there was intermarriage of the children. Within a few years, a new and unique generation had appeared, unique because of the

16

claims that were made for it: it was possessed of "divine" blood that came in unbroken descent from the loins of Quetzalcóatl himself as the Lord of Tula. This was, of course, an absurdity of the first magnitude: there was no line of either blood or culture back to Tula, nor did this new generation have any appreciable amount of Culhua blood in its veins; whatever Acamapichtli had to offer was entirely lost in the proliferating sea of Mexican genes and blood. But the claim was widely advertised with no one to contest it. Within fifty years, the new generation had become a flourishing society that in turn ran by the power of its own engine. It was a society born of a system that was calculated to produce it. These were the *Pipiltin*,* "Sons-of-Lords." It is difficult to suggest a more profound historical example of social engineering. Aristocratic distinction was now determined by posses-sion of blood and membership in a class. The older lines of genealogy and kinship were obliterated. Within the class, each individual *Pilli* was a member of royalty and well beyond the authority of the old calpulli, even though for the time being the calpultin continued to control agricultural land. For the most part, the Pipiltin were in control of the ship of state; the future belonged to them. If one is to understand the subsequent history of the Mexica, he must take into account the needs and desires of this group, for it was they who created and shaped the empire.

The spoils of Atzcapotzalco provided the Pipiltin with independ-ence from the last calpulli restraints. They took the lands of the vanquished, together with the men on them, who now became *ma-yeques*,† or "serfs," who were permanently bound to the soil. The ruling class now had its own lands and labor force. Their weapons freshly crusted with Tepanec blood, King Itzcoatl and his peers of the Pipiltin returned to Tenochtitlán and without delay proclaimed the

---

* Pee-pil-teen.
† mī-ek-kays.

perpetual servitude of the commoners, the *macehualtin*.* From this time forward, all who were not Pipiltin were considered to be commoners. The last meaningful political act of the macehualtin had been to confirm the election of Itzcoatl, who was to condemn them to perpetual servitude.[4] The imperialists were wasting no time.

Other Tepanec states, traditionally allied to Atzcapotzalco, were deeply shocked to see their capital so thoroughly and devastatingly crushed. The city-state of Coyoacán sent aid and assistance, but found it impossible to revive the slain city: the legions of the Triple Alliance had done their work too well. Watching closely, the Triple Alliance now turned on Coyoacán and gave it the same mauling, leaving it smashed and gutted. It was digested after the fashion of Atzcapotzalco and transformed into a vast patchwork of private estates, its populace, for the most part, being reduced to serfdom or slavery. With this accretion the Mexica, with their share, could now round out the nobility and set up the machinery of succession to rulership. Twenty-one titles were created for the greatest families, four of which were supreme. On succession to the throne, it was decreed that each time a new king was chosen there should also be named to specified titles four brothers or close relatives of the king, one of whom was to be his successor, and no other. In a political sense, these four great lords were the presumptive heirs of the king. None of their titles, or the crown itself, could be inherited outright through claim of blood or bequest, however. Each ruler was to be chosen on merit alone, as were his presumptive heirs. This proved to be a superbly effective safeguard against accession of an incompetent. Those four titles of highest eminence were symbolic and prophetic of the nature of the empire that was being fashioned: the first was "Prince-of-the-House," followed by the "Butcher-of-Men," "He-Who-Claws-Shedding-Blood," and "Lord-of-the-House-of-Darkness." [5]

* mahsay-wal-teen.

The prosperous city of Xochimilco, a southern neighbor of Coyoa-cán and an old Tepanec ally, was next on the list for conquest. Legions of the Triple Alliance attacked, working a vast and terrible slaughter until the survivors, pleading for mercy, surrendered all their lands and properties and pledged themselves to perpetual servitude. For ease of tribute collection and administration, the conquerors ordered the Xochimilca to construct a southern causeway to Tenochti-tlán, which was fast becoming the capital of the Triple Alliance.[6] The king of Cuitlahuac, whose capital was situated to the east of Xochimilco, recognized the growing peril and immediately sought aid from Chalco, the last independent power on the lake. The Chalca, with an empire of twenty-five towns, apparently felt secure. Their king listened to the blandishments of Itzcoatl's ambassadors and appeared willing to turn his back while Cuitlahuac was being raped. In despair, the lord of Cuitlahuac capitulated, even as the enemy was bearing down on his city. Cuitlahuac disappeared in the realms of the Triple Alliance. Chalco's turn came soon enough; it was a long and bitter struggle, although the outcome was never in doubt. Chalco was crushed in 1465, and now the legions of the Alliance were free to spill over the rim of the central plateau in conquest of the rich lowlands, the coastal provinces, and to exploit the exotic wealth of the *tierra caliente*.[7]

The division of lands taken from Xochimilco seems to have been rather typical of the manner in which the lords of the Triple Alliance distributed and invested their new wealth. First shares went to participating lords, each one receiving a parcel of approximately 222 acres. This grant included the services of the people who happened to be living on the land; they now joined the mayeques as "people who belong to the household and palace of the kings and lords." Such properties were usually converted into landed estates that were subject to entail. The Pipiltin were particularly avid developers of latifundia.[8] As a new and powerful class, they were anxious to bolster their social and political pretensions with substantial economic foundations. Plebeians who distinguished themselves in combat also won a share of the spoils, ordinarily consisting of 111 acres and military status as proven warriors. Frequently these parcels of land were not populated, or scantily so, in which case the new proprietors usually got refugee commoners to work as *renteros* on a crop-sharing basis.

A second slice of land and labor was set aside for support of the growing imperial officialdom: treasury officials, tribute agents, justices, administrators, and functionaries of all kinds. Every position carried with it a salary computed in produce from the land and personal service of the tenants, to which were commonly added various perquisites and privileges. Such income was enjoyed only during tenure of employment by the state. Not unlike the Roman idea of usufruct, the holder might enjoy the fruits but he must not dissipate the principal. A third portion of imperial plunder was used to support and extend the Mexican clergy.[9]

Rich in lands and tribute and in unchallenged control of the state, the Pipiltin proliferated grotesquely. Each Pilli had one wife who bore his "legitimate" heir, that is to say, the person who would inherit his estate; otherwise, there was no distinction between his many children, whoever their mothers might be. In addition to his principal wife, the lord had as many sexual favorites as he could afford; they were usually counted by the score, even to hundreds by the great lords. These unofficial wives were, as in the beginning, drawn from the families of his peers and from homes of the plebeians, whose more attractive daughters were liable to claim by the nobles as tribute. The production of children was staggering by any standard of comparison. During the first five years of life, the children lived in the lord's harem, being cared for by their mothers and wet nurses provided by the state; at the age of six, girls were commonly advanced to boarding schools run by older women who had been retired from the lord's harem, or sent to religious temples for devotional exercise and training. Boys were sent to the local *Calmecac,* a preparatory school and college combined, where they were trained in rhetoric, history, religion, and astrology. This training was essential for those who wished to enter the priest-hood or the civil bureaucracy; many also graduated to careers in military service. Those intellectually deficient or emotionally unpre-pared for the Calmecac could return to their father's old barrio *Tel-pochcalli,* a military preparatory school primarily intended for sons of the macehualtin. Although they reigned supreme, the lords of the Pipiltin never lost touch with their old clan associations; the calpulli continued to serve many functions and purposes. Most of the sons, however, took their training and went on to military careers; one captive taken in war earned knighthood; two or more captives pro-vided entry to the military caste, with eventual membership in higher ranks of the central bureaucracy. With this kind of success, the young Pilli took a wife and harem and emulated his father, producing scores of sons. The cycle was endless. On the other hand, all those who failed in war, regardless of their training or paternity, were forced to renounce their inheritance and enter the macehualtin, there to spend the rest of their lives in anonymity.[10] It appears obvious that over an extended period of time the calpultin were gradually deprived of the best genetic stock; it is equally obvious that the social system was predicated upon the assumption of a constantly expanding empire, the plunder, labor, and taxes of which supported the entire complex.

As the daughters of the Pipiltin matured, they too entered imperial service; their fathers married them to the lords of subject provinces and cities. Precise birth records were maintained so that years later the issue of such unions could be identified. Within the empire, only the sons of these Mexican mothers were considered legitimate and there-fore qualified to inherit landed properties. Elder sons not in this category were dispossessed the moment the Mexica assumed sover-eignty in a province. This constituted a tight system of hereditary control throughout the provinces; in effect, the women of the Mexican state produced a ruling caste that in turn controlled the empire.[11]

The ruling group within the Pipiltin was much smaller than its accomplishments would indicate. There was Itzcoatl, who came to the throne in 1428 and was to rule until his death in 1440, aided by his five half-brothers; Nezahualcoyotl,* his nephew, who mounted the throne of Texcoco in 1428, there to reign for forty-four years, during which time he partially Mexicanized the kingdom; Montezuma, another nephew who was to succeed Itzcoatl and rule until 1469. All were members—by blood and marriage—of a dozen or so great families, great because of their position and possession of divine blood, although Itzcoatl himself was living proof of the emptiness of the blood boast. In his declining years Acamapichtli had been enflamed by a beautiful Tepanec slave girl; the return of his youth lasted long enough for him to sire Itzcoatl, but only a short time before his death.

The mad mélange of blood and genes that characterized the formation of Pipiltin society seems to have produced a highly effective leadership, so carefully yet swiftly was the empire created and organized; virtually nothing was left to chance. But the genetic jungle also produced aberrant forms, and out of it there stalked a brilliant psychopath who rose to prominence in 1429 as hero of the Tepanec war: he was Tlacaellel,† nephew of Itzcoatl and half-brother of Montezuma.[12] Named Prince-of-the-Armies after the fall of Atzcapotzalco, he assumed command of the legions of the Triple Alliance. As commanding general, he wielded vast authority; yet this proved to be one of his lesser powers as he gradually assumed control of Mexican destiny, which he was to hold for the next sixty-eight years.

After Atzcapotzalco had fallen and the macehualtin had been subjected to servitude, Itzcoatl and Tlacaellel issued an edict: Let the

* Netz-a-wal-coy-ōtl.
† Tla-cal-yel.

world take note that Huitzilopochtli is guiding the destiny of the Mexica. It necessarily followed from this that all who should oppose them would be opposing divine destiny. As soon as Coyoacán had been swallowed and digested, they issued another edict, this one more pointed than the first: It is the divine mission of the Mexica to bring all peoples and nations to worship of Huitzilopochtli by force of arms. These pronouncements may have brought smiles of contempt to the faces of powerful lords residing in nearby capitals; what could those upstarts be thinking of? For the lords of Tlacopan and Texcoco, however, it was no cause for mirth. The Mexica had issued a unilateral declaration with the most profound implications: they were pledging the blood and treasure of the Triple Alliance powers, who were now bound to use their armed might to impose upon others a deity that they themselves neither recognized nor worshiped.

Acting under the latter edict, Itzcoatl sent emissaries to the lords of Xochimilco demanding that they furnish building materials for a new temple that was to be built for Huitzilopochtli. Since these were items for which the Mexica formerly bartered, the Xochimilca refused. Nor did they appreciate the new Mexican hauteur. In anticipation of refusal, the general had his forces in readiness; the attack was swift and devastating. Hundreds of captives were taken back to Tenochtitlán and sacrificed to Huitzilopochtli, their breasts slashed open and their beating hearts wrenched from their bodies. This lesson was not lost on the king of Cuitlahuac, who was next "invited" to bring his lords to the capital and worship Huitzilopochtli. He saw the situation in a realistic light and sought alliance with powerful Chalco. Meanwhile, he could not hide his contempt from Itzcoatl's emissaries, who waited for his reply. "Do you realize what you are saying? Are my sons, brothers, and relatives, and the lords of Cuitlahuac creatures of your god that they should hasten to sing and dance at his pleasure?" Contempt turned into rage as his reply became a tirade, climaxed by his oath that he would not permit even his whores to dance before

Huitzilopochtli. As if to document their train of thought, Itzcoatl and the general declared Cuitlahuac to be in a state of rebellion and dispatched forces to control the situation. Failing to get help from Chalco, the king chose voluntary submission over extinction. Warned of the approach of a Mexican force, he went out to meet it bearing rich gifts and presents for the general. In the middle of the road, before his peers, he groveled and begged forgiveness, offering himself and his lords as "vassals of Mexican majesty and servants of the great god Huitzilopochtli." Tlacaellel made an immediate levy of sacrificial victims as a price for dallying; this initiated a regular levy of such victims for Huitzilopochtli on all conquered and subjugated peoples that was never relaxed until the fall of Tenochtitlán to Spanish invaders.

Upon their return to the capital, Tlacaellel and his troops were greeted and hailed by the Pipiltin. Priests in Huitzilopochtli's service, rapidly achieving pre-eminence, came out to the city's gates and conducted the heroes to his temple where they held formal ceremony of thanksgiving. Meanwhile, the prisoners were stripped of all their clothing and placed in file before the base of Huitzilopochtli's temple. As a signal was given, they were prodded and dragged up the temple staircase where, at the top, death awaited them. As the prisoners' eyes cleared the top step, they fell on a large convex slab of polished stone, around which stood six priests, each with his head and arms stained black, his hair tied in tight coils and held in place by a leather band, his forehead crossed by a row of tiny colored disks, held by a string; their bodies were draped in flowing dalmatics that originally had been white, with black designs, but were now drenched with the crimson of fresh blood. The victim had time to register little more: he was quickly seized by four of the priests, one on each limb, and flopped over the sacrificial stone; a fifth priest slipped a hook around his neck and choked off his screams while the officiant raised the great knife and let it fall. A good, clean stroke nearly bisected the victim, so that it was then easy to reach through the welling blood into the thoracic cavity and tear out the still palpitating heart. The carcass was unceremoniously dumped from the slab and kicked over the edge of the platform. The levy of sacrificial victims, the greeting of the heroes and formal thanksgiving at Huitzilopochtli's temple, the ensuing blood bath, all were made custom and rigidly observed at each imperial victory, the only change being one of degree: as the empire grew, the victory fete became increasingly lavish and burdened with esoteric symbolism.[13]

When the Mexica spilled over into tierra caliente, they found their merchants, the *Pochteca,* most valuable. Centered in Tlatelolco, they were deeply rooted and widely established before the empire was formed; hence they were of great usefulness when the juggernaut began to roll. Each advance was led by so-called Vanguard Merchants, who were imperial spies. "When they entered lands with which they were at war, and went among people who were far distant, they became like their enemies in their garments, their hair-dress, their speech [that they might] mimic the natives. And if they came to an evil pass, if they were discovered, then they were slain in ambush and served up with chile sauce." [14] Successful conclusion of the mission, however, brought rich rewards back in the capital. Acting on the intelligence supplied by their merchant-spies, the Mexica sent ambassadors to distant courts with ultimata for the ruling lords: Install and venerate Huitzilopochtli and other Mexican deities; recognize and accept Mexican sovereignty; pay tribute; and produce a regular levy of sacrificial victims for Huitzilopochtli. If the lords so approached complied without delay, they were permitted to retain their old deities on a par with Huitzilopochtli. If, on the other hand, they caviled, or if the Mexica thought they were too slow in accepting, they were forced to pay great sums in penalty and in the end to comply. Those who refused were visited by the legions that came and slaughtered until the survivors cried out for respite, which proved to be costly. The conquerors confiscated valuable properties, enslaved and sacrificed a large segment of the population, destroyed their religious temples and carried their gods back to Tenochtitlán, where they were put in a special prison for captive deities. The survivors ended up by worshiping Huitzilopochtli even as they sought some means to avoid his sacrificial slab. In all of their conquests the Mexica invariably demolished and set fire to the enemy's religious temples. This practice was not Mexican invention; it was rather a Mesoamerican tradition wherein the dethroning of local deities and burning of their temples was taken as an unmistakable sign of defeat—so ingrained was the idea that the Mexican glyph for defeat of an enemy was a demolished and blazing temple.[15] What this tells us, of course, is that in the minds of the Mexica, sovereignty and religion were inseparable.

What does appear to be Mexican innovation is the calculated use of human sacrifice as a functional instrument of statecraft. The immolation of men to gods had been going on in Mesoamerica for centuries, just as it has been known in some form or other by all primitive societies. It seems apparent now that the question of human sacrifice was a stormy issue during the later years of the Toltec empire and may even have been a significant factor in its decline. Intestine struggle was waged between two contending groups of priest-philosophers, the leaders of Quetzalcóatl * cult opposing the followers of Tezcatlipoca,† both of whom were ancient *cultus* focuses. Quetzalcóatl, whose real identity is locked in the secret of Teotihuacán, founded a religious system peculiarly like Christianity in that it stressed peace, love, mercy, and compassion as positive moral values; its followers practiced oral confession, baptism, and mild forms of ascetic denial as they sought to approximate the founder's sublime moral sense and ethical code of conduct. Later generations held Quetzalcóatl to be a god-man

* Ket-zal-cō-atl.
† Tetz-cot-lee-pōka.

26

who gave life by mere laying on of hands; who invented agriculture, the calendar and astrological sciences, weaving, and the arts; he forbade human sacrifice and instituted bloodless offerings. He was a culture hero who authored the golden age of Toltec civilization, a time when cotton fabrics grew ready-woven and dyed in many colors; the air was filled with the sweet song of birds; turquoise was washed from stream beds; the arts flourished; there was no hunger; it was a time of plenty. But one day, as the legend goes, evil appeared in the form of Tezcatlipoca, who was Quetzalcóatl's sworn enemy. A conspiracy was drawn for Quetzalcóatl's downfall that succeeded: he was given an intoxicating liquor and then seduced by a harlot. In deep disgrace, Quetzalcóatl left Tula and made his way to the gulf coast where he departed, promising that one day he would return. Back in Tula, Tezcatlipoca celebrated his victory by sacrificing all of Quetzalcóatl's partisans.[16] From our vantage point we assume this classic story of good struggling with evil to be in reality a description of a power struggle between two politico-religious factions in Tula. At any rate, it does document a basic Mesoamerican neurosis: to kill or not to kill. It was a question that was never definitively answered. The sources leave small doubt, however, that it was during the early years of the Mexican empire that human sacrifice leapt into such prominence on the central plateau. Andrés de Olmos, who did the most extensive research on the question in the sixteenth century, concluded that the Mexica were solely responsible. Durán's sources show that it was Tlacaellel and his peers who promoted human sacrifice as a political instrument.[17] Apparently, Tlacaellel and his aides were dipping back into the past for certain historical elements that they were combining in new and untried forms. Certainly their handiwork is identified by the fact that the new vogue of human sacrifice was wedded to Huitzilopochtli cult, which was undeniably an imperial invention.

The religious base fashioned by the Tolteca had cracked during the fall of Tula and shattered with the diaspora; its fragments, through isolation and the lowering of speculative levels caused by barbarian intrusion, became acceptable entities in themselves, exaggerated caricatures of the idea of which they had once been a part. By the time the Mexica came to power, the Mesoamericans had reconstructed the basic religious formulas of the Tolteca, although there still remained a bewildering spectrum of confused and distorted philosophical and religious notions. According to reconstructions of the Mexica, there were twelve heavens, in the highest of which dwelt Ometecutli with his wife Omecihuatl. They were male and female, or positive and negative, dual aspects of a single deity; hence they were called "Lord of the Dual Essence." This was the creator of the primordial field of force that in turn provided the ultimate essence of all matter and phenomena. One is struck by its similarity to the Chinese Yan and Yin. This, too, was the Lord of Creation, "he who breathes the breath of life itself into the belly of woman." The other gods were born of this essence, and they played a more immediate role in the lives of men; for it was they who created the earth and everything upon its broad surface. But from this point on, it was every philosopher for himself.

Texcoco held the proud distinction of being the cultural capital of Nahuatl civilization; it was ever the center for polished Nahuatl poetry and speech; its archives were rich in history; its artists were supreme. Religiously, the Texcocans cherished myriad deities and local demigods, as did all dwellers of the central plateau. Among its thinkers, however, there lived an apparently small but dedicated group that sought to promote a monotheistic concept. Beyond the twelve Toltec heavens and the Lord of the Dual Essence they visualized a holy force, called Tloque Nahuaque, reigning alone over the universe; it was formless and omnipotent; all other gods were held to be false, and human sacrifice was recognized as empty placation rather than genuine worship. The sources are so meager that we cannot say more. But on the face of it, this appears to be a survival of ancient

Quetzalcóatl cult that, even among the Mexica and in spite of their craze for blood sacrifice, remained as the moral basis of society and a point of philosophical departure. The cult enjoyed powerful support among some of the nobles, King Nezahualcoyotl being one of its staunchest advocates.[18]

These people could not but recognize Huitzilopochtli cult as a piece of barbarous fakery, nor could they fail to resent Itzcoatl's and Tlacaellel's employment of Triple Alliance forces to uphold the cult and serve their private ends. The Texcocan nobility was heavily infiltrated with Mexican blood, largely as a result of the intermarriage that had occurred for many years. Nezahualcoyotl was himself a Mexican and married to Itzcoatl's sister who, by the vagaries of Mexican genealogy, was also his aunt. But like many of his kind, he was culturally a Texcocan, and was consequently suspicious of the motives of the Mexican lords. Indeed, he could recall that just a few years ago, when the Mexica were still vassals of Atzcapotzalco and he was striving against their opposition to gain political power, Itzcoatl had on more than one occasion plotted against his life. Most of all he feared Tlacaellel, the master strategist and the man who seemed to stand at the center of the new Huitzilopochtli cult.

Itzcoatl's death in 1440 unleashed a train of events that were to bear out Nezahualcoyotl's darkest fears. When the four titles of presumptive royalty had been created, Tlacaellel had taken for himself that of Prince-of-the-House, whereupon he began to conduct himself in the manner of heir apparent. Montezuma had become Butcher-of-Men, while two of Itzcoatl's brothers assumed the other titles.[19] Election of the successor was in the hands of the kings of Texcoco and Tlacopan acting in council with the most influential imperial lords. Although inconclusive, internal evidence suggests that Nezahualcoyotl was forced to make the most disastrous of concessions in order to swing the election to Montezuma rather than Tlacaellel. From the moment of Montezuma's election, Nezahualcoyotl and Texcoco were required to pay an endless reckoning. First, Nezahualcoyotl was required to go to Tenochtitlán and recognize Montezuma as "Supreme Lord and Monarch of the World," and pledge himself and the kingdom to unqualified vassalage. When this had been done, Montezuma convened his council of peers, informing them that "The King of Texcoco, our kith and kin, pledges and subjects himself to the favor of our god Huitzilopochtli." Tlacaellel rose to his feet and voiced objection: The Mexica must subdue all nations through the pain and blood of war; therefore, this peaceful surrender to the sovereignty of Huitzilopochtli can not be accepted. The Texcocans must fight a sham battle in which they will be defeated by the Mexica, and King Nezahualcoyotl must personally set fire to the main temple as a sign of abject surrender. "Only then," he concluded, "shall our fame and honor remain without blemish, [the Texcocans] without injury or malice, the common folk subjected to our service when we require it, and the other provinces and cities terrified with the knowledge of our having destroyed [the temple of] Texcoco." The entire farce was acted out with a cast of thousands. Nezahualcoyotl set fire to the central temple, after which he was required to swear fealty to Huitzilopochtli and assume all the obligations of a conquered city, which included payment of sacrificial victims as tribute—all of which was done in public ceremony. A new temple was constructed on the site of the old one, and Huitzilopochtli moved in to stay. Only now could Tenochtitlán, as demanded by the general, be the undisputed seat of empire "from whence the god Huitzilopochtli reigns and holds dominion." [20]

If Nezahualcoyotl had bargained to curb Tlacaellel's bid for power, he lived to see himself the loser on every count. Deprived of the throne, Tlacaellel made himself his brother's keeper: he assumed the title of *Cihuacoatl*, or "Vice-Ruler," and had fashioned a duplicate throne that he promptly placed beside Montezuma's. From now on Tlacaellel assumed the role of oracle of the empire; he enjoyed the power of majesty with none of its restraints. The sources say that "nothing was done in the realm without his orders, and thus he used the tiara and insignia of the king." [21] Perhaps there is some exaggeration here, but there is no doubt of his growing power within the ruling presidium. As Cihuacoatl, one of his first acts was to establish a new coronation ceremony called *motlatocapaca*, literally, "the washing of his feet [in blood]." It was decreed that each newly elected monarch, beginning with Montezuma, must personally lead armed forces in battle to garner an appropriate number of sacrificial victims with which to grace the public coronation ceremony. At the sacrifice the king was to wield the sacrificial blade, at least until his feet were awash in the blood of Huitzilopochtli's victims. The fete was duly initiated and observed as immutable law. [22]

With Montezuma's accession, plans for a new and more elaborate temple for Huitzilopochtli were laid. Subject cities and provinces were assigned matériel and labor quotas. Chalco, still independent, received an invitation to contribute huge stones from its quarries. Chalco's refusal gave Montezuma the excuse he needed for making a coronation haul at their expense. He took his prisoners in a brief campaign that proved to be the opening skirmish of a long and bloody war. For a time it appeared as though the Mexica would win easily, but the Chalca turned the tables and inflicted heavy casualties on the invaders. Notified of the losses, General Tlacaellel took personal command and made a vow: all captives taken in this war would be offered to Huitzilopochtli in a newly contrived fete that he called the "fire sacrifice." He had set in the earth before Huitzilopochtli's temple a huge brazier, later named "Divine Hearth" by official mythologians. In possession of 500 Chalcan captives, he ordered the new sacrifice to begin. The victims were cast onto the brazier and permitted to writhe in agony over the glowing coals for a reasonable period of time before being fished out with long hooks, whereupon they were cast onto slabs and their hearts torn from their charred bodies. The hearth steamed with the welter of blood, its smoldering stench reminding one and all that it was impolitic to refuse Huitzilopochtli anything. [23]

Huitzilopochtli continued to be developed as the symbol of imperial

31

sovereignty as the Mexica relentlessly extended their dominion. Te-peaca, located on the southeastern rim of the central plateau, had been conquered early as an important gateway to tierra caliente and the gulf coast. Under the weight of tribute schedules, the people revolted, but not for long. Mexican legions quickly arrived and burned Tepeaca and neighboring Cuauhtinchan, Tecalli, and Acatzinco. Residents were slaughtered until the survivors agreed to submit and pay double tributes, plus a sur-levy of sacrificial victims for Huitzilopochtli pay-able every eighty days. The first instalment was taken on the spot. Placed in marching order, the plebeians had their hands tied behind their backs, a choker line about their throats; together with their lords, they were marched back to the capital. At the gates of Tenochtitlán they were inspected and incensed by joyous priests, who then led them to Huitzilopochtli's temple where they were made to do rever-ence before his altar. From there they were led to the royal palace where they paid the same reverence to Montezuma and Tlacaellel seated on their twin thrones. Next, the nobles were brought forward; in Huitzilopochtli's temple they offered rich gifts; before the altar they bled their tongues, legs, and ears; they were shown how to squat before the altar—the Mexican form of obeisance—and with a mois-tened finger to dip some earth and place it in their mouths, a gesture that the Spaniards later characterized as "eating dirt." Now they were led before the twin thrones, where they performed the same adoration. The lord of Tepeaca, having been coached by a priest, now recited the following piece: "I come to worship Huitzilopochtli, who gathers unto himself all nations; and now, as his creature, I come to serve him, bringing all my vassals and servants that they too may adore him and recognize him as their lord." This ceremony was enacted without variation every time a new city or province fell or a rebellion was put down.[24]

One of the most impressive creations of the Pipiltin, as they es-tablished administrative councils, treasury agencies, judicial courts, military garrisons, and the other bureaus of empire, was the imperial church. In every major city and provincial center that entered the Mexican orbit, or as Huitzilopochtli "gathered unto himself" all the peoples and nations, striking changes were wrought. In the exact center of the city a large square was leveled and paved and surrounded by a crenellated wall with gates facing the four cardinal directions. Within the enclosure of the wall, a number of temples were built, larger towns having perhaps twelve or fifteen. The central pyramid was invariably the highest and most elaborate, since it belonged to Huitzilopochtli. It was large enough to furnish commodious apartments for his priests, quarters for acolytes and penitents, and the omnipresent Calmecac. The gates to the enclosure were flanked by armories and barracks where imperial troops were frequently stationed during times of unrest. Huitzilopochtli's pyramid had twin chapels on its summit, one housing a representation of the imperial symbol, the other housing the local deity, or, if it happened to be imprisoned back in the capital, Tlaloc was usually put in its place. The four gates opened onto the four roads that approached the town. If they were not straight when the Mexica took over, they were made so for a distance of four or five miles, so that all roads of the province—indeed, of the empire—converged in straight lines on the central enclosure, meeting at Huitzilopochtli's temple. As it worked out, roads passing through outlying communities came to an end at the great pyramid that stood in the absolute center of the largest town. Once through the gates, the road seemed to climb the massive staircase to the top of the pyramid, which, from its base, appeared to vanish into the heavens. From the summit Huitzilopochtli's priests could survey the entire countryside and luxuriate in a sense of presiding power. Toribio de Motolinía measured the central pyramid of Tenanyocán, which was of medium size, and found it to be some 90 feet high and 240 feet at the base on each side. As the elevation increased, the ledges were skilfully tapered inward, producing an illusion of greater height; a person standing at

33

the base saw the steps rise and disappear in the clouds. The summit platform had twin chapels with the indispensable sacrificial slabs placed before their doors so that the deities could witness the immolation.[25]

As the imperial church and its clergy expanded, growing wealthy through land holdings, the fruits of *corvèe,* and almost unlimited tribute, Huitzilopochtli's annual feast day, called *Cohuaichuitl,* or "Feast of all Peoples," was proclaimed a universal festival in all areas under Mexican domination, with a standing demand for 1,000 sacrifices in each of his temples. During the four-day fete, fasting was required of everyone until the thousand victims had been dispatched; when one considers the rivers of gore that would by then be running down the temple staircase to the edification of the plebeians huddled below, it hardly seems that the prohibition would matter. In order to assure proper adherence to its official cult, the state provided a ratio of one priest per five of population.[26]

Tlacaellel's virtuosity was most apparent in his variations on the symbolism and modes of human sacrifice.[27] As the imperial legions speared into the southwest, they encountered an ancient form of Xipe Totec cult that was closely identified with fertility and spring rites. In classic form, a victim was trussed up to a rack and shot with arrows, the dripping blood symbolizing spring rain; the body was then flayed and the fresh skin donned by a priest in representation of the fresh mantle of spring. While the Mexica thrust Huitzilopochtli upon the people of the area, Tlacaellel did not fail to see the sacrificial possibilities of Xipe cult. Probably because of its fundamental relationship with simple folk and the growing of maize, which gave it universal significance, Xipe Totec was incorporated in the Mexican calendar as the focal deity of the second month, *Tlacaxipehualiztli,* or "Festival-of-the-Flayed-Ones." It was at this time that the calendar appears to have assumed the character it had when the Spaniards arrived, the only subsequent modifications being those caused by the steady encroachment of Huitzilopochtli in rites and fetes where he previously had neither role nor function.[28] In his assimilation of Xipe cult, the general ordered a huge, round stone to be cut, nine feet in diameter, its edge to be sculpted and painted with scenes portraying the victory over Atzcapotzalco. This was to be the famous *Temalacatl*. When completed, it was laid flat, like a wheel, before Huitzilopochtli's temple on a low platform of masonry and rock. In use, a captive warrior was tied to its hub with a short rope securing one ankle; the victim was given a *macana,* or broadsword, from which the obsidian edge had been removed and replaced by feathers, and a few short sticks with which to defend himself against his tormenters. When all was in readiness, the prisoner was attacked by four Eagle and Tiger knights, who used their regular battlefield equipment. Their procedure was to attack one at a time, seeking to maim and exhaust rather than kill outright. When the victim could no longer keep his feet, waiting priests slashed him open and wrenched out his heart, flayed him, and performed in his skin. This sacrifice, first inaugurated in 1458, became immensely popular among the Pipiltin as a spectator sport and was widely imitated over the central plateau.[29]

Simultaneously, Tlacaellel appears to have been working closely with learned mythologians in fabrication of a philosophical justification for the homicidal nature of domestic and imperial policies. Their efforts resulted in the well known "cosmic mission theory," according to which the world was in darkness until one of the gods created the sun by casting himself into a brazier of live coals. He rose again as the sun, but could not move across the heavens in daily journey without proper nourishment, which, it was determined, was a magical substance found only in the hearts and blood of men. It therefore became the divine mission of the Mexica to feed the sun, thereby guaranteeing daily continuation of the universe. Since the gods had sacrificed themselves in order to initiate the process, it was held that man must sacrifice himself in order to maintain it. It was now that the Pipiltin began to call themselves "People of the Sun." It is noteworthy that the blood that nourished the sun was also held to nourish Huitzilopochtli.[30]

With this mythology well in hand, Tlacaellel and his aides undertook intensive development of ceremonial symbolism, the possibilities of which were virtually endless. He ordered a second stone carved, in size and shape closely resembling the Temalacatl, except that its center was carved to form a basin which was drained by a small drilled pipe. The basin, of course, represented the sun as it caught the blood that gushed forth from the victims gaping breast. This was the famed "Sun Stone." [31] Paired with the Temalacatl, the two stones became the focus of the Festival-of-the-Flayed-Ones, rapidly being boomed as one of the empire's greatest fetes. Used in tandem, the fallen warriors, having been beaten down by their adversaries, were transferred from the Temalacatl to the Sun Stone for the final act. On the occasion of its first public showing, all the lords of the empire were commanded to attend so that they might "see what the sacrifice signified." Montezuma and Tlacaellel officiated as high priests; their bodies stained black, bejeweled and brilliantly plumed, they both wore golden crowns and ocelot sandals on their feet; robes of majesty covered golden bracelets from elbow to shoulder; they both wore the insignia of Huitzilopochtli's high priest. Significantly, this was the first time that majesty and godhead were united. The visiting lords went home impressed.

After this period of formulation, the sources indicate increasing refinement of sacrificial symbolism. Freshly drawn hearts are held aloft and offered to the sun; the victim is frequently stained red, the solar color; slowly he mounts the eastern staircase, like the rising sun, reaching the slab precisely at high noon; the blade falls and the sun gets a drink; the drained corpse is tumbled down the western side in sprawling emulation of the setting sun. People of the Sun. Whatever the mythologians made of it, Tlacaellel never lost sight of first principles: he seldom failed to use the Festival-of-the-Flayed-Ones and other sacrificial spectaculars to gain political ends. Not only were provincial lords made to attend, but the lords of cities and states yet independent were enjoined to come, with the avowed purpose of intimidating them and gaining their submission.[32]

The ruling lords of the Pipiltin never confused symbolism with practical sovereignty. When a provincial lord died, the capital took note. A successor was "elected" by the state, which meant that his genealogy was searched to be certain that his mother was a Mexican Pilli. Once confirmed, he was taken to Huitzilopochtli's temple where he made obeisance and received his robes of office and instruction in his responsibilities by the high priest; after being anointed with Huitz-ilopochtli's sacred balm, the new lord entered four days of seclusion and contemplation within the temple, after which he "carried himself and acted as Lord and was so feared and obeyed that one hardly dared look into his face, unless it was a peer or intimate friend." Those who succeeded to provincial overlordship were required to go to Tenochti-tlán and repeat the ceremony in Huitzilopochtli's great temple. Similar but less elaborate ceremonial was prescribed for elevation of a commoner or entry of a young Pilli into the orders of knighthood.[33] In any case Huitzilopochtli's was the dominating presence.

Twenty years after the fall of Atzcapotzalco, the fabrications of the Pipiltin were exerting considerable influence beyond imperial borders, especially in those relationships between land, man, and society. Neighboring states had become accustomed to the ruthless expansion of the empire; some peoples were so utterly "conquered" that they disappeared without leaving a trace; rebellion or failure to pay tribute occasioned unbelievable cruelties in retaliation; growing numbers annually perished on sacrificial slabs until, at mid-century, the blood mania appeared to be getting out of hand.[34] With its inception, the empire had been founded on a principle of divided society that emphasized degradation of the macehualtin as it simultaneously exalted

37

the Pipiltin. Domestic policy was inseparable from imperial policy during the formative years; and as the structure gradually took shape, the differences between commoner and noble were increasingly fortified. Economically, it was a basic division between producers and consumers, the former being rigidly exploited to keep pace with the growing appetites of the latter. The Nahuatl language itself bore witness to the distinctions that were growing ever more sharp and absolute: in addition to special forms of address for persons of rank, even nouns, pronouns, verbs, and prepositions were affected by the rank of the person to whom applied, and to his material possessions. There were less pronounced social and economic reflections of like nature in the Otomí, Zapotec, and Mixtecan languages and dialects, indicating that the Mexica, if not the authors of the trend, were in the forefront of its refinement.[35] Larger independent states, Tlaxcala, Cholula, Huexotzinco, and Michoacán, were creating domestic patterns much in the fashion of Tenochtitlán, and in so doing were approaching the logical and ultimate conclusion of a quasi-feudalism that had been under development in Mesoamerica since the fall of Tula. The Mexica, while caught in the grip of the same inexorable force, were by virtue of their imperial sway asserting a subtle but forceful control over the eclectic process involved in interpretation of the next predominant variant of hallowed Tula and ancient Teotihuacán.

By 1450 the lords of rival states had more in common with each other than they had with the plebeians of their own cities and provinces. Their social and political status structures, in large part dependent upon warfare and the capture of sacrificial victims for distinction and advancement, provided them with obvious avenues of mutual interest. So intense had the pursuit of status become by mid-century, especially for the Mexica, that irregular warfare against rival powers or occasional rebellion in distant provinces could not suffice to keep the system going. The Mexica were running out of ready foes, and conquered peoples, in fear of genocide, were no longer prone to rebel.

For the Pipiltin it posed a major crisis: the biological intermedium had overtaken the empire and could not be contained. Crisis was deepened by a coincidental problem of much shorter run. From 1451 to 1454, there had occurred freak climatic phenomena and natural disasters making for lean crop years; the macehualtin, already disillusioned with the course of empire, were facing starvation. Unrest and disease were rampant.[36] Identical problems, in varying degrees, were plaguing other powers of the plateau. By late 1454 emergency was general.

A solution was sought by a Congress of Lords, held on neutral ground. The Triple Alliance was represented by Montezuma and the general, accompanied by the other eleven lords of the ruling presidium.[37] They met with the rulers of Tlaxcala, Huexotzinco, Cholula, and Atlixco. The sources do not begin to tell us what we should like to know about the discussions that took place in the meetings, even though some of their resolutions are reported by the chroniclers. According to them, it was agreed that the powers of the Triple Alliance would meet the others in prearranged military engagements at regular intervals, the purpose of which would be to provide a testing ground for aspiring youths and to provide captives for sacrificial purposes. Such appears to have been the origin of the famous *Xochiyaoyotl*, or "Flower Wars." According to Tlacaellel's arguments, as they are reported, these engagements would be most acceptable in serving the Mexican status system and nourishing the gods, for the barbarous Chichimeca were too far away for ready exercise, besides which their flesh was coarse and stale by the time they had been dragged all the way back to the capital for sacrifice. But these fresh, youthful victims, especially the "most luscious and exquisite" Tlaxcalan warriors, would be "like bread hot from the griddle, soft and delicious."[38] The truth of the matter was that the Chichimeca were too hard to defeat; the Mexica never succeeded in breaking their frontiers. One must also suspect that the flesh of tax-evaders and common felons who were sacrificed on the same slabs for the same ends was equally unfit for the gods.[39] Tlacaellel gave the opposing powers the sobriquet of "Enemies-of-the-House," and offered further refinements: the wars should be confined to the given time and place, and in reality would be sham because the great lords would in time of need come to the other's aid, the "time of need" presumably meaning rebellion of the masses. The general was here apparently anticipating refinement of his diplomatic strategy of conquest by intimidation, hence, "Although there is enmity between us wherein the [Flower] Wars are concerned, there is no reason why they should be excluded from our fiestas and solemnities, for we are all one, and during these times [of festival] it is fitting that there should be a truce and intercourse between the lords." It was further agreed that the commoners and lesser gentry were not to be made aware of these secret arrangements, nor were they to be informed of the resolutions agreed upon by the lords. In order to maintain security, it was arranged that henceforth all unauthorized movement from one province or state to another was to be universally forbidden under pain of summary sacrifice. As the congress disbanded and the nobles returned to their capitals, guarded frontiers were erected, ending free movement for the macehualtin. As for the starving populace, the lords agreed to open their granaries and to barter plebeian children as sacrificial victims to the Totonacs for maize.[40]

Tlacaellel hastened to use the newly ordained Flower Wars to shore up the sagging status system. Shortly after his return to Tenochtitlán, he issued an edict: Henceforth, for each prisoner taken in the "military fairs of Tlaxcala," the captor was to be rewarded from the state treasury and awarded certain distinctions of dress and privileges; no person, whatever his lineage, was to wear any article of attire or badge of distinction beyond that allowed to plebeians unless he had earned the right through participation in a Flower War; all who should not go to war, or fail therein, were to be cast from the Pipiltin, regardless of birth or family connection. This decree was issued as *summum jus* under pain of sacrifice to the person who might disobey or contest it.[41] Of extreme significance, this law restricted future membership in the Pipiltin to those who would conform utterly to the system; no weaklings or deviationists were to be admitted. Those already possessed of status within the system were of necessity exempt, although from now on veteran warriors who went into battle and failed to bring home a captive were held in contempt and confined to their quarters for sixty days, during which time they were forbidden customary luxuries and forced to live in the manner of plebeians; they were not restored to their former positions until they had returned to war and taken a victim for Huitzilopochtli.

The compact entered into by the nobles proved effective; it fed the system and kept the ranks of the Pipiltin swollen with properly hardened servants. Where propaganda was concerned, it proved to be one of Tlacaellel's most brilliant triumphs. On the occasion of every big state sacrifice, ruling Enemies-of-the-House were invited to attend. They were spirited across frontiers at night and brought into Tenochtitlán before daylight so that " . . . the brave Mexica will not guess that there is stealth and secret concord between the two [sides]." [42] On some occasions the hostile lords of Michoacán were persuaded to come, as were the rulers of unconquered cities and provinces. Lodged in secret chambers of the royal palace, they lounged in fabulous luxury behind a wall of security measures that would do credit to a modern state. At the sacrificial spectacular, which is what Tlacaellel really brought them in to see, they were dressed in Mexican garb—a new outfit for every occasion—and seated in special spectators' boxes that were covered with lattice work and thousands of roses; the screening was perfect in that they could see without being seen. The box seats were large and roomy, almost effeminate with their fancy hangings and floral designs; the floors were strewn with aromatic sedge root that, with the roses, tended to disguise the odor of blood and death that pervaded the place. From their boxes the distinguished visitors

observed while the kings of the Triple Alliance rewarded the out-
standing heroes of the latest Flower War; shield, weapon, and insignia
were bestowed individually, then a crier droned their newly won
privileges: they might attend royal banquets and dances in the palace;
they could wear fine cottons and sandals, drink cacao, smoke tobacco,
eat human flesh; they might drink intoxicants and have as many
women as they chose; they were exempted from all taxes, tributes, and
service dues. Then came the sacrificial games, with all the color of the
Roman coliseum; the Temalacatl and Sun Stone became drenched in
blood.

> And when one showed himself strong, not acting like a woman, he
> went with a man's fortitude; he bore himself like a man; he went
> speaking in manly fashion; he went exerting himself; he went strong
> of heart and shouting, not without courage nor stumbling, but
> honoring and praising his city. He went with firm heart, speaking as
> he went: "Already, here I come! You will speak of me then in my
> home land." And so they were brought up [the pyramid temple
> steps] before [the sanctuary of] Utzilopochtli. Thereupon they
> stretched them, one at a time, down on the sacrificial stone; then
> they delivered them into the hands of six priests, who threw them
> upon their backs and cut open their breasts with a wide-bladed knife.
> And they named the hearts of the captives "precious eagle-cactus
> fruit."

There was no need for anyone to spread the word in the victim's
homeland; his rulers were watching from behind the rose screen,
relaxed and sampling dainties in enjoyment of the spectacle.[43]

After the show, the visitors were ushered back to the palace where
they attended a gay dancing party; attendants, carefully drilled in
their duties, lowered the lights each time one of them took the floor,
raising them again when he disappeared into the shadowed sidelines.
If the party was given by some lord in celebration of his son's victory
in war, which was very likely, the guests were treated to a special dish

prepared from the captive's flesh cooked with squash. The last day of the visit was usually spent in nibbling sacred green mushrooms and playing at orgy. With nightfall, the sated guests were secretly transported out of the city and deposited behind their own frontiers, laden with gifts from Tlacaellel and the king. As explained by one of Durán's sources, this extraordinary procedure was necessary "to avoid suspicion by the commoners, the soldiers, and captains that their king and lords were fraternizing and making friends [with the enemy] at the cost of their lives and the spilling of their blood." [44]

Refinements in organization of the Pipiltin and their social and political systems failed to alleviate an economic problem that was gradually assuming threatening proportions. In spite of imperial expansion, the Pipiltin, through fondness for latifundia, were engrossing more land than the domestic economy could tolerate. The calpultin, still serving as the fundamental agency of land administration for the macehualtin, were finding it impossible to satisfy both the spiraling demands of the lords and the needs of the plebeians. In spite of occasional crop failures and subsequent famine, the central plateau was experiencing one of its periodic population explosions, the most striking evidence of which was the unheard-of volume of human sacrifice that could have been supported under no other condition than one of surplus. For the first time in Mexican history, there were substantial numbers of freemen who had no land, a problem that was to defy the Mexica, survive the Spanish conquest, and persist to the present day. When a landless freeman entered a noble's lands as a rentero, or simple tenant, he lost the identity and protection of the calpulli; it was only a question of time until he and his family became mayeques. The whole trend of imperial development was inimical to the old standard of equity as it was upheld by the calpultin, or so it must have seemed to the macehualtin.

The land problem was considered by the Pipiltin as a matter of surplus population, rather than one of uneconomical distribution; the lords had no intention of halting their quest for landed property, nor did they feel inclined to deny the voracious appetites of the bureaucracy and the clergy. The problem consequently grew more acute with the passing of time. Opportunity for solution consonant with the aims of the Pipiltin came early in the reign of youthful King Axayacatl,* who succeeded Montezuma in 1469.[45] Leading forays into Xiquipila, Oquila, and Malinalco, he proved his mettle to the satisfaction of his peers and provided abundant victims for a spectacular coronation fete. For some time Tlacaellel and his imperialist companions had been casting about for a suitable region for conquest. The Pipiltin and the system were in need of more prime agricultural land, and surplus plebeians had to be located. The valley of Matlatzinco, better known by its post-conquest name of Toluca, loomed as the logical answer to the problem. Forming the western flank of the valley of Mexico, Toluca was the upper arm of the Lerma River basin; it was extremely fertile, one of the most important agricultural zones of the plateau. But the people who lived there were fearsome enemies, as were their immediate neighbors the Tarascans of Michoacán. Yet, it was in this direction that the empire must now expand.

A kindly fate intervened, giving the Mexica the opening they required. In the course of dynastic struggle King Chimal, seeing his throne lost to a hated rival, fled the valley and went to Tenochtitlán in search of aid. At first, the Mexica refused to believe him sincere; but once convinced, they turned and gave Chimal what we would today call a thorough brainwashing. Three years later—in 1472—he guided Axayacatl and a huge imperial army into Toluca; there ensued a ferocious fight with Axayacatl coming off the winner, although he walked with a limp for the rest of his life. In flight before the slaughter, the Matlatzinca took refuge behind Tarascan frontiers, leaving the entire valley depopulated. Toluca was divided between

* Ash-a-ya-katl.

44

conquering lords and the imperial state. Chimal was set up as titular lord of the valley behind the protection of a powerful garrison. Aside from the large grants of land given to the leading nobles, each captain received a smaller piece, so that the valley now had absentee lords whose properties were administered by *calpixques*, or "overseers," and resident lesser lords, some of whom remained in military command. Commoners were shipped in from cities and towns of the Triple Alliance as mayeques and tenants. Fruits of the land were divided equally between the new lords and the state, produce being stored in hastily constructed granaries for periodic shipment to the capital.[46] For the time being, the Pipiltin's land hunger had been appeased.

The conquest of Toluca having succeeded so brilliantly, it was probably now that Tlacaellel began to consider invasion of Michoacán, a venture filled with challenge and great risk, but one offering raptured contemplation for the general. But his reveries were rudely shattered by sudden appearance of imminent peril from a most unexpected quarter: conspirators in Tlatelolco were plotting to usurp the center of imperial authority. From the time that Tlatelolco was founded in 1337, there had been arguments and periods of strained relations between the Tenochca and Tlatelolca, especially in political affairs. The Tlatelolca remained aloof and named their own supreme lords, if not their own king, and steadfastly refused to recognize the suzerainty of Tenochcan majesty. More pointedly, they organized their own Huitzilopochtli cult and erected a temple every bit as sumptuous as that maintained by the Tenochca. Every time the central temple was enlarged or enriched they did likewise, measure for measure. To the growing embarrassment of the Tenochca, who considered themselves the very heart of the Mexican empire, there were in reality two central temples and two distinct Huitzilopochtlis. Moreover, the Tlatelolca maintained independent military forces and jealously guarded their overlordship of wealthy and important towns. Over the years, their commercial networks had given them vast

45

wealth, so that now they were a power to be feared. The military lords of Tenochtitlán must sometimes have wondered where the Tlatelolca would draw the line, or if they would have to be stopped.

They got their answer in 1473. The time seemed auspicious: Tlacaellel was now seventy-five years old and apparently failing in health; he might even be dying. Axayacatl was young and inexperienced; more importantly, he and the flower of Tenochcan military forces were in Toluca mopping up after the recent conquest and were strategically committed in respect to possible conflict with Michoacán. They could not withdraw without risking loss of the entire western flank. Without warning, Moquiuix,* the titular lord of Tlatelolco, declared himself sovereign in the name of Huitzilopochtli. In haste, he sent ambassadors to the capitals of the Enemies-of-the-House in search of alliance against the Tenochca. His arguments were concise: he accused the Tenochca of waging perpetual war as a means to keep their sacrificial slabs and cooking pots filled at the expense of the so-called Enemies-of-the-House. But there was a way out: let the Enemies join with Tlatelolco in military alliance, for only by this means could they escape their ultimate fate. The lords of Tlaxcala and the others doubtless listened carefully, for this was no trifling matter. While they were probably growing weary of watching the immolation of their young men as part of a political gesture intended to intimidate them and of being bribed with their own tribute, they were also wary of a trap. They could recall the "war" between Tenochtitlán and Texcoco, even the firing of the temple, which had been faked; they understood the duplicity and deceit of diplomacy; but most of all they suspected and feared the wolfish cunning of the general. And so most of the lords politely refused the offer and sat back to watch the result. Apprised of diplomatic failure, Moquiuix conscripted every male twenty years of age and over and put into motion a prearranged

* Mōk-wee-weesh.

46

strategy, the kernel of which was a surprise assault to be carried out under cover of night. Perhaps through the general's intelligence, or even Moquiuix's wife, who was Axayacatl's sister, the planned attack was leaked to Tlacaellel, who promptly arranged an ambush for the attackers. They were massacred. At this point Tlacaellel, having recalled King Axayacatl in haste, offered amnesty to the plotters in return for subjection, unmistakably revealing how weak the Tenochcan position was at this moment. He was in fear that intestine conflict would invite rebellion in the provinces; it could very well tip the balance of Tarascan judgment, sending powerful Michoacán into the fray, a course already being urged by the Matlatzinca. Seeing the strength of his position—perhaps even deceived by it—Moquiuix peremptorily refused the terms of amnesty and reaffirmed his claim to sovereignty by swearing that he would sacrifice Axayacatl to Huitzilopochtli. Upon Axayacatl's return a major engagement was joined along the border, both sides effecting the most wanton cruelty and rapine. The chronicles say that the waters of the lake were stained red with blood. Gradually, the Tlatelolca were forced to give ground until, in a last stand, they were pushed into the courtyard of the great temple. Once the Tenochca had stormed the walls, it was all over but for the coup de grâce. Moquiuix fled to the top of Huitzilopochtli's pyramid, hotly pursued by Axayacatl; at the summit they closed in desperate struggle, king against king. Those below could not see the duel as it was fought, but suddenly a body was hurled from the temple's platform; tumbling crazily as it caromed off the descending ledges, it sprawled in a lifeless heap at the base. It was Moquiuix.

As soon as surviving conspirators had been rounded up and executed, the final reckoning was drawn: Tlatelolco must pay all the tributes of a conquered people, including the usual levy of sacrificial victims to be paid every eighty days. The Tlatelolca were to lose all privileges within the empire and must henceforth demean themselves by carrying Tenochca baggage on military campaigns and providing the royal household with menial service. Since they did not have extensive land holdings, most of their wealth residing in commerce, their famous market place was cut into portions and doled out to the victorious lords, who now began to collect a 20 per cent sales tax on every transaction within a given area of possession. Tlatelolco had to take down and surrender its image of Huitzilopochtli, and was forbidden to have another; the temple was ordered heaped with garbage and excrement and declared to be a public latrine forthwith. The city was to be ruled by the *Tlacochcalcatl*, Tenochca's Prince-of-the-House.[47]

The Pipiltin had risen to their second great challenge and carried the day; there was to be no further threat to their system or to Huitzilopochtli's dominium until the arrival of Hernando Cortés and his lusty *condottieri* with their image of the Virgin Mary bearing the Christ Child in her arms.

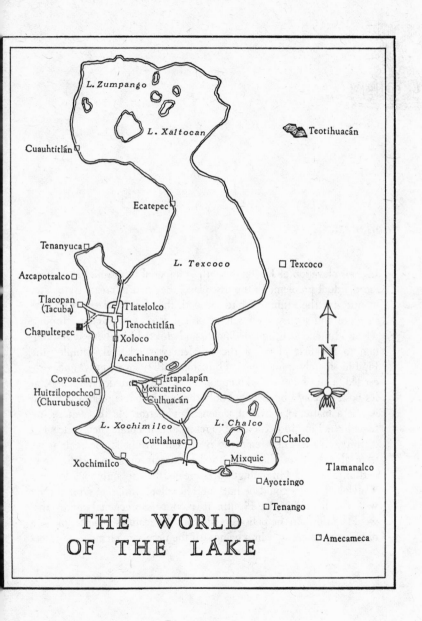

L. Zumpango

L. Xaltocan

Teotihuacán

Cuauhtitlán

Ecatepec

Tenanyuca

L. Texcoco

Texcoco

Azcapotzalco

Tlacopan
(Tacuba)

Tlatelolco

Chapultepec

Tenochtitlán

Xoloco

Acachinango

Coyoacán

Iztapalapán

Mexicatzinco

Huitzilopochco
(Churubusco)

Culhuacán

L. Xochimilco

L. Chalco

Chalco

Cuitlahuac

Mixquic

Tlamanalco

Xochimilco

Ayotzingo

Tenango

N

Amecameca

THE WORLD
OF THE LÁKE

Chapter III

Mythogenesis

In their elevation of Huitzilopochtli as imperial factotum, the Mexica faced a dual problem. In the first place, they had to create status and identity for the Hummingbird. Second, they felt it necessary to substantiate and justify their self-appointed role as the agents through whom Huitzilopochtli made known and effected his divine will. Solution to the first phase of the problem was relatively simple: the Pipiltin merely proclaimed Huitzilopochtli's sovereignty and proceeded to annihilate all who opposed it. Once asserted, Huitzilopochtli's position could be disputed only through recourse to armed might; it was a matter of physical violence and terror. As the empire unfolded, the Pipiltin needed but to refine and elaborate their concept of divinity, all the while removing rivals, both symbolic and real; as we have already seen, this went to the extreme of a competitor from within, a second Hummingbird as created by the ambitious lords of Tlatelolco. There could be but one Huitzilopochtli, one symbol. Nor was it difficult for the Pipiltin to produce cosmogonal myths that would conform to the political and economic realities which formation of the empire brought into being. All the necessary elements lay close at hand in the Toltec heritage; the mythologians needed but to reach and select. This is how Coatlicue, the widely venerated earth goddess, older by centuries than the Mexica, was chosen to be Huitzilopochtli's mother. As the story came to be told, Coatlicue was one day performing her daily task of sweeping the patio of the temple when a ball of feathers floated down from the sky. She caught it and thrust it into her bosom, thinking to remove it when she finished her sweeping. But look as she might, the feathers were not to be found; and from that moment on, she was pregnant. Her many children, all living in this same sierra of Coatepec, were publicly shamed and embarrassed over her condition, for it was obvious that she had secretly sinned. In righteous wrath they determined to slay her. Led by the eldest daughter, they closed in for the kill; but at that moment, Huitzilopochtli leaped fully armed from her womb and slew his brothers and sisters. From that moment on, he was taken for a god who was born of woman without man.[1] More to the point, and certainly more persuasive, was the forced association of Huitzilopochtli and human sacrifice with ancient sun cult, the whole garishly adorned with pageantry and symbol. Beneath the disguise, however, human sacrifice was the instrument that gave substance to the Mexican system of rule by terror. As the system matured, people were induced to fear rather than belief, so that the decision of whether to accept the Hummingbird or to deny him ultimately implied a political rather than religious choice. That is why the question of Huitzilopochtli's sovereignty was invariably decided with reference to physical force and violence.

The second part of the problem, that of substantiating Mexican possession of Huitzilopochtli's mandate, was not so easily solved. Terror backed up by force can make people say and do things, but it cannot compel them to believe. And like all totalitarians in their beardless youth, the Pipiltin suffered a morbid compulsion to be believed by those whom they deceived. Simple resignation to the Hummingbird's supremacy was to them unpalatable victory; even as they applied brute force, they longed for acceptance and affirmation. Now the successor states, over whom the Pipiltin were rapidly extending mastery, always had a deep historical imagination; from the days of Teotihuacán there had existed a strong attachment with the past. As newly risen conquerors, the Mexica, more than anyone else on the lake, needed a proper background. Did their own people really believe in the Pipiltin as having divine blood and exercise of Huitzilopochtli's mandate? Would the macehualtin follow them if terror and force were relaxed? How, indeed, could the Pipiltin convince Culhuacán and Texcoco, whose knowledge of the past was unrivaled, of their historical right to rule? They obviously had to have a history to prove it. Sovereignty in the lake world of the central plateau invariably sought its identity in the past.

Histories there were in abundance. Texcoco had a vast archive filled with codices, maps, and genealogical records, most of which were to be tragically destroyed when Cortés' Tlaxcalans burned the archive in exuberance over the conquest of Tenochtitlán that was in progress. Culhuacán may also have had substantial historical wealth, although it is likely that its official archives were sacked and burned following defeat by Atzcapotzalco in 1348. But at the time under discussion, both Texcoco and Culhuacán cultivated an extensive knowledge of the past. As we have seen, the Mexica were illiterate when they entered the lake community, although they quickly learned the art of glyphs and began to record the present in which they lived. They also tried to recapture their past, as far as it could be recalled. The *Mapa de Sigüenza,* if its original is correctly dated at about 1300, may well be a typical attempt. If so, it would be representative of the very few Mexican documents of the preimperial period that survived. The Mexica doubtless produced many accounts of their origins during the years prior to establishment of the empire, but none have come down to us, largely, as shall be explained, because the Mexica themselves destroyed them.

52

Fortunately for the curious of later centuries, Spanish colonial administrators early recognized the need for a comprehensive history of the Indians; and so in 1533 commissioned a Franciscan friar, Andrés de Olmos, to prepare such a work. Fluent in many Indian languages and dialects and the most accomplished Nahuatl scholar of his day, Olmos was possessed of a brilliant intellect that he now brought to bear on the task at hand. Through patient and diligent research he compiled voluminous manuscript sources from Mexico-Tenochtitlán, Texcoco, Tlaxcala, Huexotzinco, Cholula, Tepeaca, Tlalmanalco, and other unidentified towns. This may well have been the most comprehensive collection of such sources ever made. With the aid of Indian *sabios*, "learned elders," he interpreted the glyphs, accumulating a vast amount of data. In order to solve contradictions and add depth to his sources, he employed what is now considered to be the modern technique of interviewing informants who have been selected on critical bases. Using comparative techniques, Olmos combined his data to draw a synthesis of the Mexican past up to the advent of the Spanish invasion. The finished opus—perhaps the equal of Sahagún's work—has long since been lost to us, a tragedy mitigated in part by the fact that it was extensively used and in some areas quoted by Gerónimo de Mendieta in his classic *Historia eclesiástica indiana*.[2]

A fellow Franciscan, Bernardino de Sahagún, following hard on Olmos' heels began to research his own *Historia* about 1540. In Tepepulco, a large dependency of Texcoco, he began to collect and study native manuscripts. Aided by a dozen or so informed elders and four Indian research assistants who had been trained at the Franciscan Indian College of Santa Cruz, he spent two years exhausting Texcocan sources. From Texcoco he moved with his assistants to the college in Tlatelolco, where the same investigative procedure, including personal interview and critical appraisal of sources, was carried on. On the basis of sources studied at Tlatelolco, the work completed in

53

Texcoco was further criticized and revised. At the central Franciscan convent of the capital, known everywhere as El Grande, Sahagún spent three more years in organizing and writing his first draft, which, after further critical review by Indian scholars, was set down in Nahuatl. This work represented the widest synthesis yet drawn of preimperial history.[3] A third source for study of the early Mexica is afforded by the Texcocan historian Fernando de Alva Ixtlilxochitl, who enjoyed access to innumerable sources now lost.[4]

The works of these few scholars, then, represent the only known histories of the early Mexica that were drawn from manuscript sources that can be dated *prior* to establishment of the Mexican empire. They have certain revealing features in common: they all describe the Mexica as the last of the barbarian "squadrons" to come down out of the north, wandering aimlessly without definite destination. They had a totemic deity that talked to them, presumably giving advice, as did most tribes moving southward.[5] They arrived in the lake world and stopped in Chapultepec, thence to captivity in Culhuacán, finally taking up residence in the wetlands of the lake. They appear to have chosen the swamp because there was no other place for them to go. Seeing the nest of a red-tailed hawk and its abundance of bones and wildfowl feathers—the lake being situated on one of the great continental waterfowl flyways—they calculated the abundance of game and saw a likelihood of trade in furs, feathers, and fish. The natural defensive features of the swamp were also to be counted; and so they settled there. It was from such humble beginnings that they rose to power. Such is the picture given by these historians, one in which there is nothing to distinguish the Mexica. More significantly, not only is the famous promise of the Hummingbird lacking, but none of the three even mentions the name of Huitzilopochtli.

That is probably why Itzcoatl and Tlacaellel, having declared Huitzilopochtli to be sovereign of the world and the Mexica his enforcers, thereupon ordered the writing of a new interpretation of the Mexican past. The royal historian, Cuauhcoatl, was placed in charge of the project. Sedulous canvass of repositories turned up most of the earlier manuscripts, which were now reinterpreted in the light of imperial necessity. A new official state history was then drawn and widely disseminated. Older histories and manuscript sources, having served their purpose, were carefully gathered and burned, forever closing the door on a too-humble past.[6] A few escaped the flames, however, one of them being used by Ixtlilxochitl, who tells us that his history of the Mexica is based upon "an ancient history of this land, the original of which I have in my possession." [7] It ended abruptly during the reign of Itzcoatl. The burning of old histories and their sources was to become a constant of imperial policy; every time a temple was destroyed as the mark of submission, its archives were set aflame, presumably so that history might begin anew under the sovereignty of Huitzilopochtli.

We have no pure copy of the official history, but it was closely followed by the compiler of the *Códice Ramírez*, who refers to it in his text. It was also extensively employed by the compilers of the *Anales de Tlatelolco* and the *Códice Azcatitlán*. Olmos and Sahagún doubtless read it; but I believe that their critical method of research and analysis clearly indicated its true nature, and for this reason it was probably rejected by both of them. Subsequent writers, less critical in method and further removed in point of time, made wide use of the official history, and it became one of the major post-conquest sources for the pre-Columbian past. The works of Juan de Tovar, Tezozomoc, Durán, and Acosta afford prime examples of its use. But they are not alone. Nearly every secondary reconstruction by modern scholars is distorted to the extent that its author relied on the veracity of the official history as reflected in the *Códice Ramírez* and other works primarily based upon it. So striking is the interpretation of the official history that Radin considered the *Códice Ramírez* to be "a political pamphlet written in the interests of Mexico-Tenochtitlán." [8] Alfredo

Chavero, one of the first to make a critical appraisal of the *Códice Ramírez,* also concluded that it was a pointedly Mexican interpretation of history.[9] But neither realized that he was seeing nothing more than a projection of the official history.[10]

When the royal historian and his assistants searched through the old histories, they encountered a congeries of myths and legends, some representing the earliest Toltec racial memories, a dreamworld past. One persistent legend told that all the tribes moved together under the guidance of a single deity who was omniscient. Landing near what is today Tampico from a veiled limbo in the direction of Florida, they wandered the gulf coast south to Guatemala, where they went inland to a place called Tamoanchan. After many years had passed, their god took notion to leave them and through his priests made the following farewell:

> Our Lord goeth bequeathing you this land; it is your merit, your lot. He goeth, he goeth back, but he will come, he will come to do his duty, he will come to acknowledge you. When the world is become oppressed, when it is the end of the world, at the time of its ending, he will come to bring it to an end. But [until then] you shall dwell here; you shall stand guard here. That which lieth here, that which spreadeth germinating, that which resteth in the earth, is your merit, your gift. He maketh it your birthright. For this you followed him here. . . .[11]

After their god had departed, the Tolteca, still living as a single tribe, moved north and settled in Teotihuacán where they built the great temples of the Sun and Moon. Later, the legend continues, they went to Aztlán where the tribes split up, each one following the others in migration to the lake world of the central plateau; the Mexica were the last to leave.

It seems apparent that the court historian selected certain elements of this legend for reinterpretation: the deity is reduced in scope, becom-

the problem to them. "Oh Lord, Oh King, let them go to the nearby hills of Tizapán," was their response. "Very well, let them go thither. They are notorious rogues; perhaps they shall be eaten by the serpents that infest the place." [14] Upon arrival the Mexica found that the neighborhood did indeed swarm with snakes, of which they were terrified until Huitzilopochtli came to their aid with the practical advice to devour them. Shortly thereafter, a few strolling lords of Culhuacán passed by to see what had happened to the Mexica; they were chagrined to find the last of the snakes in their cooking pots.

The Culhuaque hastened home to report to the king: the Mexica were thriving and had built a temple for their god. Now the great lords decided that it was time to pay their respects; after examining Huitzilopochtli's temple carefully, they climbed up on the altar and evacuated themselves, and then left without a word. Undismayed, the Mexica went to see the king, requesting permission to seek small game on his lands for sacrifice to their god. Coxcoxtli gave his approval and suggested they go in the direction of Xochimilco. Meanwhile, he sent swift runners to warn the Xochimilca of pending attack by the Mexica. His strategy worked perfectly, and they became embroiled in a savage fight. But contrary to expectation, the Mexica won it and came away with scores of prisoners whom they now planned to sacrifice. As though to set precedent, the official historian had the Mexica invite the lords of Culhuacán to witness the sacrifice. They haughtily refused, but King Coxcoxtli couldn't resist the opportunity to see what the Mexica were up to. He arrived just in time to see the bloody immolation of the Xochimilca on the Hummingbird's altar. At the height of the sacrifice, the sky suddenly darkened and thunder began to roll in swirling heavens; suddenly a great eagle flew down and perched on the temple roof. King Coxcoxtli returned home in deep thought. Apprehensive of what he had seen, he called his lords in council: "I have told you before that these people are highly favored by their god and that they are evil and cunning in their designs; leave them alone and do them no harm, that unprovoked they might remain quiet." [15]

The Mexica now began to prosper in the hills of Tizapán; but as in Tula, Huitzilopochtli did not want them to become softened as a result of easy living, for then they would be unfit to withstand the hardships and suffering that creation of the empire would demand. One night he appeared and spoke at length to one of his priests:

> We must find a woman who shall be called the woman-of-discord, and she is to be known as "my grandmother" in the place where we shall finally reside, for this is not the place where we are to make our home.[16] The place I have promised you is farther on, and it is necessary that our excuse for leaving be made on account of war and death. Thus we must raise our weapons and give the world to understand the worth of our people. Begin, then, to gird your loins against our enemies and seek the reason whereby we may leave this place. It shall be thus: go to the King of Culhuacán and ask him to give you his daughter for my service. He will give her to you, and she is to be the woman-of-discord, as you shall see.[17]

Since Huitzilopochtli, in full control of the drama, left him no choice, King Coxcoxtli agreed to the request and was pleased that his daughter was to be deified and made queen, or so he was led to believe. Now the Hummingbird returned to his priest:

> I told you that this woman would be the cause of discord between you and the Culhuacanos. In order to bring this about, kill the girl and sacrifice her in my name, and from this day on I will accept her as my grandmother. After she is dead, flay her and have one of your youths dress himself in her skin, and over the skin put on the girl's dresses. Then invite the king, her father, to come and worship the goddess, his daughter, and to offer her sacrifices.[18]

Huitzilopochtli's instructions were followed to the letter, and even as King Coxcoxtli and his lords traveled the hot and dusty road to Tizapán his daughter was sacrificed and flayed. While the king rested and refreshed himself, a youth wearing his daughter's skin was taken to the temple and seated beside Huitzilopochtli. On Coxcoxtli's approaching the temple, he was met by the high priest. "If my lord be pleased, he may enter and see our god and goddess, his daughter, and do them reverence by making his offerings." The inner temple was a windowless chamber whose semidarkness was made black by the king's entrance from the bright light of noon. He called out his daughter's name, but got no response. Fumbling, he twisted the head from a quail and sprinkled its blood on the dimly perceived altar before the idols; he layed out gifts and flowers; now his eyes could see well enough to grasp a brazier filled with coals; he cast into it a fistful of copal incense that momentarily flared in livid flame. In that flash he saw the skin-draped figure and recognized his daughter's eyeless face: dropping the brazier, his hands clutching his face, he fled screaming from the temple. His peers returned with large forces and drove the Mexica to the lakeshore and into the swamp.[19]

Finding themselves deep within the fastness of their watery refuge, the Mexica stumbled upon a marvelous spring that was bordered by pure white willows; they saw a white frog and a white snake. What was this omen? Aztlán itself was the "white place," "land of the great white heron." What did this mean? All doubts were dispelled when Huitzilopochtli came to a priest in a nocturnal vision:

> Now you shall be satisfied that I have told you nothing that has not turned out to be true, and you shall see and know the things that I promised you come to pass in this place where I have brought you. But wait, for there is even more for you to see. You will recall how I ordered you to kill Copil, son of the witch who was said to be my sister, and to tear his heart out and throw it into the reeds of this lagoon, which you did. Know, then, that the heart fell upon a rock and from it there grew a Tunal so large and beautiful that an eagle nested in it, and there resides, maintaining himself and feasting on the most exotic of birds; there he spreads his great and beautiful wings, enjoying the warmth of the sun and the freshness of morning.

Go there tomorrow and you shall find this handsome eagle on the Tunal and around it you will see a great quantity of green, blue, red, yellow, and white feathers of the elegant birds on which this eagle dines. To this place where you shall find the Tunal with the eagle above it I have given the name Tenuchtitlán.[20]

Early the following morning, the priest summoned his people and informed them of his audience with the Hummingbird. He recounted their past trials, pointing out the many boons granted by Huitzilopochtli. Bringing his tale up to the present, he continued:

In this place where the Tunal grows we shall find our happiness, our peace, our rest. Here the name of the Mexican nation is to be exalted and praised. From this place shall spread the fame of our powerful arm and the courage of our hearts, with which we are to conquer every nation and territory, subjugating from sea to sea the remotest provinces and cities. We shall be the lords of gold and silver, of jewels and precious stones, feathers, and rich mantles, and other things. In this place we are to reign as lords of all peoples, of their possessions, of their sons and daughters; they are to serve us and pay tribute. On this very spot is to be built the famous city which is to be Queen, the ruler of all others. Here shall we receive kings and lords; here shall they repair and submit, as to a supreme court. Therefore, my children, let us seek this place where the Tunal grows among the reeds and canebrakes in the fastness of this lagoon. Our god says that it shall be so, which is beyond any doubt because everything he has told us we have found to be true.[21]

Separating into small groups, they began the search. Those who returned to the white spring discovered that it had changed color; now the two rivulets that drained it were running red and blue. Excited by this new omen, they pressed the search, and not far away they spied the eagle stretching his wings and taking the warmth of the morning sun; he held a brilliantly plumed bird in his talons. Hesitating, they slowly approached and bowed to the eagle as to a divine being; the eagle bowed back. Now there was a spontaneous eruption of joyful weeping and shouting: "How can we deserve such good fortune? By whom are we made worthy of such grace, excellence, grandeur? We have seen that which we most longed to see; we have found that which we most desired to find. We have found our home, our city, thanks to the Lord of Creation and our god Huitzilopochtli." [2]

Under their first king, Acamapichtli, the Mexica flourished and prospered. According to Olmos, there were several earlier kings, but the official history avoids mention of them, probably because only with Acamapichtli does the myth of divine blood begin. Moreover, it is doubtful that the monarchy achieved an authentic identity before this time. At any rate the lords of Atzcapotzalco showed no concern until Acamapichtli was enthroned, at which time their king took positive measures:

> You have noticed, Atzcapotzalca, how the Mexica, after having occupied our lands have chosen for themselves a king. What are we to do about it? We overlooked the former injury, but we should not countenance the latter, for after we are dead and gone they might try to subjugate our sons and successors and thereby become our lords, to whom we [as a nation] would be tributaries and vassals. Given this beginning, it seems to me that little by little they will grow more arrogant and bold. In order to forestall this, we should go and command them to pay double tribute as a sign of submission and subjection.

The lords did so go and command, adding for good measure the stipulation that the Mexica must bring to Atzcapotzalco fully grown junipers and willows for transplanting, and must also construct on the lake's surface a planted field that could be floated about like a raft; in it were to be planted the vegetables most favored by Tepanec taste. In essence, the king was demanding immediate invention of the chinampa.

Acamapichtli and his lords were stunned and made fearful by the outrageous demands. But that night, as the official history relates,

63

Huitzilopochtli appeared to his priest: "I have seen the anguish of the Mexica and their tears; tell them to still their grief, for I will deliver them safely from their hardships. Let them pay the tribute and tell my son Acamapichtli to be of good cheer. Have them deliver the willows and junipers, and tell them to build the raft on the water, planting in it the fruits and vegetables that are ordered, for I will make the whole thing simple and easy." They followed instructions and made good the demands. True to his word, the Hummingbird showed them how to construct a chinampa, at which the king of Atzcapotzalco and his courtiers were aghast. Filled with consternation, their king remarked, "My brothers, this feat appears to me superhuman; when I ordered it done I thought it to be impossible. In order for you to be assured that I was not mistaken about these people, summon the Mexica here that you may of your own experience understand that they are favored by their god and because of this are destined to rule all nations." The Mexica obediently appeared at court, where the king ordered them to produce yet another chinampa like the first one, except that it must also contain heron and duck eggs that were to hatch precisely at the moment of delivery. This command was given under pain of death for failure, and the Mexica were again terrified. But as before, Huitzilopochtli flew to the rescue, appearing to his priest:

> My father, be not afraid and do not be intimidated by their threats. Tell my son, the king, that I know what needs to be done; leave everything to me. Tell the king to do everything they command, for all these things are to be paid for with the lives and blood of his enemies . . . who shall either be dead or his captives before many years have passed. Therefore, let my sons suffer and bear [these humiliations] for the present. The day of reckoning is not far off.

As previously, Huitzilopochtli provided everything, including the eggs that hatched on schedule.[33] The lords of Atzcapotzalco now grew cold with fear.

In its extensive treatment of the war against Atzcapotzalco, the official history makes no mention of the contributions of the allies, nor does it adequately acknowledge the part played by those beyond the innermost circle of ruling Pipiltin. Tlacaellel emerges in brilliant detail as the greatest of heroes. In spite of the fact that he was standing at the royal historian's elbow, his role was probably not greatly exaggerated. The macehualtin received small mention beyond explanation of how and why the plebeians lost their political and social privileges that had always existed under the old calpulli system of government. According to the official historian, the plebeians lost courage when war appeared inevitable. In full flush of cowardice they attempted to surrender themselves and Huitzilopochtli to the mercies of their Tepanec overlords. Tlacaellel it was who took prompt action and saved the day: striking a bargain with the plebeians, it was agreed that should the nobles lose the war, they would turn themselves over to the macehualtin to be slain and eaten. But if they won, then the plebeians were to pledge themselves to perpetual servitude. Of course, no such bargain could have been made. The commoners were not then or later permitted to eat human flesh, a privilege jealously guarded by the nobles. In the event of defeat, most of the nobles would have been slain or reduced to servitude and the plebeians with them, so that by no stretch of the imagination could the commoners have envisioned any kind of gain to themselves that would come by way of the alleged pact, no matter who won or lost.[24]

According to the official history, Huitzilopochtli does not speak, appear to anyone, or intervene in Mexican affairs after the accession of Itzcoatl and institutionalization of the Pipiltin. The past had caught up with the present, and the myth as interpretation of history had come to an end. The Hummingbird had been enthroned, and there was no further need.

The official history was unleashed as a potent piece of propaganda bearing a pointed message: the Mexica are invincible because they are backed by omnipotent deity. In human affairs nothing succeeds like success, and the overweening posture of the Mexica must have induced many to belief, especially among the masses. But to some the apologia must have appeared crassly ridiculous. Colonial researchers of a later day, like Sahagún and Ixtlilxochitl, pointedly refer to "the many fables and fictions that infest the history of the Mexica," and it appears likely that such judgments were guided by the non-Mexican sources and commentaries they were using.[25] As it turned out, there was sufficient contemporary criticism to force Tlacaellel and Montezuma into temporary retreat and search for substantiation of their mythology. They first made public claim that Huitzilopochtli's mother, Coatlicue, was still alive and residing in Aztlán. As might be expected, announcement of a formally organized expedition followed closely, one charged with the task of finding her. In the Sierra of Coatepec the searchers encountered a sorcerer who offered to aid them; he raised a demon who in turn wafted the expedition to Aztlán by means of visions. Somewhere beyond Tula, they visited and chatted with Coatlicue, who gave them a new robe and sash for her son. Returning to Coatepec as they had come, the searchers triumphantly entered Tenochtitlán and presented the robe to Montezuma and the general who, with studied aplomb, draped it over Huitzilopochtli's cold stone body and ordered up a fresh batch of victims for his slab.[26] Let the scoffers beware.

Chapter IV

"I am already king. . . ."

As Montezuma grew older and felt the great cold gathering about his bones, he leaned ever more heavily on Tlacaellel, who, though counting the same seventy-one years, seemed possessed of a boundless vitality. In imperial affairs the general was indeed the indispensable man, and in recognition of this fact Montezuma named him to be his successor. Early in 1467, just after approving plans for a new royal vacation palace to be built at Cuernavaca, Montezuma fell ill and, sensing the approach of death, ordered his image carved in the Gallery of the Kings at Chapultepec. The king's thoughts continued to dwell on morbid themes, in which he was joined by Tlacaellel who hovered over the royal litter like death itself. The general ordered his own figure to be cut beside Montezuma's, so that the two of them should be preserved together in the minds of posterity. The images were sculpted in the broad stone surface of a cliff that faced east, looking out over the lake almost directly at the capital from the Chapultepec park. The rising sun cast its rays directly upon their figures, done in high relief and vividly painted, to produce a dramatic and startling effect. As soon as the work had been completed, Montezuma and

68

Tlacaellel journeyed to see themselves memorialized in the living rock.[1] Not long thereafter Montezuma died, was cremated, and his ashes interred in the midst of vast pomp and ceremony.

The electors offered the throne to Tlacaellel, as ordained by Montezuma; but he declined, choosing in his stead Axayacatl, a younger son of the late king. As uncle to the king and vice-ruler in his own right, the general was already de facto monarch of the empire. Axayacatl proved to be an excellent choice. Although still in his teens, he slew with fury to the beaches of the Southern Sea, becoming the first king of the Mexica to measure his realm from sea to sea. His coronation fete was the most splendid yet staged; the Enemies-of-the-House were staggered by its scale of human slaughter.

There was considerable consolidating to be done following Montezuma's death; it thus became Axayacatl's immediate task to seize the choice agricultural districts of Chalco-Amecameca and convert them into an appanage of the imperial throne. He further consolidated control of the south by placing trusted allies in command of Tlalmanalco, Xochimilco, Tenanco, and Chimalhuacán.[2] With the south secured, Tlacaellel now felt safe in initiating the Tolucan campaign, which, as we have already seen, was carried to brilliant conclusion in 1472. Although maimed and exhausted by his victory, Axayacatl was forced to return to the capital and fight a civil war against Tlatelolco. Fortunately for him, the conquered provinces failed to realize how serious the rebellion was until it had been quelled; but even then, there were scattered uprisings in every quarter of the empire, each one forcing Axayacatl to the field once again.

Meanwhile, the general was planning his next imperial adventure, the conquest of Michoacán, of which the Tolucan campaign had been the opening maneuver.[3] The legions of the Triple Alliance stood in readiness; the general, effusing confidence, ordered a new and more splendid Sun Stone to be carved in time for sacrifice of the Tarascans of Michoacán. Axayacatl led the vanguard of the invading force, some

24,000 of the best imperial troops. Poised in Toluca, he hurled his spearhead at the enemy's frontier. It was met by 40,000 Tarascans who simply devoured the invading host. Axayacatl limped back to Tenochtitlán at the head of 200 survivors. Tlacaellel's reaction to defeat was stunned disbelief, then mortal embarrassment, for he had already commanded all imperial lords and the Enemies-of-the-House to witness his scheduled sacrifice of captured Tarascans on the new Sun Stone; it was much too late to call it off. The guests were already arriving in the usual manner, being spirited into the capital under cover of darkness and lodged in the royal palace. But in place of the promised Tarascans they saw their own people sacrificed, some 700 captives from the Flower Wars whom Tlacaellel had tucked away for just such an emergency. Axayacatl took his place beside Tlacaellel as executioner and, gripping the great blade, struggled through the carnage; but hardly had the rose-covered boxes emptied of spectators "when the king collapsed from the exhaustion of the sacrifice and the overpowering odor of blood which was, according to the history, a foul, acrid smell. . . ." [4] Axayacatl did not long survive; after a reign of but twelve years he died, a haggard veteran not yet thirty years of age. Tlacaellel's ambition had consumed him.

Axayacatl's younger brother, Tizoc, was chosen to succeed him. Again Tlacaellel leaned toward youth, apparently determined to have a king who could maintain the pace he demanded. Sources for Tizoc's reign are painfully scant, so that it is difficult to generalize. Even so, it appears that Tizoc proved to be a failure from the very beginning. When he attacked Meztitlán for his coronation haul, he suffered humiliating defeat, permitting more victims to escape than he brought home. Consequently, his public coronation was a rather dull affair. Thereafter, he failed to lead; apparently, it was only at Tlacaellel's insistence that he initiated construction of a new temple for Huitzilopochtli, the cornerstone of which was laid in 1483. [5] Tlacaellel and the presidium showed patience, but not without end. The sources suggest that the king was quietly poisoned in 1486. He received an enormous state funeral.[6]

Now the chronicles portray the ruling lords as being uneasy. Tlacaellel appeared determined to enthrone yet another youthful king, even though Axayacatl had buckled under the weight of the imperial crown, and Tizoc had had to be discharged. Ahuitzotl, a third son of Montezuma, was Tlacaellel's choice, but the lords of the presidium dared oppose him. Demanding that a seasoned veteran mount the throne, they insisted that Tlacaellel himself wear the imperial crown. Tlacaellel stood firm, and the lords began to give way: they would be willing to accept Ahuitzotl as "apprentice" ruler under the general's tutelage. Tlacaellel spoke gently but firmly, reminding them of his de facto rule since creation of the empire. "Calm yourselves, my sons, and do my bidding. I am already king, and king I shall be until I die." They submitted gracefully, and Ahuitzotl was crowned.[7]

Tlacaellel and the rulers of the Pipiltin were ever mindful of the Mexican image abroad. In view of Tizoc's disgraceful coronation, it was determined that Ahuitzotl's should be sufficiently spectacular to remove any doubts that might exist. While the king was in Chiapa securing an army of victims for the slaughter, quotas were laid on every community within the empire for a special tribute of goods and services under penalty of death for failure to comply. Every nerve was strained to produce a staggering display of opulence for the visiting lords and kings of enemy states. The quotas were filled and the coronation, with its grand blood bath, was an impressive success.[8]

The year following Ahuitzotl's coronation saw completion of Huitzilopochtli's new temple. Tlacaellel was now eighty-nine years old; it was twenty years ago that he and Montezuma had had themselves carved in stone at Chapultepec. During those years, he had seen three more kings occupy a throne that in reality he alone possessed. Twenty years! A new generation had come of age, one he could take pride in, for these Pipiltin had grown up under his hand, had risen within the system for which he bore such heavy responsibility. They were his people. In celebration of the opening of the Hummingbird's new temple they were to make 1487 a year never to be forgotten. The occasion was to be highlighted by a bloodletting of unprecedented magnitude; every lord in the empire was commanded to attend and bring sacrificial victims in numbers befitting his rank and station. As the lords filed into the capital, the Enemies-of-the-House, the rulers of Michoacán, Meztitlán, Yopitzinco, and other hostile provinces and states were secretly brought in under truce and lodged in the palace. Over 200 picked security guards formed a human wall behind which they retained anonymity. As for Ahuitzotl's coronation, special tributes had been levied for the fete with the result that tribute mounted in unbelievable volume before the eyes of the honored guests. The roads remained choked with traffic as the opening day approached; this was to be the greatest mass of humanity ever assembled in Tenochtitlán.[9]

The new pyramid was the one the Spaniards were to marvel over and, eventually, to destroy. It was indeed an imposing pile of stone, its five terraces, or stories, rising over 100 feet in the air; the platform on its summit was graced by twin chapels, the upper portions of which were handsomely carved in aromatic wood. Inside, the pyramid was a labyrinth, with countless apartments, rooms, and shrines, all connected by a maze of corridors. It was said that several thousand ecclesiastics dwelt within its polished halls. Huitzilopochtli's temple was the center of a vast complex of lesser temples and buildings, over seventy in all, the whole being enclosed by the famed *Coatepantli*, or "Serpent Wall." This was the seat of empire, with the Hummingbird's temple situated on the very spot where Copil's heart sprouted the cactus and where the Mexica first saw the eagle. Or so the guests were told.[10]

Well before daybreak of the opening day, legionnaires prepared the victims, who were put in close single file down the steps of the great pyramid, through the city, out over the causeways, and as far as the eye could see. For the average person viewing the spectacle from his roof top, it would appear that the victims stretched in lines to the ends of the earth.[11] The bulk of the unfortunates were from hostile provinces and the swollen ranks of slavery. On the pyramid's summit four slabs had been set up, one at the head of each staircase, for Tlacaellel and the three kings of the Triple Alliance, all of whom were to begin the affair as sacrificial priests. All was in readiness; the lines of victims were strung out for miles, with great reservoirs at their ends, thousands of trapped humans milling about like cattle, awaiting their turn in the line that was about to move. Suddenly, the brilliantly arrayed kings appeared on the platform and silence fell over the city. Together they approached Huitzilopochtli's chapel and made reverent obeisance. As they turned to join their aides at the four slabs, great snakeskin drums began to throb, announcing that the lines could now begin to move. The lambs were slaughtered with machine-like precision; as the knife wielders fell exhausted, they were replaced by fresh priests who lifted the heavy blade and let it fall in precise and measured stroke until their arms grew weary; others stepped in without losing a beat. A refinement of mass sacrificial technique was apparent; it took but seconds to dispatch each victim. Under such circumstances ceremonial and symbolic niceties were ignored. Rivulets of blood became bright red streams washing over darkening clots, like boulders in a stream; the freshets became rivers of blood, gradually breaking off huge clotted chunks and carrying them down stream as though in height of springtime flood. At the pyramid's base far below, priests wallowed and skidded about as they removed the bodies that tumbled down in ceaseless order. Others rescued hearts by the ton. Still others bailed up blood in jars and cups that were then carried by runners to the barrio temples where the faces of the idols were smeared and painted.

The holocaust went on unabated for four days and nights, with tens

73

of thousands perishing on the slabs. Most of the sources claim that over 80,000 were sacrificed during those incredible ninety-six hours.[12] It is impossible to be certain because accurate tallies were not kept. The stench grew so overpowering, the revulsion so general, that there was an exodus from the city.[13] When the full impact of what was happening hit the guests, the rose-covered boxes were deserted in haste, as were other seats of honor, the guests joining the plebeians and the mass of the Pipiltin in panic-stricken flight. According to some of the sources, Tlacaellel and his sturdier partisans stuck by their knives, and by the end of the ceremonial month it was estimated that they had butchered over 100,000 people in Huitzilopochtli's honor.[14]

Anything Tlacaellel did after this would of necessity be anticlimax, which may be why he seems to fade from the annals. He is seldom mentioned in the sources after this time. Even his death was anticlimax, coming in 1496 at the age of ninety-eight. Mourned by his eighty-three children, he was given the most sumptuous funeral in Mexican history.[15] Chimalpahin, dredging in sources now lost, came up with a succinct but eloquent epitaph:

> There were many great kings who inspired fear far and wide, but the one who was the most courageous, the most illustrious in the state, was the great captain, the great warrior Tlacaellel. . . . It was he also who established the worship of the devil Huitzilopochtli, the god of the Mexicans. . . .[16]

Chapter V

Montezuma II

When Ahuitzotl ascended the imperial throne in 1486, he had among his qualifications one not previously possessed by a Mexican monarch: Where predecessors had frequently worn the insignia of priesthhood during ceremonials, Ahuitzotl was in fact Huitzilopochtli's high priest when he was elected to the throne. This was one more evidence of the growing proximity between the Hummingbird's cult and the sovereignty of the state, between king and deity.[1] Not long after his coronation, Ahuitzotl took a significant step toward eventual merger. In the past there had always been clear distinction between Ometecutli, the Lord of the Dual Essence, and other deities, the former being the acknowledged author of the universe and its phenomena. But now in public prayer, which was also a form of political address, Ahuitzotl began to address Huitzilopochtli as "All powerful Lord of Creation, Lord by whom we live, whose vassals we are; Lord of Night and Day, Air and Water, with whose strength we sustain ourselves. . . ." Leading into a detailed narration of the official history, replete with red and blue flowing water, the eagle on the cactus where Copil's heart once lay, he concluded that ". . . this wondrous marvel, worked by thee alone [was intended] to teach us the greatness of thy power and of thy will to make us the Lords of that which we now possess. . . ." [2] For fifty years following the reign of Itzcoatl, the official history had been repeated over and over again in every Calmecac of the empire until the official past had become a part of the present, but with one change: the Hummingbird had been promoted.

Huitzilopochtli had also made substantial advances in his encroachment on other deities and their cult. When he toured the empire's temples early in his reign, Ahuitzotl made the same obeisance before other deities as he did before Huitzilopochtli, so generalized had state cult become. In Texcoco, Chalco, Iztapalapán, Mexicatzinco, and Huitzilopochco, which had been centers of Tezcatlipoca cult, Huitzilopochtli had taken over, wearing a "smoking" mirror in his feathered headdress, a similar neckpiece, and a breast jewel just like Tezcatlipoca's. And one of Tezcatlipoca's old fiestas, *Teotleco*, was now celebrated as Huitzilopochtli's birthday. The whole of Sahagún's *Libro* II gives detailed evidence of studied infiltration by the Hummingbird in ceremonials and fetes of other deities, whether by direct intrusion, through his priests being involved, his symbolism being employed, or his temple used. In defiance of logic and in absence of traditional relationships, one finds Huitzilopochtli everywhere in the ceremonial calendrical year.[3] Even in Cholula, a traditional locus of Quetzalcóatl cult, the Hummingbird was making inroads, assuming a part of his cult and position.[4] On the other hand, the *Tonalamatl*, or "Sacred Almanac," shows Quetzalcóatl under the war sign, holding a sacrificial victim with one hand and excrement, the symbol of sin, in the other; at the bottom is a basket of hearts supported by skulls.[5] Thus where Quetzalcóatl was not suppressed, he was forced into an image more compatible with Huitzilopochtli. This is why the priest who wielded the blade in human slaughter was given the title of Topiltzin, which was another name for Quetzalcóatl. In curiously Mexican fashion Quetzalcóatl, the welling spirit of humanity who

77

forbade human sacrifice, was made to become its agent. As religious consolidation progressed under Ahuitzotl's hand, Huitzilopochtli loomed ever larger on the scene, always the symbol of majesty and the power of the state.

With Tlacaellel's departure from the scene, Ahuitzotl became the first king to really savor the full flavor of imperial power. Since the Tarascan frontier had been closed as an outlet for domestic and imperial pressures, he unleashed fresh aggressions on less resistant fronts. But it seems doubtful that he could put Michoacán out of mind; it was a perpetual threat and source of danger. In view of this, Ahuitzotl determined to strengthen Tenochtitlán by supplementing its water supply. The springs at Huitzilopochco, today Churubusco, could be dammed and piped into the capital, thus providing an auxiliary supply to the source at Chapultepec. The lord of Coyoacán, who ruled the area as imperial deputy, cautioned the king against the plan lest he alienate the powerful lords of the district whose estates were dependent upon the springs. Ahuitzotl replied by sending assassins who strangled him to death for offering unsolicited advice. As ordered by the king, the springs were diverted to a basin behind a dam while an aqueduct was laid to the capital. By miscalculation, or perhaps by design, the water flow was too great and the southern part of Tenochtitlán was flooded. Dikes were immediately raised, but they eventually created sufficient back-pressure to push out the dam, causing a sudden tide that inundated a large part of the capital. Many were trapped and drowned, and there was panic and terror over what appeared to be an unexplainable rising of the lake. Ahuitzotl happened to be dallying in low-lying gardens when the water rose. Racing for his life, he struck his head on the lintel of a low doorway. Dragged to safety by servants, he was treated by his physicians who removed pieces of his shattered skull; lingering for a time, the king finally died, apparently from a subdural hematoma.[6]

Nezahualpilli,* the king of Texcoco, met with the king of Tacuba and the presidium to choose a successor. Even though Ahuitzotl's sudden demise had come in the seventeenth year of his reign, he was still a young and vigorous man and had therefore not yet indicated his preference for a successor. The leading candidate was Macuilmalin-altzin,† Axayacatl's eldest son and now the husband of Nezahualpilli's daughter. Popular with his peers and noted for chivalrous love of combat, he was the Hotspur of the imperial court. Nevertheless, his candidacy was strenuously opposed by a faction of the presidium that insisted the successor must be possessed of sacerdotal eminence. For their tastes, Macuilmalinaltzin was much too flamboyant in nature and bearing. With the electors disagreed over the candidate, there was no recourse but to look beyond him to a younger brother, Montezuma, who seemed to have every qualification. Respected for military leadership and courage displayed early in youth, he was now high priest in Huitzilopochtli's service. His gravity of bearing and wisdom were legendary; he seldom spoke, but when he did men listened because of his great clarity and sagacity of mind. Greatly revered as a holy man, Montezuma had his own private chamber in the labyrinthine depths of Huitzilopochtli's pyramid where it was rumored that he frequently communicated with the Hummingbird. He was also a philosopher of note, spending much time in plumbing the depths of Nahuatl poetry and philosophy. Probably from the beginning he was the candidate of those who favored the priesthood. The presidium was divided between contending factions, both seeking to fill the vacuum left by the death of Tlacaellel; one sought military supremacy, the other hegemony for the priestly caste. It was a fateful crossroads in evolution of the imperial system. Deadlock was broken by compromise, although it

* Netz-a-wal-pee-lee.
† Mac-weel-mal-eenalt-zeen.

was evident that the priests had bested the generals. Montezuma was chosen to rule and Macuilmalinaltzin was confirmed as his successor. As was customary, the electors went to tell the new king of his election and to convey him to the sacred brazier where he would privately take his oath of office. But they could not find Montezuma. Led by the vice-ruler, one of Tlacaellel's sons, they finally located him in the Black Room, as his private shrine was called. With his peers, Montezuma climbed to Huitzilopochtli's altar where he squatted and bled his ears and legs and accepted the burden of majesty. This day appears in the chronicles as *Toxcatl* 9, by Christian reckoning May 24, 1503. Through odd coincidence, this was the same day that his grandfather, Montezuma the Elder, had stood before the altar and taken the same oath sixty-three years earlier.[7]

Montezuma quit his speculative pose and again took up the implements of war. As Tlacaellel's tradition dictated, he could not be publicly crowned until he had gone into battle and emerged with an abundance of victims for Huitzilopochtli and a foot bath for himself in their blood. Leading an imperial force of 60,000 men, he attacked the provinces of Nopallán and Icpatepec, lately rumored to be rebellious. Taking 5,100 prisoners and leaving carnage in his wake, he began his triumphal march home. This was an imperial victory, since his forces were drawn from every quarter of the empire. No longer was it a Triple Alliance. On the way back to Tenochtitlán Montezuma began to test his ground. Ruling lords of provinces, rather than their young sons, were required to fetch his fingerbowls and perform the other menial tasks his service required. None but lords of the greatest families were permitted to approach his person. Such became the pattern in every provincial town. Returning at the head of a victorious army, its carriers heavily burdened with tribute and plunder, with thousands of captives in tow, he approached Tenochtitlán. Tens of thousands poured out over the causeways, as the chronicles tell us, "to receive and adore him almost like a god."

The ensuing coronation was by far the most elaborate yet staged. Distinguished guests included, besides the Enemies-of-the-House, the rulers of Michoacán, Meztitlán, Tliliuquitepec, the Huasteca and Yopitzinco. Everything was afforded in lavish measure; 1,000 *tamemes* were daily employed in carrying food and delicacies to the capital from all corners of the empire. On the fourth day Montezuma was crowned by the king of Texcoco, this duty remaining as his only imperial function, just as it was the king of Tacuba's to act as witness. The 5,100 prisoners were duly slain, whereupon the guests quit the crimson scene and repaired to the palace, where they abandoned themselves to sensual extravaganza. Montezuma did not join them because he was now too close to divinity. But he did arrange for the Enemies-of-the-House to visit Tenochtitlán on three festive occasions each year.[8]

Once enthroned, Montezuma openly prepared for his own deification. Where Ahuitzotl had merely edged closer by elevating Huitzilopochtli to a level with Ometecutli, then making the Hummingbird engulf and become the Lord of Creation, Montezuma now placed his own person on equal footing with deity, needing only to take the final step of becoming Huitzilopochtli. Plebeians had never been permitted to look upon Huitzilopochtli, nor, for that matter, had lesser nobles. The godhead was not for vulgar gaze. Now Montezuma proclaimed that any plebeian who dared look into his face should die; all commoners were to prostrate themselves at the sound of the conch shell trumpets that warned of his approach, and were to remain with their faces pressed into the earth until he had passed. Nor were nobles to look directly into his face; to meet his eyes was to die. Furthermore, his edict continued, any errors of protocol committed in the royal palace, any miscues or blunders of whatever category, were to be treated as though they had occurred in Huitzilopochtli's temple, for henceforth the imperial palace was to be called "the House of God." Therefore, death should be meted out to all offenders by reason of irreverence. Montezuma was god, and no mortal might err in his presence or temple and live to tell of it. His personal seal was now carved in the likeness of Huitzilopochtli. The proper words were set down and put into the mouths of his one-time peers:

> Although you are our friend and fellow, son and brother, we do not count ourselves as your equal; nor do we consider you to be a man, because you are now possessed of the person, appearance, the familiarity of our lord god, who speaks to us and teaches us through you; his mouth is your mouth; his tongue is your tongue; his face is your face; his ears are your ears. He endows you with authority and gives you fangs and claws, that you may be feared and held in utmost reverence.[9]

It was further claimed that Montezuma, like Huitzilopochtli, drew eternal life from the sacrifice of unfortunates who were dispatched under certain augural day signs.

There were some who early got the drift of this curious evolution and were found in opposition to it. The trend had begun with Ahuitzotl, who conducted himself in arbitrary fashion even before Tlacaellel had died. Many of his decisions were unpopular; and with distressing frequency, he ignored the presidium entirely, being guided by his own whims and fancy. His seizure of the springs at Huitzilopochco was a case in point. When he had the lord of Coyoacán killed, he alienated the king of Tacuba, a close relative of the slain lord, and the king of Texcoco, whose intimate he had been. In fear of the narrowing margin between king and deity many had opposed election of another high priest, especially one of Montezuma's stature. But the priestly caste had forced the issue and won. Now, with Montezuma's plans unfolding, there was cause for alarm. The lords had not missed the point when Tlacaellel's son, in direct violation of the code, was invested with all the general's titles and privileges merely because he was in line to inherit. And now, with Montezuma's approval, he took the title of *Tlilpotonqui Cihuacoatl,* which added a divine surname to his title of vice-ruler. And when the emperor's brother went to war, Montezuma gave him the device of a god for his shield.

Whatever his enemies might have thought about it, Montezuma's election victory was not merely the result of priestly conniving or persuasion. It marked the emergence of a new and formidable power structure within the imperial system. For generations kings and lords had endowed the church with landed properties, until it had become a vast feudatory, holding innumerable tenants and serfs and not a few lords as vassals of sorts. Each major temple also held varying numbers of towns as tributaries, the temple of Texcoco, for example, holding thirty, many of which were large population centers. All of this was in addition to the communal holdings, the *teotlalli,* that were worked by the capultin for the support of their local temples, so that in addition to regularly assigned communal contributions, the church claimed tributes and first fruits, received landed estates in endowment and other valuable gifts, and developed extensive agricultural holdings that it owned and operated outright. As Montezuma's election indicated, the priestly caste now controlled vast economic and political power.[10]

The question of Montezuma's election also reflected a rift in the Triple Alliance that seemed to be growing more serious with the passing of time. Although the ruling stratum of Texcoco had been more or less Mexicanized through intermarriage, there were still many powerful lords who resented Mexican hegemony and all that it implied. Especially humiliating was the fact that Texcoco was still required to send a regular levy of sacrificial victims to Tenochtitlán, and, like every other subject province, had been required to produce its quota in support of the massacre of 1487. Montezuma's brother Macuilmalinaltzin lived in Texcoco, aligning himself with his wife's kin rather than his own. Enjoying the intimate comradery of the Texcocan lords, he was their candidate by popular choice. As political currents began to polarize after Montezuma's coronation, Texcoco loomed as a center of anti-Montezuma sentiment.[11]

If the emperor was hated by many Texcocans, they in turn were despised by him. Many years ago, a young sister, Chachiunenetzin, had been given in marriage to Nezahualpilli by their father, Axayacatl, who sought to strengthen Mexican hold on the Texcocan throne. It was her duty to bear the successor. In respect to her extreme youth Nezahualpilli gave her a luxurious palace with a staff of 2,000 servants and time in which to mature. In spite of her tender years—she was scarcely in her teens—she already experienced the incessant demands of nymphomania. And so she had a parade of paramours brought to her chambers in secret session night after night. As though to prove the female the deadlier of the species, she had her lovers slain as soon as they had fulfiled their function; and then, in what may have been psychotic fancy, she had icons made of each one that she kept as morbid souvenirs of her secret trysts. Nezahualpilli, during occasional visits, noted that the palace was becoming filled with statuary. It happened that one inamorato so delighted her that she could not bear to have him slain. This proved to be a mistake, although it seems doubtful that her secret could have kept indefinitely. In bestowing gifts on her Lothario, she erred in giving him a jewel that the king distinctly remembered having given to her. Meanwhile, she had discovered two other talented courtiers and was now closeting herself with all three in regular orgiastic revel. Goaded by suspicion, Nezahualpilli himself investigated his young queen's secret life and succeeded in catching her in the act of adultery. She and her paramours were jailed and the household staff, over 2,000, strong, was held as accessory to the deception. Going over Axayacatl's head, Nezahualpilli notified all cities within the empire of the pending trial and even invited the Enemies-of-the-House to attend. The city of Texcoco swarmed like an anthill on the day of trial. The queen and her lovers were found guilty and thereupon garroted and burned in full public gaze. The household servants were likewise slain for their complicity and buried in a common grave.[12] Neither Axayacatl nor his sons could do anything but bite their lips and hate, for Chachiuhnenetzin had flagrantly violated tradition and law.

Montezuma's overt bid for deification set the wheels of opposition in rapid motion. His enemies no longer had reason to doubt their most exaggerated suspicions when the emperor himself gave them substance. The lines were clearly drawn, with Texcocan lords leading in contention as they rallied around Macuilmalinaltzin. Montezuma understood perfectly: his own assassination would put his brother on the throne, since he already had undisputed right of succession. Keeping a vigilant eye on Texcoco, Montezuma sent messengers to Huexotzinco and prepared to deal with his foes. In routine manner the Flower War against Huexotzinco was announced, with Texcoco getting the call to lead the defense of imperial honor. When Macuilmalinaltzin and his Texcocans reached the plain of Atlixco where the contest was to be joined, they were set upon by superior enemy forces. Contrary to traditional form wherein small squadrons sought to capture their opponents, the Enemies-of-the-House attacked en masse with intent to kill. Where the battlefield of the Flower Wars was ordinarily dry, this day the bosom of the earth was drenched in blood. Macuilmalinaltzin, his two brothers, and 2,800 lords were slain, most of them Texcocans. Nezahualpilli made bitter accusations, and Montezuma's treachery became the subject of popular song and verse. Acting swiftly while his opponents were stunned and shaken, the emperor struck a telling blow: he dissolved the presidium, fired the ruling lords of the bureaucracy, demoted the generals, and removed those provincial lords who were not in his camp.[13] It was a clean sweep. Montezuma was ready to become the living god, and he intended to rule like one.

With the Pipiltin purged and none but his own partisans in positions of authority, Montezuma turned his attention to the macehualtin. He began by slamming shut the door of the Calmecac to all but sons of preferred lineage; henceforth, all higher education was to be the exclusive privilege of inheriting sons, so that in the future only the landed elite might govern the state and church. And from now on, the priesthood was to be filled from selected lineages. Montezuma's next move was even more disquieting: he summarily discharged every bureaucrat and functionary who stemmed from plebeian stock, regardless of experience and ability. Even the most menial position was to be held by a certified Pilli. He rounded up Ahuitzotl's old palace staff, including all who had ever served in any capacity, and had them put to death, presumably because they had been around before majesty became deity and had seen more than they should. He also had his own children's tutors and nurses slain for the same reason. Meanwhile, from all quarters of the empire sons of the ruling lords journeyed to the capital, many entering the emperor's personal service. They wanted to ingratiate themselves, and Montezuma liked to have them handy for retaliation against possible mischief by their fathers. As they swept and polished floors and filled their sundry tasks, Montezuma set down a long list of rules governing demeanor, speech, dress, and morality for all who entered the royal precinct. Any departure from the code merited death by burning alive. A crank for details, Montezuma frequently lectured his household and made unscheduled inspections, just as he periodically donned disguise and ventured abroad in the city to see if his laws were being obeyed.[14]

While Montezuma's tactics secured to him a more absolute control over the capital, it was essential that he strengthen his hand by gaining full mastery over the ramparts of empire; and in this he needed the aid of the Pochteca, the merchants of Tlatelolco. In a show of largesse he therefore restored Tlatelolco to its former status within the empire. All penalties imposed by his father after the civil war were now withdrawn and privileges restored, and the Tlatelolca were given permission to reopen their temple. The only reminder of their past disgrace was continuation of tribute dues, which Montezuma demanded as a symbol of submission to his rule. In this manner he earned the gratitude and support of the merchant princes, which in some measure balanced the losses he suffered in Texcoco as a result of the betrayal of his brothers. Although many of his enemies had perished, Texcoco and its fifteen subject provinces continued to nurture conspiracy and resistance against his designs. But Tacuba and Quauhtitlán were fast in the emperor's grip, as was the entire southland through his control of Coyoacán. From all the capitals and provincial centers he forced the great lords to come to Tenochtitlán for certain periods of each year. From their ranks Montezuma selected an "Honor Guard" of 600 lords, each with three or four armed retainers. He had, therefore, some 3,000 men in daily attendance, with many times that number in the capital at all times. They were all hostages. The Honor Guard was as stringently regulated as any other department of the imperial household; there was no fraternization permitted between differing ranks; rooms and halls in the palace were clearly designated for persons of certain rank; the penalty for entering a room reserved for superiors was summary execution. All ranks were held to uniform regulation of dress and insignia. In addition to these nobles who served as hostages against the actions of their kin at home, thousands of plebeians from subject provinces were kept under guard in lakeshore communities for immediate sacrifice if such reprisal should be indicated for any reason. Out in the provinces themselves the emperor maintained military garrisons and fiscal officers in 100 cities; in the event of rebellion, officers had standing orders to execute all adults over fifty years of age, presumably for having misled the young. These forces were backed up by a standing army of 150,000 men with as many more in ready reserve.[15]

At the same time Montezuma extended Huitzilopochtli cult with vigor; in this he was aided to considerable extent by the merchants of Tlatelolco. Alternating between gifts and blandishments and the mailed fist, he thrust Huitzilopochtli upon local lords; the *Coacalco,*

Tenochtitlán's prison for captive deities, was filled to overflowing.[16] Conquest of the Mixteca was largely seesaw; the emperor made significant gains, but was frequently beaten back. Advances in the Totonac area were somewhat easier, although a regional "Goddess of the Heavens" forbade human sacrifice and so gained new stature as a refuge from which the Hummingbird could be opposed. Her priests stood firm against Montezuma's pressure, but human slaughter made heavy inroads through the influence of Mexican merchants and local lords who, following instructions, tried human sacrifice as a means to maintain social and political discipline and found it good. It was Montezuma's ambition to install Huitzilopochtli from Tehuantepec to Pánuco, from Honduras to the Lerma River. In his mind *Anahuac,* the exotic, tropical crescent that held the central plateau between its points as a jewel in a mount while its body tapered far to the south, that populous land which made the empire rich and gave it identity, was to be expanded until it embraced *Cemanahuac,* the entire earth. Montezuma was to be its god and king.[17]

If some of the lords now regretted having backed Montezuma in the election, none had more reason for self-reproach than Nezahualpilli, who had supported the notion that priesthood was an indispensable qualification for election. Perhaps befuddled by abstract ideals, he violated his own interests when he opposed Macuilmalinaltzin. It is also entirely possible that he, like many others, had been completely deceived by Montezuma's demeanor. Bearing his own hatred and his daughter's grief at loss of her husband, Nezahualpilli waited patiently for revenge. Months after the disaster at Atlixco, toward the end of 1508, Nezahualpilli seized an opportunity to make payment against the debt. Montezuma's father-in-law, Tezozomoc, was one of the powerful lords of Atzcapotzalco. Under circumstances that are not clear, he was publicly exposed in commission of adultery, a crime for which the penalty was death. On the face of it this seems odd, inasmuch as the entire structure of Pipiltin society rested on sexual license and, for the males at least, unhampered promiscuity. The crime, of course, lay in the fact of notoriety. The plebeians were rigorously denied any sexual latitude and were punished with death if caught in adultery. Although the nobles could drink and wench to heart's content, they must do so in absolute privacy. Under the law Montezuma had to take action against Tezozomoc, who was tried and found guilty. But the judges merely banished him from Atzcapotzalco and pulled down his palace instead of exacting the required death penalty. Dissatisfied with the sentence, his Tepanec enemies cut off the end of his nose as a mark of infamy. Nezahualpilli loudly proclaimed the judges to be derelict in their duty and on that ground presumed legal jurisdiction in the case. The accused was tried *in absentia* and sentenced to death. Nezahualpilli's assassins sought him out, and he was strangled and burned. Montezuma's rage was choleric, but he could say nothing; even the plebeians knew all about that law. As if to add insult to injury, Nezahualpilli now had his killers stalk and slay one of the emperor's favorite nephews.[18] It was becoming a classic vendetta.

These events were watched with more than passing interest by subject provinces and the Enemies-of-the-House. When Montezuma conspired to have his own forces slaughtered at Atlixco, word spread like fire before the wind: The Mexica had suffered major defeat, the worst since Axayacatl's ill-fated invasion of Michoacán. Spontaneous uprisings followed the news in the Mixteca, the rebellions in Zolán and Yanhuitlán having major significance. Montezuma had to send a huge expeditionary force to restore order, but after exacting a terrible revenge and raising the tribute scale, the enforcers were faced with yet another rebellion.[19] The people of Yanhuitlán, already paying one-third of all produce and manufacture, could not meet the new demands. Imperial forces returned and burned the city, putting both sexes of all ages to the knife. In other Mixtecan rebellions of the time Montezuma's troops went so far as to wipe out entire towns, leaving

89

nothing but silence and the sighing wind. Elsewhere, communities were decimated by carrying off live victims for Huitzilopochtli; 12,210 were taken from Tlachquiauhco alone.[20]

Meanwhile, the Enemies-of-the-House seemed no longer convinced of Mexican invincibility; they brazenly challenged the emperor to schedule Flower Wars more frequently. And when they did meet in combat, they no longer minded the rules; they killed more than they captured, with the result that the Mexica frequently found themselves bested. For the Enemies-of-the-House it was the beginning of a protracted struggle for independence and power. Montezuma's betrayal of his brothers had been the spark that set it off. Seeing most of his troops slain and himself captured and slated for sacrifice in Huexotzinco, Macuilmalinaltzin broke from his captor's grasp and, seizing a weapon, flailed about until the enemy was forced to kill him on the spot. Such was his escape from the slab. His two brothers, like the bulk of the defeated, had been slain with their backsides to the enemy.[21] The cowardice shown by the imperial army made sensational news.

Open hostility between the Enemies-of-the-House and Montezuma broke out in 1510. In the course of his machinations Tlacaellel had made one of the ancient Mesoamerican goddesses, whom the Mexica called Toci, become the mythical woman-of-discord. Tying an old deity to official myth, he created a new role in which Toci became something of a national heroine and her fete one of the Mexica's biggest patriotic celebrations. The sacrifice bore Tlacaellel's trademark: the victims were divided into thirds, the first meeting death on the slab, the second by slow roasting alive on the Divine Hearth, while the third group was tied individually to the pillars that held up Toci's stage and then shot with arrows to commemorate those who perished in the flight from Culhuacán. Montezuma erred in using prisoners taken in a recent Flower War for this Mexican fete. The lords of Huexotzinco heard of it, and, although not directly involved, set up a ringing protest. They charged that Montezuma had deliberately departed from tradition by employing calculated cruelty in place of the customary quick death on the slab, and all for a ceremonial of dubious validity. Unable to vent the whole of their displeasure and contempt verbally, the Huexotzinca sent agents across the Mexican frontier who during the night set fire to Toci's temple. Upon hearing of it, Montezuma flew into a rage and ordered the arrest of Toci's priests, blaming them because they were obviously sleeping when they should have been up for devotional exercise. Locked in cages not large enough to stand or lie in, their floors strewn with razor-edged obsidian chips, the priests were condemned to death by slow starvation. The emperor saw them almost daily, haranguing them on the responsibilities of priesthood. At the same time, real war was unleashed against Huexotzinco, all captives being turned over to the priesthood for Toci's sacrifice. After having been dispatched, the prisoners were flayed and their skins given to street beggars who put them on to give their importuning a patriotic note. With rebellion so general throughout the empire, Montezuma found that he could not afford to mass his forces for unlimited war against the Huexotzinca; as it dragged on, the war proved costly for the Mexica, the enemy frequently giving better than they received. Holding many great nobles among their prisoners, they now invited Montezuma and his lords to come and witness their sacrifice to Camaxtli, a rough counterpart to the Hummingbird; and as added incentive, the lords promised to emulate the now famous "triple threat" feature of the Toci sacrifice. Montezuma stonily refused to attend, but insisted that some of his lords go. And so for the first time the tables were turned, and the Mexica sat behind rose screens and observed the slaughter of their comrades in arms. The experience was sufficiently shocking to evoke voluminous complaint, to which Montezuma responded, "Why do you complain? It is for this that we are born and for this we take the field; this is the blessed death of which our forbears taught us and to which they left us so deeply committed." [22] Somehow the emperor's reply lacked the ring of conviction, perhaps because his late brothers had taken the coward's way out in preference to that "blessed death" on the slab. And everyone knew it.

It was also at this time that dangerous pressures began to mount among the macehualtin. Montezuma's elimination of all hope of betterment was but the final act of a declination that had begun three-quarters of a century earlier with the victory over Atzcapotzalco. Gradually, the calpultin had declined, which meant that the fortunes of the commoners did likewise, for they had inseparable existence. In the early days of empire, appreciation of loss was somewhat obscured by apparent gains: the barrios were theoretically entitled to share in the plunder that fell to Mexican forces, and there is little doubt that for a time—perhaps a generation or so—the standard of living for the plebeians was appreciably raised by this means. Such rise may well have been reflected in the population growth that occurred with expansion of the empire. Also, the commoners' daughters, when taken to wife by a lord, automatically rose in status, their children becoming members of the Pipiltin and accordingly reflecting back on their own lineage. A plebeian's son, if successful in war, could become wealthy and influential, and do much for still humble parents and family. Perhaps even greater potential awaited the son of a macehual who succeeded in the Calmecac. Above all, the Mexican masses could take deep pride in the fact that their nation was achieving such eminence in the world of the lake, an emotion to be taken not lightly in the affairs of men. And so, even though they had been deprived of all political voice and subjected to the will of the state, channels of social and economic mobility had been created where there were none before. In this respect, the growing empire was hailed by the macehualtin, as were the sure-footed rulers who so deftly led the imperial march. As for the new religious practices and ideas that simultaneously appeared, what of them? The macehualtin had their own folk cult that served to get them through life's crises; they knew nothing of state cult or its conception of orthodoxy; therefore, how could they question it? Or why? How could the plebeians deny that human sacrifice, as practiced by the state, was good? It did not directly concern them.

But gradually things worsened for the masses in spite of the growth of the empire and its apparent affluence. There never seemed to be enough land; as the calpultin strove to maintain what they had, they were increasingly set upon by grasping lords who sought to enlarge their holdings at calpulli expense. Plainly, imperial expansion could not keep pace with the appetites of the Pipiltin. By the time Axayacatl ruled, the plebeians had to be circumspect lest they find themselves shipped out as *colonos* to far away territories. Oftentimes, the state sent them as mayeques, as in the colonization of Toluca, wherein they lost all identity with their ancestral calpulli and even lost the status of freemen. Under the old calpulli system of land management there could be no serfs; yet, by the time Montezuma II came to power, almost one-third of the total population, exclusive of slaves, had become mayeques.[23]

Under Montezuma's administration tribute collection was overhauled and made more efficient. All those liable to taxation who owned productive lands or industry were required to pay at the rate of one-third of production every eighty days. With inexorable collection, tributes mounted in unprecedented scale, requiring over a million tamemes to carry it to the capital at every levy. But the barrios saw precious little of it; gold, jewels, cacao, feathers, and all precious commodities were claimed by the emperor and his lords. All food products were likewise deposited in state storage facilities, it being illegal for a plebeian to have a granary or other repository. The state no longer permitted the independence that food surplus might nourish. As the Pipiltin established themselves, the plebeians had had much to learn about the price of corn. Indeed, as the empire waxed rich, the macehualtin were subjected to increasing demands: more labor, more service, more informal levies of tribute for special religious or political occasions, the endless demand for *comida y servicio* itself growing as burdensome as regularly scheduled tributes. Renteros, or sharecroppers, usually paid their landlords by the year, but by Montezuma's reign had fallen so deeply in debt that they were actually called slaves and used as such. This was the beginning of debt peonage in Mexico, which lingered in various forms until the revolution of the present century, and may exist yet today. In the midst of plenty the commoners found themselves severely rationed, sumptuary legislation being extended to cover even their daily diet: the macehualtin might have only meager and frugal fare, to be eaten from none but rude clay dishes; clothing was restricted to uniform dress made of coarse agave fiber; they could wear no cottons or sandals on their feet; by law they were confined to small and dingy homes, windowless and of not more than one story—all of which led Oviedo to remark that the Mexican macehualtin were the poorest folk yet discovered in the Indies. Considering his wide personal experience in the Caribbean, that was saying quite a lot. What happened to the wayward macehual? He was sentenced to death for overtaking a strolling noble, or for looking directly into his face; he was slain for tax evasion or accidental underpayment; he was put to death for incest, adultery, abortion, theft, rape, homosexuality, homicide, second offense drunkenness, for wearing a garment or status mark above his station, for daring to enter a lord's palace, for entering a woodlot belonging to a noble or the state, for felling a tree for fuel; if detected in treason against a lord or the state he was tortured to death, his family and descendents enslaved to the fourth generation, his fields sown with salt, his house pulled down. If none of these sufficed, there was a catchall statute under which any plebeian could be summarily sacrificed to Huitzilopochtli for "insubordination." [24] It is not difficult to comprehend how this society could function without public prisons.

94

As the screw tightened on the macehualtin, they did what people must do under such circumstances—they sought an anodyne against the pain of existence. *Octli*, better known by its post-conquest name of *pulque*, became indispensable. As soon as alcoholism became a problem, the fermented agave sap was outlawed by the state, but that stopped neither illicit manufacture nor consumption. Evidence of the onset of the problem is painfully sketchy, essentially because plebeians seldom put themselves on record. But it is clear that Montezuma the Elder was forced to acknowledge a growing problem of alcoholism among the plebeians. Sahagún gives so detailed a description of acute alcoholism, its etiology and prognosis, that one must conclude the Mexica studied it intensely, doubtless out of necessity rather than choice. By the time of Montezuma II, the macehualtin could count over 400 folk gods of intoxicants and drunkenness. The state finally sought to control the problem by making public drunkenness a capital crime on second offense. Elder citizens in retirement were permitted to freely drown their sorrows, probably because there was no way to stop them. But the workers of the Mexican world had to be protected against themselves, and so prohibition was enforced. On the other hand, whenever the state found itself in the midst of large construction projects, it judiciously used alcoholic beverages to wring additional effort from its laborers, so that prohibition had rather extensive economic implications.[25] Nevertheless, the fundamental problem presented by a poverty-stricken, repressed peasant and his jug was not solved, even by punishment of death; nor has any succeeding Mexican government solved it, including the present one.

Under Montezuma's hostage system there were thousands of nobles in the capital at all times, which necessitated large scale construction of palaces for their use. The plebeians, of course, were required to build them. Most of southern Tenochtitlán, the area flooded during Ahuitzotl's reign, was now rebuilt by Montezuma to suit this purpose. These were the magnificent palaces that so captivated and impressed the Spaniards. The burden of maintaining the palace complex, together with the appetites of its tenants, was also placed on the straining macehualtin, and not gently.[26]

The most terrifying aspect of the plebeians' declension was the way in which the gods turned upon their own people and began to devour them. The first four months of the ceremonial year were dedicated in motif to the coming of rain and ancient fertility rites. The great god Tlaloc and lesser rain deities, the *tlaloque,* were focal, although Huitzilopochtli was by no means absent. This vernal season was marked by sacrifice of children; from February until the rains came, small children and infants were wantonly immolated. If they cried as they were being slain, the priests rejoiced: it would likely be a wet spring. Every year a larger crop of victims was required, especially after the sacrificial mania got out of hand. The state solved the problem of supply by simple means: it requisitioned children through its agents who "purchased" children from their parents. Any plebeian child with a double cowlick or who had been born under a favorable astral sign was taken, parental protests and tears notwithstanding. The sources do not tell us what the payment was, but it could not have been consequential. Refusal on the parents' part was insubordination, for which they could themselves be sacrificed to Huitzilopochtli. By the time Montezuma II came to power, the sacrificial engine was forging ahead at frantic speed. Zumárraga's guess that 20,000 children were sacrificed annually pales beside Ixtlilxochitl's estimate that one child out of every five was so slain. A lot of nonsense has been written to show that this sacrifice of children was voluntary, that parents were willing, even anxious, to give up their children for the good of the greater number, just as they themselves almost hastened up the pyramid steps to fling their bodies down on the slab, secure in the knowledge that they were casting away their own lives for the benefit of others. Unfortunately, the sources make it abundantly clear that no such socialized altruism functioned, or was even conceived of by the sobbing mothers from whose breasts the infants were wrenched.[27] To accept the indigenista nypothesis is to agree with the imperial state that the Mexican masses were so unfeeling as to be something less than human. In view of the fact that the indigenista is attempting to enhance the image of his indigenous past, this must be one of the greatest of all ironies.

The nobles did not escape unscathed; they too were tightly locked within the system by its unyielding discipline. Corrupt justices were slain, as were public officials and administrators who failed in their responsibilities. Military leaders who erred in judgment were executed; leaders of youth in the war colleges were slain if corruption was detected in their schools or dormitories; ecclesiastics who transgressed were put to death; public executioners who bungled a job were themselves given the garrote; noble youths who fled the harsh discipline of the Calmecac were slain, as were those who mistakenly entered lordly precincts in the royal palace.[28] Death was lurking everywhere. The big difference, however, was this: the nobles had frequent release from their restraints, while the macehualtin almost never did. The nobles monopolized the ceremonial calendar and its fetes. Careful reading of the sources indicates that the plebeians were seldom participants and oftentimes were not even spectators. Every twenty days, which made a calendrical month, the nobles put on huge fiestas that coincided with the religious calendar. They were elaborate affairs, hosting thousands of guests who were lavishly sated and entertained. Professional choreographers were engaged to contrive dances for each occasion; poets likewise composed verse; each noble sought to outdo the other in affording his guests elegant diversion and, if they wanted it, riotous bacchanal. The plebeians could afford nothing like this, nor could they be permitted to watch the revelry of their lords. Aside from the formal social calendar, the nobles had frequent occasion for merrymaking: elevation to overlordship, marriage, military promotion, or any similar excuse. Their parties usually lasted forty-eight hours and were made as impressive as the lord could afford. If the nobles had their restraints, they also had their releases. In spite of this, Sahagún and other sources give evidence that many aristocrats could not tolerate the system, and, like the plebeians, turned in desper-ation to alcohol. Any lord who failed to witness a sacrifice to which he had been summoned, or who blanched and showed fear, was subject to summary sacrifice himself; any priest or noble who should turn his head at the sacrifice of children, or who should refuse to take part therein, was by imperial mandate to be broken, declared infamous, and cast out of the nobility.[29] It is anyone's guess how many lords sought solace in a bottle.

Through the years the lords of the Pipiltin had proliferated until they became a grotesquerie of nature. Nezahualcoyotl and his 2,000 concubines produced sixty sons and fifty-seven daughters; his son and successor, Nezahualpilli, fathered 144 children. Montezuma II was one of Axayacatl's 150 children, and he in turn had scores of his 4,000 concubines pregnant at one time. Others were as prolific, with the result that the Pipiltin grew so numerous that even an expanding empire could not support them. Organization and refinement were constant within the group. Where in the beginning all members of the Pipiltin were relatively equal, there were now rigidly ordered classes: the Tlatoque, or ruling lords, were supreme. Beneath them the *Tetecuhtin*, lesser lords, held positions of honor and responsibility. Still lesser lords comprised a third and most numerous class of the Pipiltin. The details of administration had long since devolved to the hands of a bureaucracy, generally peopled by *caballeros pardos,* lesser nobles of sorts who enjoyed many privileges of nobility, including tax exemption, but who were not possessed of divine blood.[30] The admin-istrative system remained remarkably stable, even as Montezuma II rocked the ship of state with his violent purge. The reason for its stability lay in that as a way of life the system was guaranteed by the upper stratum that held all prestige and authority. This was its source of strength, yet it also contained a flaw: in its omnipotence the ruling stratum had no need to question itself or the nature of its accomplish-ments or the values it established. Consequently, it did not trouble itself to see that by its rule of terror it had gradually turned the docile macehualtin into a tormented beast.

The great disparities of life could be read in popular folk belief, after death the spirits of worthy nobles became fluffy white clouds or precious gems, or exotic birds, while plebeians became weasels, skunks, and dung beetles. The peasant consoled himself in the knowledge that fiery Popocatepetl was a "mouth of hell" where evil and oppressive lords went after they died. He also understood that he and his kind "were born not for enjoyment of life, but for eternal labor." [31] It was not the disparities that were afflicting him: it was his studied dehumanization, which grew more profound with each passing year of Montezuma's reign. At their height, the Pipiltin were literally consuming the macehualtin. For every noble who died, anywhere from 100 to 300 plebeians were sacrificed as proper funereal send-off, be they freemen or slaves.[32] The epitome of dehumanization was achieved when the lords could with good appetite sit down and eat the flesh of the plebeian, both foreign and domestic. While he did not originate the practice, Montezuma II led the van, having fat and healthy unfortunates butchered daily for his table. His favorite dish, according to Bernal Díaz, was prepared from the flesh of young boys. During the ceremonial months of spring, the lords and priests ate the children who had been sacrificed like suckling pig; officers of the imperial legions in Toluca marched on parched corn and human jerky. After formal sacrifices resulting from the Flower Wars, the victims were usually served up with squash at the victory fete; when, after the Spanish conquest, human flesh was no longer obtainable, or only at great risk, the lords began eating pork because, as they declared, it tasted almost like human flesh.[33] That is why the use of pork so early became a significant status symbol in post-conquest Indian society. But it was the macehualtin of Montezuma's day who set the fashion through their degradation and despair.

Chapter VI

"There came a great light in the east. . . ."

Extensive crop failures from 1505 to 1507 set the whole of the empire astir with rebellion and unrest. In spite of drastic efforts the lords could not wring tributes from the macehualtin, nor could they enforce the usual degree of discipline. Under duress of hunger the little people were not so fearful of being sacrificed. With no apparent alternative Montezuma granted remission of tributes for a year. This may also have been a political gesture, since evidence indicates that the masses had caught on to the Flower War fakery and the state's cynical duplicity. Every time the Enemies-of-the-House were hosted, there was threat of rioting, even though security measures were manifoldly increased. All the plebeians needed was to be provoked at a moment when they had nothing to lose.[1]

Beneath the turbulent surface of popular unrest there was a contributing factor that caused growing apprehension. From the Caribbean there drifted in rumors of the appearance of strange beings, ferocious supermen from some other world. These tales were vague, shrouded in dreamlike obscurity, but they were persistent. From 1507 to 1510 the rumors were almost constant, and, as time passed, they grew more specific. As we have seen, these were the very years during which Montezuma was effecting his revolution and carrying out his purge; when the Enemies-of-the-House challenged the imperial system; when the split between Mexico and Texcoco was widening into an unbridgeable gulf; when the macehualtin were beginning to react against dehumanization. As quickly as they were heard, the rumors were interpreted and consequently became intimately associated with the emotions and desires of those who heard them. In the interpretations of the rumors we may with considerable confidence read the wishful thought of the times. Almost invariably, they were taken as omens of Montezuma's fall from power and overthrow of the empire. It becomes evident that he was the object of almost universal hatred and fear.[2] In Cholula, Quetzalcóatl's image was made to predict the emperor's overthrow by the strangers, who would also seize the empire. Nezahualpilli recapitulated the myriad interpretations precisely in 1509 when he told Montezuma "to be warned and mark this well: I have seen with utmost certainty that within a very few years our cities are to be destroyed and laid waste, we and our children slain, your vassals humbled and destroyed. Have no doubt of this, for to verify what I have foretold, and that you may know the truth of it, understand that never again shall you win the Flower Wars . . . and I say even further that soon you shall see in the heavens signs [and omens] of what I have foretold. . . ."[3]

Montezuma was already concerned about the rumors and their ominous interpretations, and now he was angered by Nezahualpilli's calm pronouncement of imminent doom. To prove him wrong, he hastily initiated a Flower War with Tlaxcala; on the field at Auayucán his forces were overwhelmed and crushed. The emperor received the news while holding court. Rising from his throne, trembling with rage, he delivered a bitter harangue on military negligence and weakness, concluding with a command for all persons to ignore the returning survivors. Thus it fell that for the first time since the empire was founded, Huitzilopochtli's warriors returned from battle unhailed and unsung. The causeways and streets were empty and an eerie silence brooded over the city. Bewildered, the beaten warriors made for the Hummingbird's temple but found no one about, thence to the emperor's palace, where the gates were swung shut in their faces. Now they understood and retired in disgrace. The following day Montezuma convened his staff and again assailed the generals, accusing them of effeminacy and dereliction of duty. Appropriate scapegoats were chosen to be stripped of rank and banished to plebeian life for a year. Montezuma's wrath and rancor were genuine enough, but they were also public bluster beneath which his secret heart, in the light of Nezahualpilli's prediction, began to know the meaning of fear.[4]

Nothing untoward happened for several months, and the emperor began to discount the rumors and Nezahualpilli's warning as idle gossip. But one night early in 1510 a penitential servant in Huitzilopochtli's temple, upon arising to relieve himself, was startled into full wakefulness by a great light rising in the eastern sky, a "light by night which lasted forty days. Those who saw it said that it was to be seen all over New Spain, that it was very large and brilliant, that it was in the east and came out of the earth and ascended to the sky. . . ."[5] The penitent roused two others from their slumber to confirm his discovery, and in the morning they dutifully went and reported it to the emperor. Remembering all too clearly Nezahualpilli's warning, Montezuma was frightened; at the same time he refused to believe their story and harshly dismissed them as a trio of fools. But nightfall found him atop Huitzilopochtli's pyramid, anxiously searching the heavens, waiting, fearing. Lo! it appeared at midnight, just as they said; seeming to rise out of the earth, it slowly ascended the eastern sky. Montezuma could not take his eyes from it. His mouth was dry; his insides churned. What did it mean? Finally breaking away, he returned to the palace and summoned his royal astrologers and seers, but they arrived still dulled by sleep and could contribute nothing. Infuriated, he condemned them to death.

Nezahualpilli's prediction began to weigh more heavily on Montezuma's thoughts. He had not won another Flower War, and now this cryptic omen had appeared in the heavens. Was the rest to follow? In full and studied possession of Texcoco's cultural heritage, Nezahualpilli was the most eminent astrologer in the empire. If the Spaniards are to be believed, his art closely approached the science of astronomy, his skills being such that the conquerors could not but believe that he was the beneficiary of a pact with the Evil One. There is some suggestion that Nezahualpilli may have understood something of the cyclic behavior of comets and used the rumors and his own science to wage psychological war on Montezuma. However this may be, the emperor was now at Nezahualpilli's mercy, for the torture of doubt and anxiety could only be assuaged by his explanation of the heavenly phenomenon. Swallowing his pride, Montezuma invited his enemy to the capital. Closeted in the imperial palace, Nezahualpilli confessed to Montezuma that he had been studying the comet since its initial appearance many nights ago, and after repeated consultation of historical and religious manuscripts had reached a definite conclusion: the light in the sky heralded the imminent return of Quetzalcóatl; Montezuma was to be overthrown and his empire lost forever. There was no hope for escape. With few words Montezuma grimly rejected what his guest had said. As though he had not heard, Nezahualpilli went on, warning that Montezuma would "soon lose his pleasure in imagining having made himself absolute lord of the empire," and was to discover how truly evanescent were the joys of possession and command. As for himself, Nezahualpilli declared that he had already canceled further Texcocan participation in the Flower Wars and had halted military aggression on his frontiers. In the little time that remained he was determined to live in peace. Obviously, Nezahualpilli was also attempting to lessen the bill of reckoning he would have to settle with Quetzalcóatl if and when he should return. It is impossible to be certain at this point if he really believed all that he was telling Montezuma, but it seems clear that he was not dismissing any possibilities. The two kings parted, each buried in his own secret thoughts.

Montezuma had retained his composure before Nezahualpilli, but no sooner had the latter gone than he was gripped by dread and foreboding. As he paced the throne room, he cursed the astrologers who had slept through the appearance of this omen. Beside himself with anger and fear, he ordered the execution of every royal astrologer and seer, their families enslaved, their houses pulled down. They would pay for their negligence, and let the public take note. But in his quiet moments, when he dared bare his breast, as later that night in lonely vigil atop the great pyramid, arms outstretched to the darkened heavens, he became a humble and bewildered man:

> Oh Lord of Creation, Oh powerful gods in whom is vested the giving and taking of life, why hast thou permitted, there having been so many kings and great lords, that the calamitous destruction of Mexico should fall my lot? That I should witness the death of my women and children? That I should see myself dispossessed of kingdoms and lordship, of my vassals, and of all that which the Mexica have conquered and won with their strength of arm and spirit? What shall I do? Where can I hide? Whither shall I go? Oh! that I could but turn into stone or wood or some unknowing thing, ere I meet that which I await with such dread [in my heart]. . . .[6]

Montezuma kept Nezahualpilli's prophecy to himself, telling no one of his fears. But the macehualtin did not need to be told; with appearance of the comet, terror and panic swept the land that, already plagued by hunger and oppression, now awaited pestilence and death. Or salvation at Quetzalcóatl's hand. As the imperial system had grown more oppressive, Quetzalcóatl had assumed the role of a Mexican redeemer, at least among the masses. That the light in the sky might be an omen of his coming gave hope to an otherwise darkly pessimistic future.

The emperor moved cautiously now, engaging in prolonged augury before taking any important action; he and his high priests spent long hours in meditation, bleeding themselves almost constantly and making sacrifices to the gods. For a time the Black Room was virtually the control center of the empire, just as the summit of the Hummingbird's temple was Montezuma's nightly haunt. As unrest mounted, he reacted by increasing sacrificial schedules until the slabs were consuming record numbers of victims. The idols were being drowned in blood. In the absence of Flower Wars the burden of supply fell upon the slaves and macehualtin. Much the same thing was happening in neighboring states, although as lesser imitators of the Mexican system their problems were less acutely felt. But the moment the Flower Wars failed to feed the system, it began to feast on its own, wherever it happened to prevail. Montezuma appointed new astrologers and fed his seers and priests sacred green mushrooms—*teonanacatl*, or "flesh of gods"—to enhance their occult powers. Those who foresaw disaster were slain, as were those who saw nothing. In childish spite the emperor slew all who reported anything that he did not wish to hear.[7]

When the year 1511 came to an uneventful close, Montezuma began to regain his composure, thinking that perhaps Nezahualpilli had been wrong from the start. Surely if the baneful comet, now long since gone, had been an omen of Quetzalcóatl's return, he would have appeared before now. Well into 1512, the emperor felt even more optimistic and seemed to have banished Quetzalcóatl from his thoughts. Apparently determined to renew his purge, he ridiculed Nezahualpilli and the lords of Texcoco because they had not engaged in a Flower War for almost four years. Nezahualpilli was already withstanding pressures exerted by his own lords who desired resumption of the wars. A whole generation of warriors had come of age, and many veterans wanted to be promoted. When Montezuma loudly inquired if the Texcocans were old women who shrank from omens and shadows, Nezahualpilli could not but agree to a Flower War against Tlaxcala, which the emperor scheduled early in the following year. Well in advance of the pending action, Montezuma secretly warned the Tlaxcalans that Texcoco was planning a major offensive to be launched under the guise of a Flower War. Taking no chances, the Tlaxcalans prepared their strategies accordingly. The net result of all these machinations was a disastrous massacre of the Texcocan army early in 1514 in which Montezuma lost a host of enemies and critics.[8] The emperor waited impatiently for news of the outcome of his carefully laid designs; Nezahualpilli would pay dearly for his precious omens and prattling tales of doom. A special messenger was ushered into his presence: the Texcocans had been destroyed by Tlaxcala. Elated, Montezuma at once dispatched his own forces to assume control of several of Texcoco's wealthiest provinces and towns. Nezahualpilli was so distraught over the loss of his legitimate son and the flower of the military nobility that he could do nothing but offer protest, which Montezuma rejected, instructing the ambassadors "to tell their master that the old days were past; if the empire used to be governed by three heads, it was now ruled by only one, and that he [Montezuma] was the Supreme Lord of Heaven and Earth, and that their master was never again to approach him in this way under pain of dire punishment." Montezuma never saw Nezahualpilli again. Withdrawing to the seclusion of his apartments, the king grieved over his loss and humiliation. In brooding reflection he recalled his father's defeat at the hands of Tlacaellel, how Nezahualcoyotl had been forced to acknowledge Mexican suzerainty and provide a temple for Huitzilopochtli. It was on the occasion of the opening of that temple, with its great blood bath, that his father had made a prediction, so often repeated in his later years, of the eventual collapse of the entire Mexican system, carrying with it the lords and the world they were creating for themselves. Nezahualpilli believed fervently in that prophecy, but he was equally certain that he would not survive to see it unfold. Within a few months the king joined his son in death, very possibly by his own hand. The question of succession was settled by the emperor, who enthroned Cacama, one of Nezahualpilli's illegitimate sons by a concubine who was the emperor's sister. With his nephew on the throne of Texcoco, Montezuma reigned without a rival.[9]

Heavy snows and freezing temperatures had substantially shortened crops in 1514, and by the following year large areas of the empire were facing serious food shortages. The weary pattern of domestic unrest and imperial repression, grown habitual in recent years, took on grimmer visage as hunger stalked the land. Late in 1515, just after Nezahualpilli's death, new and more coherent rumors began to filter in from the Caribbean. It was plainly foretold that bearded men with fair skins were coming to assume the sovereignty of the earth. Montezuma, with his ear to the ground, listened and was shaken. Myriad tales and fantasies were told and retold by city dwellers and country folk: a woman recently buried thrust aside her gravestones and went to see the emperor. "I have risen from the dead to warn you that in your time the lordship of Mexico shall come to an end, and that you are its last lord because others will come and seize power." Fishermen at work on the lake found a strange bird with a mirror in its head; when it was carried before the emperor he looked into it and saw men of war marching out of the east. Some rode on the backs of large deer-like animals and slew all before them. Countrymen heard that one of the temples atop Huitzilopochtli's pyramid suddenly burst into flames that could not be extinguished; and one day the lake rose without warning or reason, drowning many people. City folk were told that out in the country huge flights of birds blotted out the sun, making noontime as dark as night. When captured, the birds were found to lack entrails, their bodies stuffed with dirt. Everywhere voices were heard wailing in the night; flaming lights were observed. Many freaks and monstrosities were born, but when taken to be seen by the emperor, they vanished and were not heard of again. Such tales and omens were without limit or end.[10] The Spaniards and Christianized Indians who passed these stories on to us in their chronicles and codices took them literally, supposing them to be divinely oriented omens of the coming of Christianity and Spanish rule. In reality they were the product of mass hysteria, and would have been told in some form or other had there been no Spanish intervention. As stimulus for these omens and stories, the arrival of the Spaniards in the Caribbean was real, as was the flooding of the city in 1503 after Ahuitzotl's seizure of the springs at Huitzilopochco, and as were the countless natural phenomena that were magnified into prodigy. But the climate of hysteria that made possible such morbid hallucinating was the symptom of a sick and tortured society that eagerly awaited its own demise.

And so, fear of Quetzalcóatl's return came back to haunt the emperor. Casting about for a source of strength or a refuge, he thought to enlist the aid of Huitzilopochtli. Perhaps the Temalacatl should be made larger and more elaborate. Hastily, he summoned stonecutters and artists and conscripted a huge labor force. Speed was essential. The best stonecutters from Xochimilco, Cuitlahauc, Mizquic, Culhuacán, Iztapalapán, Mexicatzinco, and Huitzilopochco were sent to the quarries at Chalco to begin work. But from the start there were many delays caused by broken ropes, accidents, and most importantly, slaves and laborers who dragged their feet. The emperor threatened and cajoled; he vastly increased human sacrifice, but to no avail. The workers insisted that the stone would not leave the quarry. Montezuma's mounting wrath was checked by a message from Chalco: a voice had spoken from within the rock, refusing to go to the capital and foretelling his doom: ". . . and warn him that his dominion and office are finished, that soon he shall see and know the fate that is to befall him because he has presumed more than a god. . . ." The emperor caged the messengers and threw still more men into the task. But as the great rock was being drawn over the southern causeway, it fell into the lake. Divers claimed they couldn't find it; then it was reported that the rock had mysteriously returned to the quarry. Montezuma had raged and commanded and spilled much blood, but he still did not have his new sacrificial stone and it was obvious that he was not going to get one.[11]

The emperor's reflections on his apparent loss of power were interrupted by the arrival of carriers who had been dispatched by the governor of his most distant southeastern province. They brought with them a large trunk that had washed ashore on the gulf coast. Looking inside, Montezuma took out and examined several articles of clothing; they would fit a rather large-sized man—or god. The jewels and trinkets were carefully handled, but examination revealed no clues. The only other content of the trunk was a weapon made of some unknown metal. Obviously a sword, it was covered with a brownish, powdery scale that rubbed onto everything it touched. These strange articles were not rumors; they were real. Deeply disturbed and troubled, Montezuma thought of Nezahualpilli, now two years in his grave, and his uncanny powers of foresight. Had he been right after all? Were these the possessions of Quetzalcóatl? After much thought he divided the contents of the trunk, sending articles to the kings of Texcoco and Tacuba, explaining that they had been left by ancient forbears and should be carefully preserved. It was another way of saying that they were all in this thing together.[12]

Before he could recover from this blow, Montezuma was dealt another that removed all doubt from his mind. Into his hands was placed a folded manuscript that had just been received from Yucatan, probably from a vanguard merchant. In glyphs and pictures it told of the arrival of three seagoing temples at Cape Catoche and traced their movements around the north coast and south to Champotón. Each pyramid was white and rested on a foundation formed by a very large canoe. Temples arriving from the east could mean but one thing: Quetzalcóatl was near.[13] Without further delay Montezuma ordered his image carved at Chapultepec. As the early sun illuminated the dazzling colors of the graven gallery, the emperor stood small in the presence of all the great kings; Itzcoatl, Montezuma the Elder, his grandfather, Tlacaellel, his own father, Axayacatl, and Ahuitzotl. And now another figure had been deeply carved, his own. Slowly moving his eyes from one to the other, Montezuma quietly wept: "If our bodies were as imperishable and lasting in this life as that painted effigy will be on that rock, which will last forever, who then should fear death? But I plainly see that I am to die and only this memory shall remain of me." [14]

Varied and sometimes conflicting reports followed the first news from Yucatan. The temples housed fierce beings who fought with terrible, edged weapons, and they hurled thunder and lightning. They traded peacefully for gold, but if provoked they made war. But whoever they were, the strangers were liable to mortal pain and death; many had been slain by the people of Potonchán and two had been taken alive and sacrificed. They also found bodies of some who had died of their wounds and had been cast into the sea.

Not until he had seen his own image sculpted at Chapultepec did Montezuma convene his chief administrators and the ruling lords to tell them of Quetzalcóatl's imminent return. For the first time he revealed Nezahualpilli's predictions and their startling proofs. But he said nothing at this time concerning the arrival of the seagoing pyramids. The lords were already aware of much that the emperor told them; they knew very well what went on within the empire. But they were not unduly concerned over lights in the sky or the wild rumors and ravings of the peasantry. Theirs was the upper hand, and they held firm control of the imperial system. Unlike the emperor, they felt no cause for alarm. If they were surprised at anything, it must have been Montezuma's panic and lack of self-control. Goaded by their apparent indifference, he demanded of them, "What is to become of me? I, who am ignorant of any [occult] science—how can I evade the calamity and evil that await me?" His peers looked at each other and then gave the answer they would be expected to give: they told the emperor to put his faith and trust in Huitzilopochtli, whose throne he possessed. If he would do that, all would be well.[15] Had Huitzilo-pochtli not authored and maintained the system from the beginning?

The assurances of his counselors and peers was lost on Montezuma; he was beside himself with fear and anxiety. Turning to his dwarfs and jesters, he made them his confidants and found comfort in their sympathy. In flight before the inner storm, he planned devious escapes and indulged in other fantasies; one day he would hide in a cave; the next he would don disguise and disappear. But invariably he was forced back to reality and the agony of waiting. Why could he not take the advice given by his counselors? Why was his reason so paralyzed by fear?

The emperor was in part the victim of his training, his life, his own turn of mind; he was a philosopher-priest who was bound to seek answers where his counselors were not even aware of the questions. Life within the system had grown infinitely more complex since the early days of empire. Tlacaellel's primitive system had been sufficient, even with its negative moralization of man's role in the cosmic drama for creation of the society Montezuma and the lords now enjoyed. But the social and political structures could not simply float freely in space; they had to be held by philosophical underpinnings whose strength and quality would determine the viability of the whole. The trouble was that the philosophical foundation was no longer able to hold the structure, just as in a material sense the macehualtin were no longer able to support it. Montezuma sensed his own bankruptcy, while his counselors were the kind of men who would die fighting to preserve the system they knew without ever knowing—much less caring—why it was going under and taking them with it. It was Montezuma's bad luck to be the king in whose reign the system was to reach its apogee, when the king must become god only to discover that he cannot be god, when all ultimate ramifications are culminated and spent. The philosophy that made the empire could not sustain it, and at this moment the underpinnings began to crack. The whole system was thus made vulnerable to the threat of external force. By historical accident, that force was already in motion.

Montezuma, the priesthood, the society at large, were utterly dependent upon Quetzalcóatl cult for whatever qualities of human compassion and spirituality they knew in their daily lives, and one who reads Sahagún knows how much there really was. Theoretically, the priesthood cherished Quetzalcóatl's sublime ethic and tirelessly extolled the virtues of peace, mercy, and compassion, even though in practice they were seldom permitted to display them. And so they piously mouthed Quetzalcóatl's litanies as they wrenched out human hearts; they taught their young the humble virtues, but as adults, forbade their practice. It was as though the shadow of Tlacaellel forever darkened the human threshold.

If indeed Quetzalcóatl was now to return—and after studying the messages from Yucatan, there seemed no doubt—then Montezuma must prepare to render an accounting of his stewardship; he must expiate the guilt of all the kings and Tlacaellel combined; he now stood alone and plainly in their light. Well could he demand of the gods, ". . . Why hast thou permitted, there having been so many kings and great lords, that the calamitous destruction of Mexico should fall my lot?" That Mexico would be destroyed the emperor had no doubt. Even if Quetzalcóatl should prove to be wholly forgiving and benign in judgment, the empire was finished. Quetzalcóatl's first act would put an end to human sacrifice, which would prove to everyone's satisfaction that the cosmic mission theory had been an imperial hoax. Without the threat of sacrifice there would be no discipline, and the empire could not exist twenty-four hours without its instrumentality of terror. In the absence of fear Huitzilopochtli could not survive, and without the Hummingbird there was no sovereignty. No, there was no escape. Weary of his fantasies, Montezuma took to the Black Room and reflected on his predicament. Could Huitzilopochtli be invoked to save the empire, just as history told in earlier times of peril? Could even Huitzilopochtli stand against Quetzalcóatl? A few short years ago, Montezuma had been convinced that he was a reincarnation of the Hummingbird, but he was no longer sure.

Unable to find solace or escape in his counselors and palace creatures, Montezuma committed the great folly of turning to the macehualtin, among whom hysteria was epidemic. Summoning all barrio captains and overseers, the *tequitlatos,* he commanded them to keep vigilant watch over the old people; those who dreamed of strange beings or things concerning the emperor's future were to report them in detail. He gave his assurance that no harm would befall those who should come forth. The emperor was not kept waiting; people came in droves to relate their dreams: Huitzilopochtli's temple is in flames, his pyramid demolished, and the Hummingbird himself lies smashed to bits; the emperor's palace and Huitzilopochtli's temple are swept away in a mighty torrent of water; the city is deserted and laid waste; the lords are all dead. And so they went without end. Montezuma listened attentively to every word, then had the storytellers caged and starved to death.[16] When he had exhausted the ready supply of plebeian volunteers, he turned on the priesthood. All priests were to report their dreams and visions that touched upon strange beings, events, or other unusual phenomena. They were to be particularly vigilant in caves and other places amenable to visionary manifestation. The priests were not fools; they knew what had happened to their astrologer friends and others who had volunteered information. They discreetly decided among themselves to report nothing. Montezuma soon guessed what they had done and gave them fifteen days to reconsider his command. At the end of that time they had reported nothing of consequence, and so several of their number were imprisoned and slated for slow starvation.

Montezuma now recalled his provincial governors and ordered them to send him their best seers and necromancers and all who had knowledge of astrology and divination. Many arrived in the capital promptly, and the emperor lost no time in their examination: had anyone seen, heard, or dreamed anything touching on his reign or person? Apparently forewarned, they all replied in the negative. Montezuma raged and had them jailed. Once behind bars, some rejoiced in the happy prospect of the emperor's overthrow; and as they compared rumors, there was mirth in the prison. Montezuma's spies listened carefully and reported to him: the prisoners say that since the emperor is so anxious to know his ill fortune in advance, they have read it for him in the stars. What is to befall Montezuma is more prodigious than anything in history. One old man bitterly added that "those who are to avenge us for the injuries and wrongs he has done us—and continues to do us—are already on the march." The latter threat struck Montezuma like a thunderbolt. He had kept the news from Yucatan secret, yet this man knew something. Robes flying, the emperor rushed to the prison to question the seer himself; but when he got there, he found the cells empty. The prisoners had escaped. Insane with rage, Montezuma had their wives and children slain, their homes pulled down and the foundations excavated to the water table.[17] His reach was long, his spite boundless, his vengeance terrible.

Chapter VII

Enter Quetzalcóatl

From the time he first learned of the visit of Spanish ships to Yucatan, Montezuma had the entire gulf coast under surveillance. Although the Córdova expedition had returned whence it came, he was certain that another would come; it was largely a question of when. The following year, in 1518, suspense was ended by the arrival of four more ships off Yucatan. Following the same course, trading for gold and fighting when necessary, they slowly made their way around the Yucatacan peninsula. All along the coast inhabitants had been ordered to trade with the strangers and find out as best they could who they were and what they were after. Slowly reports accumulated in the capital: the strangers spoke the language of the Caribbean and had two Indians in their company who also knew the Mayan language, so that they could easily make themselves understood. They gave presents of precious green beads, and said that they came from a distant land beyond the sea and that they were vassals of a great emperor. They were anxious to collect gold, and advised the people that they too should acknowledge this emperor as their lord. In all, the news was more baffling than threatening. If these beings controlled thunder and lightning, it must be through their relationship with Quetzalcóatl who was the god of those forces; but who was the great emperor of whom they spoke? And what of the strangers' vulnerability to death?

Montezuma's pondering was interrupted by a messenger from the southeastern province of Tochtepec. A strange vessel had been seen in the Papaloapán River near the village of Tlacotalpan; the villagers could report no more because they had never seen anything like it before and were afraid to approach. The emperor jailed the messenger pending investigation of the report. Summoning his nephew, the Lord-of-the-House-of-Darkness, and a trusted slave named Cuitlalpi-toc, he sent them to get to the bottom of the matter at once. Following their instructions, the two raced to the nearest imperial garrison, which happened to be in the city and province of Cuetlaxtlán—soon to be renamed Vera Cruz—and questioned the governor. Yes, it was true; there was a mysterious visitor in the river. Why had the governor not reported this fact? The emperor must be made to understand that it was a long coastline with many rivers, and the province of Tochte-pec was but a frontier outpost of the empire. The governor had himself just been notified of the discovery. Montezuma's emissaries knew better than to return to the capital without seeing whatever there was to be seen with their own eyes. Journeying to Tlacotalpan, they were guided to the place where the great vessel lay at anchor. At first they crouched and hid themselves among the rocks and boulders; but after their initial amazement and fear had passed, they climbed a tree for a better look. For most of a day they observed the inhabitants of the vessel as they did their usual work on deck; early in the afternoon, a party lowered a small boat and went fishing. They could clearly hear their strange talk and frequent laughter. As the shadows of afternoon lengthened, the fishermen rowed back to the ship; and their unobserved audience, having seen enough, made for Tenochti-tlán in utmost haste. Before the emperor they poured it out: the great house in the river had many dwellers with light hands and faces, some with heavy black beards. They wore strange clothing of many colors, and some had round helmets on their heads that gleamed in the sunlight. Montezuma listened intently. When they had finished he lowered his head, saying not a word, his knuckle clenched between his jaws, his mind racing in thought. Suddenly, he lifted his head; he had reached a decision. Calling for his aides, he commanded them to bring two silversmiths, lapedaries, and featherworkers and all their equipage to the palace in absolute secrecy. Within the hour they had reported, and Montezuma put them to work fashioning certain articles that he described in detail. Working without pause, the artisans completed their assignments. Barely rested from their return journey, the emissaries were called again by the emperor, who now took them into his confidence. They were to return at once to the vessel in the river and attempt to board it. If successful, they were to present the gifts that the artisans had just made, to be followed by presentation of foods and delicacies. The purpose of this, Montezuma now disclosed, was to find out if it was really Quetzalcóatl who had returned. If the strangers accepted the gifts, it would be because Quetzalcóatl recognized his own possessions; if they ate the food, it would indicate that their palates had not forgotten the tastes of the land. If the strangers passed both tests, then the chief emissary was to tell them that Montezuma willingly surrendered everything and asked only that he be permitted to die quickly. If, on the other hand, the strangers should not be associated with Quetzalcóatl and should devour the emissaries, let them be assured that Montezuma would provide generously for their families. On that somber note they departed.[1]

Upon reaching the river, they found the ship anchored in the same place. Rowed out by local villagers, they paused at the prow to squat and bleed themselves and "eat" a fingerful of marine growth from the bow's planking, just as they would do before the altar in their temple at home.[2] Once aboard, they were greeted by the person in command, but in a tongue they could not comprehend. And it was immediately apparent that the strangers could not understand Nahuatl. Their presents were accepted with wide smiles by the commander, who also tasted the foods with evident relish. The emissaries in turn were presented with strings of green glass beads and given hard biscuits and a delicious liquor that made them a little dizzy. In the absence of lingual communication, the emissary did his best to convey Montezuma's message of surrender by signs, and with this departed. From the rocks on shore they watched the vessel raise its anchor and sail from view.[3] Arriving in the capital near collapse from exhaustion, they told Montezuma of their ordeal. Fingering the sea biscuit and the green glass beads, he cautioned them to silence and dismissed them to well-earned rest. Now the emperor called his uncle, the vice-ruler, his military chief, and one of his counselors and told them the entire story, displaying the biscuit and beads. They agreed with his decision to alert coastal lookouts for the appearance of more vessels and to await further news. There was nothing else to be done. Meanwhile, he considered the gifts to be divine things. The biscuit was handed over to priests, who placed it in a golden chalice, wrapped it in precious *mantas,* and carried it in formal procession to Tula, where it was enshrined in Quetzalcóatl's temple. The beads were translucent green, one of Huitzilopochtli's colors; the emperor buried them at the foot of the Hummingbird's altar with full ceremony. The arrival appeared to be Quetzalcóatl, but Montezuma was taking no chances. Something was amiss: the strangers could not speak or understand Nahuatl. Quetzalcóatl would never have forgotten the languages of his own land. The emperor felt a desperate need for more information.[4] In subsequent reports to the capital two more vessels joined the first in trading along the coast, but they did not tarry long enough for him to learn more about them. One day they simply vanished over the horizon.

Already haunted by doubts and fears, Montezuma's anxiety was heightened by the conflicting evidence that gradually took shape.

Were the newly arrived beings strangers or returnees? Attempting to answer this all-important question, Montezuma had his court artist paint everything as it had been seen and described by his emissaries. When finished, he sent for the glyph-writers and archivists of the capital and asked them if they had ever seen manuscripts that resembled the paintings he now showed them. The viewers were unanimous in response: they had never seen anything like them anywhere. When Itzcoatl gathered and burned the old histories and manuscripts, he had effectively cut Montezuma off from the past he now so urgently needed to explore. Mexican archives were filled with post-imperial histories and their raw materials, but the official history, for the emperor's purposes, was utterly worthless. What Montezuma was after—the historical sources that contained the answer to Quetzalcóatl's riddle—might have been found in Texcoco; but perhaps through the enmity that existed, he failed to get them in his grasp. In ever-widening circles he pushed the search—Malinalco, Chalco, Cuitlahuac, Mizquic—with no success. Then, by pure chance, he learned of an aged annalist named Quilaztli who had in his own archive scores of old Mexican histories from pre-imperial times, probably one of the few collections that escaped Itzcoatl's bonfires. Hastening to Xochimilco, royal agents bundled up the manuscripts and the old man and brought them back to the capital. After lengthy examination and comparative study, Quilaztli announced his findings: there was remarkable similarity between his codices and the drawings of the court artist. The emperor could see for himself that the helmets were almost identical. And the narratives contained in the codices left no doubt. These were not strangers; they were returning to their own land. Montezuma was stunned. But they had sailed away! Was it not likely that they would fail to come back? The old man shook his head. They would soon return, perhaps this time to stay. In anguish the emperor thanked the annalist but refused to permit him to leave; rather was his family brought to Tenochtitlán, where they joined him in house arrest. Montezuma could not put from his mind the message of the codex:

> Our Lord goeth bequeathing you this land; it is your merit, your lot. He goeth, he goeth back, but he will come, he will come to do his duty, he will come to acknowledge you. When the world is become oppressed, when it is the end of the world, at the time of its ending, he will come to bring it to an end. . . .[5]

Days passed into weeks that in turn became months. Nothing happened. Once again Montezuma began to regain a measure of optimism and composure. Gradually the idea that Quetzalcóatl would not return in his lifetime became conviction, and the emperor returned to his imperial problems. He broke the lord of Atzcapotzalco and invested a nephew with his title and estates; close friends replaced the ousted lords of Ecatepec and Xochimilco; a son was given Tenanyuca as a child might be given a toy. His pride and arrogance returned as suddenly as they had departed, and now he was beyond the meaning of fear, or so it would appear as he dethroned ancient dynasties and replaced them with relatives and partisans. The provinces were stirred to wrath, and the ranks of enmity were again swollen with recruits.[6] Everything Montezuma did was in excess measure, as though severity could disguise the weakness of self-doubt. In spite of the emperor's attempts to strengthen his position, or perhaps because of them, the Pipiltin were divided and the empire was rife with rebellion.

The sacrificial games and other diversions of Tlacaxipehualiztli, March's Festival-of-the-Flayed-Ones, were blighted for Montezuma by news from Yucatan. Several vessels had appeared off Cozumel and seemed to be following the route laid down by their predecessors. Messages relayed by runners from the coastal provinces were received almost daily, sometimes several times a day; the news was increasingly ominous: on the Island of Cozumel and everywhere the visitors stopped, their leader assumed sovereignty, forbade human sacrifice, and cast down the images of the gods. But this was not all: he replaced them with a goddess of whom he carried many images and paintings; and everywhere she was installed, his followers erected a tall timber with a crosspiece near the top. And they all spoke repeatedly of a powerful emperor beyond the sunrise, and of a deity who was the only true god.[7] Montezuma could no longer sustain his flagging hopes as fear and despair again became his constant companions. The prophecy was unfolding before his very eyes; he was fast in the grasp of inexorable fate. In preparation for the inevitable, he sent five representatives to the coast to receive Quetzalcóatl—if it was Quetzalcóatl—when he should arrive. Within a few weeks word came from Cuetlaxtlán: three vessels had been sighted sailing along the coast and seemed to be headed for the Bay of Chalchiuhcueyecan.[8] Another report followed closely: they had entered the bay and anchored. Montezuma shuddered. Now it was up to the welcoming delegation; how would it go with them?

> And when this was happening, [Moctezuma] could enjoy no sleep, no good. Never could one speak to him. That which he did [was] only as if it were in vain. Ofttimes he sighed; he was spent, down cast. He felt delight in no savory morsel, joy or pleasure.
> Wherefore he said: "What will now become of us? Who, forsooth, standeth [in command]? Alas, until now, I. In great torment is my heart, as if run through with chili water, so that it burneth and smarteth, Where, in truth [may we turn], O our lord?" [9]

Waiting was torture; would the emissaries never return? What word would they bring? Then they arrived. Without even momentary delay the five delegates were hustled to an altar where waiting priests now opened the breasts of several unfortunates. Squeezing and shaking the fresh hearts, they liberally sprinkled the emissaries with warm blood. "For this reason did they do so: that they had traveled into very perilous places; that they had gone to see—had looked into the faces and at the heads of, and had verily spoken to—the gods." [10] Now Montezuma was prepared to hear what they had to tell. The delegates had watched the ships anchor and had then rowed out. On board they were taken before Quetzalcóatl. On approaching him, they squatted and did the usual reverence; he bid them rise, whereupon they incensed him with burning copal gum. Now they took out holy raiment and offered it: "Dress thyself, O Lord, in the clothing thou anciently wore when thou lived amongst us as our god and king." After hearing them through interpreters, Quetzalcóatl permitted them to dress him in the garments and seemed much pleased at what they said. Now the delegates were given strange food and a strong but delicious drink that seemed to produce a feeling of well-being. While they so ate and drank, Quetzalcóatl asked many questions of them, which they did their best to answer. But then, of a sudden, he had them bound like prisoners and gave commands that made great *tepustles,* or "irons," hurl thunder and lightning and belch great billows of smoke that smelled strongly and burned the nostrils. All the while, his subordinates stood close by, some with gigantic and ferocious dogs at heel; there were also great deerlike animals in the temple. Quetzalcóatl put on hard and shiny clothing and brandishing a gleaming sword challenged the emissaries to combat: "And now I would satisfy my doubts. I would behold and test how strong and powerful you are." They did not know what to do, or how to answer, for they could not fight a god. After this, Quetzalcóatl released them and they returned to Tenochtitlán as fast as they could. If the emperor wanted their opinion, they were agreed that this was not Quetzalcóatl, but some powerful and cruel enemy. "And when Montezuma heard this he was filled with a great dread, as if he were swooning. His soul was sickened, his heart was anguished." [11] With recovery of composure he asked what Quetzalcóatl looked like. The emissaries responded: he was slightly larger than the average being; slender but deep of chest and broad in shoulders; very muscular and well-proportioned, so that he seemed taller then he really was; his complexion was pale, eyes large and dark, aquiline nose highly bridged and well formed; his brow was wide and high, mouth and chin firm, beard black and pointed at the chin. In all, a grave and handsome countenance and a commanding presence. But his eyes were most striking, quick and uncomfortably penetrating, like those of a falcon or some great bird of prey.

Montezuma listened and ordered another test of identity to be made without delay. Before the supermen, who had just disembarked from their temples, was spread a sumptuous repast—roasted turkey, eggs, tortillas, avocados, potatoes, luscious fruits, and other delicacies. The strangers, doubtless weary of shipboard fare, were prepared to feast. But before they could begin, several nearby Indians were flung on their backs, their hearts ripped out by priests who showered and sprinkled their blood over the banquet fare like savory sauce. "And when [the Spaniards] beheld this, their stomachs turned. They spat; they blinked; they shut their eyes and shook their heads. For the food, which they had sprinkled and spattered with blood, sickened and revolted them. For strongly did it reek of blood." [12] Spanish sources do not confirm another Indian source which states that the Spaniards reacted violently.[13] But Montezuma was answered nonetheless.

The emperor was minutely informed of everything that took place on the beach, of the religious services that were held, of the things that were said. His chief emissary, whom the visitors called Tendile,* sent pictographic accounts of everything back to the capital for Montezuma to study. Over 2,000 attendants had been assigned to Quetzalcóatl's service, and it was they who built his camp and supplied his food and necessities. But among them the emperor had many disguised priests and sorcerers. They reported that the strangers

* Ten-dee-lay

seemed to have mortal appetites and were not beyond the wiles of women, especially the pretty ones.

The capital was literally humming with news of the supermen on the beach; speculation and rumor circulated through all levels of society. Groups of plebeians huddled in the streets, expecting the worst and fearing for their children. What was to befall them? The road to the coast was traveled by couriers and emissaries night and day. Montezuma worried much and slept little; his lords were restive and impatiently awaiting his move. What would he do? In his own mind he was convinced that the one who held the beach was either Quetzalcóatl or his emissary. In either case, the empire was finished. But the lords were not so convinced. In time they would learn the truth; meanwhile, he would listen to their counsel and appear to have an open mind. Before the lords in convention Montezuma indicated the alternatives as he saw them. If the visitors represented Quetzalcóatl, they could be expected to assume sovereignty, which would put an end to the state and empire. Should the Mexica fight or submit? If they were simply ambassadors of a great lord, as some argued, and as they themselves implied, should they be admitted to the capital? Extensive debate ensued, the big question being whether or not the now famous prophecy was being fulfilled; there was no possibility of agreement, although the most influential lords rejected the whole idea of Quetzalcóatl's return. Montezuma's brother, Cuitla-huac, summed up the thought of one eminent faction: "My opinion, great lord, is that one should not admit to his house the very person who intends to dispossess him of it." Cacama, speaking as the king of Texcoco, represented another powerful party. He argued that if the strangers were truly ambassadors of a foreign prince, courtesy demanded that they be admitted. After all, they were few and the Mexica could handle any emergency that might arise. It would be much safer, he cogently pointed out, to bring them to the capital as soon as possible, before they had an opportunity to spy out the land and find out that rebellion was rife throughout the empire. If they should have plans of subversion, he warned, delay would give them ample time in which to secure allies.

After the lords had disbanded to continue debate in homes and clubs, Montezuma sat by himself and fondled the gilt helmet Tendile had sent up from the coast; it was just like the ones in the old manuscripts. The fools! Did they not realize that the supermen had already assumed sovereignty on the coast? How could the Mexica resist the force of destiny? Can man fight the gods? Yet, Montezuma could not bring himself to surrender. If only he could put off destiny. But how to win reprieve? Could the visitors be persuaded or bribed to return whence they came? If he could forestall the inevitable, even for a short time! Filling the helmet with fine gold, he gave orders for a treasure train to be delivered into Quetzalcóatl's hands with a firm but polite request to go away. Reflecting on the obvious inability of his lords to comprehend what was happening, Montezuma understood that when the supermen finally did come he would be blamed for permitting them to take over; he would be cast in the role of traitor; his family would be slain in vengeance because that was how the Mexica did things. His only hope was in delaying the inevitable.[14]

For help in persuading the intruders to depart, Montezuma turned again to his sorcerers and seers; but their ranks had been so thinned by execution that he was forced to send away to Yautepec, Oaxtepec, Malinalco, and Tepoztlán for new recruits. Their enchantments proved ineffective, at which some broached the idea that if the strangers were permitted to enter the capital they might have better success. Meanwhile, Tendile had indulged in extensive conversations with Quetzalcóatl, who by this means "requested" Montezuma to stop human sacrifice and suspend all worship of idols; he even offered to send an image of a goddess called Our Lady to the capital so that Montezuma could throw down Huitzilopochtli and replace him with her image and the cross. In the most confidential manner he assured Tendile that he carried secret messages for Montezuma from the "Lord of the World" beyond the sea, and that his lord had specifically sent him to abolish human sacrifice and worship of idols. One thing emerged clearly from these conversations: the leader of the supermen, whom the others called Cortés, was not Quetzalcóatl. Possessed of this disquieting news, the emperor could see that his attempted bribery had failed; the strangers were more insistent than before in their desire to come to the capital. And now it was entirely in the open: they sought to overthrow Huitzilopochtli. And if this was not enough, there was the menacing fact that the one named Cortés was interminably asking questions about the emperor. What did Montezuma look like? What were his habits? How did he conduct himself? "And when Moctezuma had heard that earnestly he was inquired and asked about, [that] the gods urgently wished to behold him before their eyes, he felt torment and anguish in his heart. He would flee; he wished to escape. Flight was [his] desire; departure was [his] wish. He would hide himself; he would vanish; he would take refuge and conceal himself from the gods. . . ." In desperation he implored the seers to tell him where he might hide; they told him of many places and buoyed up his hopes, rather cruelly it seems, for "Unverified and unfulfilled were the words of the soothsayers, through which they had changed his mind, provoked him, turned his heart, and taken vengeance upon him by seeming to be wise in knowing [the way] to the places named." [15]

Now Montezuma took the only action left to him, as he understood the situation. He abruptly severed all relations with the intruders and withdrew services and supply. While this created certain hardships, it did not force them to leave. The emperor could not know that Ixtlilxochitl, one of Nezahualpilli's sons who had been passed over by Montezuma when he placed Cacama on the throne of Texcoco, had already approached Cortés as an "enemy of tyranny" and offered alliance against the emperor. And five ambassadors from Cempoalla had also sought out the strangers and proposed alliance against the Mexica. From these sources Cortés had informed himself of the nature and state of the empire and of the growing precariousness of Montezuma's position. Precisely those things of which Cacama had warned in council had come to pass.[16]

The emperor felt even worse when he learned that the supermen had wrecked their ships. What better proof of their invincibility could be offered? Who could doubt it? And when he learned they had permitted the Cempoallans to abuse and imprison his tax collectors, he was utterly confused. Why, he asked himself, should the successor tolerate and even encourage rebellion in the empire that is soon to be his? But all was resolved in black despair when he received word that the invaders had left the coast and were marching on Tenochtitlán. Packing his belongings, Montezuma now vacated the royal palace and returned to his ancestral home to await the end. Keeping close watch on the invaders' progress, he was stunned when they defeated the Tlaxcalans in battle; even though convinced of their invincibility, it was too much to believe. His lords and Huitzilopochtli's priests were almost riotous in their demands for direct action; the invaders had allied themselves with Tlaxcala after the defeat, and it could be expected that the other Enemies-of-the-House would likewise be enlisted. Perhaps unable to withstand the pressure of their demands, Montezuma agreed to contrivance of a trap for the supermen in Cholula, which happened to be the locus of Huitzilopochtli cult in that area and, therefore, the occasion of the first meeting between Huitzilopochtli and the invaders. The emperor held little hope for success and was not at all surprised when Cortés turned the tables and slew the Cholulans. What did aggravate his tortured mind was Cortés' seeming omniscience: after Cholula, he received a message from him with a warning to stop listening to the advice of the idols. This sent him into the Black Room for eight days of attempted consultation with the Hummingbird.

In desperation Montezuma repeatedly sent emissaries with bribes and promises to do almost anything if the supermen would but return whence they came. With word that Cortés had left Cholula, Montezuma called for a noble who looked enough like himself to be a twin. Dressing him in his own royal raiment, he was sent to meet Cortés on the road to see what would happen. But many of the Tlaxcalan nobles in the van had attended imperial fetes and knew Montezuma quite well; on their intelligence Cortés sent the imposter to his master with humiliating effect, which Montezuma suffered as another indication of the invader's omniscience. Failing in all else, the emperor again increased sacrifices to the Hummingbird; blood ran in gutters and the macehualtin approached ignition point, especially when they heard of the Cholulan massacre:

> For all the common folk went in uproar; there were frequent disorders. It was as if the earth quaked, as if the earth quivered—as if the surface [of the land] circled in tumult.

> There was terror.

> And when death had come to Cholula, then [the Spaniards] started forth in order to come to Mexico. Marshaled together, in a concourse, they came stirring up the dust. Their iron lances, their iron halberds glistened [from afar], and their iron swords moved in a wavy line like a water [course]. Their iron shirts and iron head gear jingled. And what some wore was all iron; they came turned into iron, gleaming. Hence they caused astonishment; thereby they aroused great terror. Because of it they were regarded with much dread—they were greatly feared.

> And their dogs came ahead, they went before them. As the vanguard they came, in the lead. They came at their head. They came panting, foam dripping [from their mouths].

In the town of Quauhtechcac, beneath towering Popocatepetl, Montezuma's emissaries again presented the invader with a treasure of gold.

> And when they had given them the gift, they appeared to smile, to rejoice exceedingly, and to take great pleasure. Like monkeys they seized upon the gold. It was as if then they were satisfied, sated, and gladdened. For in truth they thirsted mightily for gold; they stuffed themselves with it, and starved and lusted for it like pigs.

This bribe failed like the others before it. And the invaders were much closer now. In a desperate attempt to forestall destiny, Montezuma called on the last of his sorcerers to go out and block the road. Within a few hours they returned with an amazing tale for the emperor: they had encountered a drunken peasant on the road who was really Tezcatlipoca in disguise; he told them to stop where they stood and look back on the capital. They did and saw it lying in rubble and flames. This, the peasant said, was how it would soon look, and as for Montezuma, "Too late has he come to his senses; it has already been determined to deprive him of his kingdom, his honor, and all that he possesses for the gross tyranny he has held over his people. He has not reigned as a lord, but as a tyrant and traitor."

> Moctezuma, when he heard it, only bowed his head; he stood with his head lowered. He hung his head; he stood with his head downcast. He did not then speak, but only remained full of woe for a long time as if beside himself.[17]

The emperor went into seclusion to await the end. Cacama broke in and made a plea for action: let Montezuma free the generals to use the legions and meet the peril that hourly grew more terrible. As the invaders approached, they were assuming sovereignty and gaining powerful allies; soon they would be beyond challenge. The Mexica must fight now and win victory or death! But Montezuma was unmoved. "What good is resistance when the gods have declared against us?"

In the face of the emperor's unyielding resignation the lords had no alternative but to receive the invaders gracefully and await future developments. As the invaders approached the lagoon, Montezuma sent Cacama and many of the great lords ahead to receive them. When the Spaniards reached Acachinango, the place where the southern causeway branched off to Coyoacán, the emperor prepared to meet his fate. Reluctantly stepping aboard his ornate litter, he was carried out through the gates of the capital. He could see the supermen coming with Cacama and the others. His legs felt weak; he wanted to flee, but the whole empire was watching. There was no escape. The two columns were closing now; the one in the lead, who had just dismounted from his beast—was he Cortés? Yes, there was no question of it. He looked just like the sketches, and those searching, penetrating eyes! Motion stopped; the litter was still; aides extended their arms as canopy bearers moved in to shield him from the sun. Other great lords swept the earth before him that his golden sandals should not be soiled; a carpet was laid. None dared look at him, but Cortés stepped forward and looking into his face fixed him with piercing eyes: "Is this not thou? Art thou not he? Art thou Moctezuma?" His breath caught in his throat; he felt faint; he made deep obeisance, almost as reflex, which Cortés acknowledged. "It is so; I [am he]." Another mutual reverence. Now Montezuma found his tongue and blurted out in hasty recital:

O our lord, thou hast suffered fatigue; thou hast spent thyself. Thou hast arrived on earth; thou hast come to thy noble city of Mexico. Thou hast come to occupy thy noble mat and seat, which for a little time I have guarded and watched for thee. For thy governors [of times past] have gone—the rulers Itzcoatl, Moctezuma the Elder, Axayaca, Tiçoc, Ahuitzotl—who, not very long ago, came to guard

131

[thy mat and seat] for thee and to govern the city of Mexico. Under their protection the common folk came here. Could they, perchance, now find their descendents, those left behind? O, that one of them might be a witness to marvel that to me now hath befallen what I see, who am the only descendant of our lords. For I dream not, nor start from my sleep, nor see this as in a trance. I do not dream that I see and look into thy face. Lo, I have been troubled for a long time. I have gazed into the unknown whence thou hast come—the place of mystery. For the rulers [of old] have gone, saying that thou wouldst come to instruct thy city, [that] thou wouldst descend to thy mat and seat; that thou wouldst return. And now it is fulfilled: thou hast returned; thou hast suffered fatigue; thou hast spent thyself. Arrive now in thy land. Rest, lord; visit thy palace [that] thou mayest rest thy body. Let our lords arrive in the land.[18]

Cacama and the other lords of the Pipiltin listened and were made ill.

Chapter VIII

The Invaders

The average Spaniard who lived early in the sixteenth century could no more readily distinguish between religion and sovereignty than we of today can confuse them. It is largely on this account that we so often fail to read—or succeed in misreading—the Spanish conqueror's thoughts and the actions they provoked. Yet, we must understand how and why he happened to be doing God's work, his prince's, and finally his own, and all simultaneously. What constituted the imperial ideal?

Dualism was inherent in the sixteenth-century concept of sovereignty because it had both religious and political progenitors. Throughout the Middle Ages popes had been called upon to arbitrate temporal dispute; they could and frequently did settle international conflicts by confirming sovereignty or denying it. Now, in the western tradition, sovereignty always involves property of some sort. In fact, it is almost as difficult to imagine sovereignty without ownership as it is ownership without property. While the princes of the church acted as arbiters on the basis of Petrine inheritance, there were ancient Roman laws that secular rulers could invoke to secure their ends. Thorny questions of sovereignty contributed substantially to the divisiveness of the sixteenth century, much of which could be attributed to secular princes who were reviving Roman legal principles in their bid for political and ecclesiastical power in the newly centralized states. And so when it came down to the problem of sovereignty and possession, there were two avenues of approach.

It was, of course, the great Discovery that made the Spanish empire and gave it identity. It also gave rise to the last and most colossal papal "donation," and provided the ultimate test of the Roman principle of *Occupatio*, or "occupancy," which for centuries had guided feudal lords in formation of their estates and in more recent years had given the new monarchs a ready instrument for creation of their national domain. Occupancy, one of the time-honored "natural" means of acquisition, was broadly inclusive; it governed unoccupied lands, gems and subsoil riches, abandoned moveables, the bounties of nature, and lands newly discovered. In the Roman tradition these things comprised *res nullius* and could be claimed by the one who first took permanent possession. Ordinarily such properties were considered *res nullius* when they had no apparent prior owner or had clearly never been owned. But the property of an enemy could also be considered *res nullius* under certain conditions, so that in war all was made available to the victor. This was the legal engine of the Spanish *Reconquista* and was firmly rooted in the conqueror's mind when he invaded the western hemisphere. Indeed, it had become a part of his thinking. In order to properly lay claim to *res nullius*, it was necessary to make clear the act and intent with a formal ceremony. And so midway in the battle for Tabasco, which was Cortés' first major engagement in his attempt to conquer New Spain, Bernal Díaz relates how the commander mustered his troops in the central plaza:

> . . . And there Cortés took possession of that land for His Majesty and in his royal name. It was done this way: with bared sword he cut three slashes as a sign of possession in a large tree called a *Ceiba*

which grew in the courtyard of the great square, proclaiming that if anyone should object to his act, that he would defend it with his sword and shield. All of us soldiers who were there answered, crying out that he was right in taking possession in His Majesty's name, and that we would support him should anyone say otherwise. This act was done in the presence of the royal notary.[1]

Lest we suspect Cortés of indulging in a Romanized "finders-keepers," it should be understood that this same principle of *Occupatio* also justified physical capture in war and subsequent claim of dominium and all that sovereignty implied. Traditional interpretation of the principle of occupancy held that warfare rendered prior jurisdictions null and void, so that private property and sovereignty itself became *res nullius* in the course of just war. The conqueror's idea of what constituted just war was clearly defined in the *Requerimiento* first used by Alonso de Ojeda at Cartagena: All mankind stemmed from Adam and Eve and therefore constituted one great family under the authority of the pope who was "lord, king, and superior of the universe" by virtue of the Petrine inheritance; in papal confirmation of Spanish discovery and occupation of the Indies, part of this great power was ceded to the Catholic Monarchs who now assumed sovereignty; therefore, all peoples must accept the Spanish crown and its holy faith. Refusal to do so was cause for just war. One sees this basic idea in Cortés' mind as he requested "that his Holiness may approve and allow that the wicked and rebellious, being first admonished, may be punished and chastised as enemies of our Holy Catholic Faith, which will be an occasion of punishment and fear to those who may be reluctant in receiving knowledge of the Truth; thereby, that the great evils and injuries they practice in the service of the devil, will be forsaken."[2]

One consequence of the conquest of the Spanish Indies was a painful questioning of the principle of occupancy—primarily by Spaniards themselves. European rivals attacked Spain's advantage

more than they questioned its rationale. While English attitudes varied, as did those of other Europeans, the principle of *Occupatio*
remained as a constant in English thought. It was, in fact, to be the
means whereby large portions of the globe would become British
empire, or, as Sir Henry Maine put it, "Occupancy was the process by
which the 'no man's goods' of the primitive world became the private
property of individuals in the world of history." [3] Thus when we listen
in on a town meeting of Milford, Connecticut, in 1640, we hear the
following resolution:

> Voted, that the earth is the Lord's and the fulness thereof;
> voted, that the earth is given to the Saints;
> voted, that we are the Saints." [4]

A corollary of occupancy as employed by the Puritans became a
cardinal point in Blackstone: the earth and all its fruits are the
property of mankind by virtue of divine cession. It was but a short step
to a frankly secular theory of effective occupation that England made
its own, a theory in which the right of possession depended upon the
ability of the occupant to militarily defend his claim. Such was to
become the fundamental prop for European imperialism throughout
the great colonial age.

Spain's conquerors had an equally vivid if less direct idea of divine
largesse. "Who does not know," asked Oviedo, "that God created
terrestrial things for our use?" He might well have added "and ownership," for such was the implication and the reality. The Spaniard's
mission in the New World was divine just as it was selfish; he was the
servant of majesty and God and expected to be rewarded by both. In
his mind the Spanish empire was unique; it was ludicrous to imagine
that there could be more than one empire and one emperor. Menéndez Pidal has called this a revisitation of the old Roman vision, which
seems quite fitting. The conquest was an imperial mission whose
motive was to unite all men in one family with one faith; the empire

was unquestionably the most perfect form that human society could assume.[5] The throne, the people, and the empire comprised a *corpus mysticum* against which no earthly force could prevail. It is no wonder, then, that the conquistadores were contemptuous of indigenous empires, however powerful, and of native religions. Traditional interpretation of Ostiensis held that although pagans enjoyed natural rights of liberty, possession of property and sovereignty, these rights were forfeit with the advent of Jesus Christ and were passed over to St. Peter's successors in Rome who held full power of disposition. By virtue of the Alexandrine documents and through its physical presence, the Spanish crown claimed sovereignty over its share of the newly discovered Indies of the Ocean Sea. Its conquerors saw to it that the Indians swore fealty to the crown and accepted Christianity, all in a single breath. To do one without the other was unthinkable to all but a few friars in the Caribbean who, in 1512, began to differentiate between political sovereignty and religious conversion. But to the conquerors, this union of political and religious submission had the full force of *jure divino*. However much Las Casas and other critics were to attack this union, they could not shake the imperial ideal.

Before he ever set foot on the vast continent that was to become New Spain, Cortés had many notions concerning its nature. But how much did he really know? The gulf coast had been observed from above present day Tampico to Yucatan's Cape Catoche, and from there to the Spanish Main. Ponce de León had coasted the peninsula of Florida, and there were doubtless voyages and preliminary explorations of which we know nothing. Cortés had been in the Caribbean a dozen or so years and had talked endlessly with crewmen and pilots, so that he had a precise idea of the lay of the land. Like everyone else, he knew that the Indians of the mainland were savage fighters; their cultures were varied, showing a wide spectrum of accomplishment. The Córdova voyage had disclosed superior stonework, good cottons, refined agriculture, and considerable use of gold. The Grijalva expedition in turn gave evidence of still greater wealth and refinement and, more importantly, held out the promise of a much higher civilization somewhere in the west. Jewelry and articles received in barter at the Río de Banderas were intricately worked and suggested a culture superior to any yet encountered. The impact was sufficient to send Diego de Velásquez, the governor of Cuba and chief impresario of mainland conquest, in search of a worthy captain to lead a new venture. But it seems probable that Velásquez did not receive all the information and treasure that derived from the Grijalva voyage; the items presented to Pedro de Alvarado by Montezuma's emissaries in the Papaloapán River were apparently omitted from the lists of items received in trade, nor are they mentioned in the sources again. It may well be that Velásquez never learned of their existence.

Following a period of heavy weather, Grijalva had been forced to put into the Tabasco River to repair a broken yard and other damages his vessel had suffered. Meanwhile, Alvarado, who captained the "Trinidad," continued north, expecting the others to follow as soon as repairs had been completed. Just as Grijalva's and the other two vessels prepared to leave the river and resume their coastal voyage, the coast was struck by a savage norther that blew for two weeks, thereby extending Grijalva's stay in the Tabasco River to a period of approximately three weeks. In flight before the same storm, Alvarado sailed up the Papaloapán and his unwitting meeting with representatives of the Mexican empire. When he sailed back down and took to the open sea, he met Grijalva and the other vessels in anxious search. Alvarado was summoned aboard the flagship where he found Grijalva intemperately angry over his unscheduled journey upriver. Heatedly rebuked, Alvarado returned to the "Trinidad," counting Grijalva a friend no longer.[6] The four ships sailed around to the next river, which they named Río de Banderas because Indians posted at its mouth beckoned them in with white banners tied to long poles.[7] Following Montezu-

ma's orders, the people of Cuetlaxtlán gave every sign of friendliness
and co-operation. The Spaniards were taken aback by this show of
cordiality, so much so that some began to talk of establishing a permanent settlement. The trade was brisk, and in a few days had netted the
Spaniards a considerable amount of gold. Grijalva was apparently a
man of small imagination; he resisted all arguments in favor of settlement and tried to put an end to them by moving his little fleet out of
the river entirely. Juan Díaz, the chaplain of the voyage, was one of
those who wanted to stay. They had all seen a meteor rise in the
eastern sky and fall in the west, and this he interpreted as a sign that
God too favored the project. At San Juan de Ulloa the question was
argued again, but to no avail. Rather abruptly on June 24, but apparently with permission, Alvarado took his ship and headed for Cuba,
presumably because she was in need of repair. Bernal Díaz later said
that Alvarado was ill and no longer interested in the expedition.
However it was, Alvarado was the first one back with news of the
voyage. Did he also report his experience on the Papaloapán River? It
appears doubtful. The items gained in trade were not solid gold, at
least those that were reported. But it seems that the articles sent down
by Montezuma were of fine gold and exquisitely wrought, especially
Quetzalcóatl's wind staff and throwing stick. Be that as it may, Governor Velásquez was furious when he learned that in the face of welcome invitation Grijalva had failed to depart from his orders and
establish a settlement. Hastily he cast about for a new captain, one who
could think on his feet and more successfully lead a new expedition.
The problem, of course, was to find an effective leader who would do
the job without casting off the governor's authority and taking it for
his own, just as he himself had seized control of Cuba from the
Columbus family.

In answer to the governor's needs, his chief accountant, Amador de
Lares, proposed the name of Hernán Cortés, who also had the support
of the rich and influential merchant Andrés de Duero. Cortés got the

appointment and set out at once to organize the expedition. There has always been some question as to whether or not Cortés had full access to Grijalva's reports before his own sailing. I believe this to be quite beside the point. He did have access to Alvarado, and the two of them were cheek by jowl in preparing for the voyage. It is not at all unlikely that they exhausted many an hour and bottle together pondering the civilization that had produced those remarkable gifts of the Papaloapán. If there was such a conspiracy between Cortés and his backers and Alvarado, they had ample time in which to work out its details; Alvarado returned early in July, and Cortés was not appointed until late September.[8]

Cortés probably knew more about the Indians' religious practices than any other aspect of their culture. He had heard many times about the temples with their bloody sacrificial stones, of cannibalism, of priests clad in long robes not unlike a friar's, with long and stringy blood-clotted hair, and how they stank of death, of copal incense, of hideous idols. The men of the Córdova expedition had used a temple for refuge when attacked at Cape Catoche; within they had seen many idols and sculptures, some portraying the act of sodomy. When they returned to their ship, the chaplain, Gonzáles, carried with him a number of small idols and figurines, and they became inspiration for raucous humor in ship's hold and camp. From now on the Spaniards tended to consider every native priest a sodomite.[9]

If these are some of the things Cortés knew, or thought he knew, what were the tacit assumptions against which they would be weighed? First, it becomes obvious from his letters and utterances that he believed divine providence to be at the helm of discovery and invasion; conquest was a part of the "mystery and miracle of God." He was eternally reliant upon his God for safety and victory, as he promised his men at Cape San Antonio, the Cuban staging area for Mexican conquest: "[This day] we undertake just war and one of great fame. Almighty God, in whose name and faith we wage it, will give us victory." [10] In a very real sense Cortés was here announcing a crusade. In his own thought, as in that of most enlightened men of his age, the earth was governed by two forces: the Christian world by God, the non-Christian world by Satan. Wherever the cross prevailed, the Evil One was forced to flee. But he stubbornly resisted, employing three weapons against intrusion of the cross. These were Judaical perfidy, Mohammedan falsity, and idolatrous blindness. In all areas of the world where the word of God was not preached, there Lucifer had his seat and center, his dominion; and there one would find perfidy, falsity, or idolatry rampant, or perhaps all three. But God had chosen the kings of Spain to oust the devil from the Indies, to destroy his power over the Indians, to cleanse them of his idolatrous contamination. It was Lucifer who held sovereignty, not the kings or priests; it was he who must be banished from the land. And Cortés was the emperor's strong right arm through which the deed would be done. These propositions were the essence of a reality beneath which all others could be subsumed.

In this light it is more clearly seen why Cortés felt compelled to take possession of New Spain at Tabasco, even though Grijalva had done so the year before at the Río de Banderas. The great difference lay in the fact that Cortés was leading the last of the great crusades. Before the fight at Tabasco, which in Cortés' mind was *the* battle for New Spain, he was meticulous in following official formula. With the enemy's forces spread across the field, Cortés deployed his own troops accordingly, and in a last minute parlay made the following demands upon the Tabascans: they must permit the Spaniards to land and take on water in peace; they must permit them to speak about God and king; if they resisted or refused, then war would consume them and the fault be theirs alone. [11] Through interpreters the message was perfectly understood and promptly spurned by the Tabascans. After his victory, Cortés took possession; and from this point on he considered Charles V to be the legitimate sovereign, not only of Tabasco, but of the whole New Spain. This was a colossal arrogance in view of the fact that he had no idea of the real size of the continent or of what it might contain. But it was consistent with the other attitudes that characterized crusading Christianity.

The Conqueror also displayed what amounted to an automatic response to native religious practices. Beginning on the Isle of Cozumel, Cortés forbade human sacrifice and cannibalism, rolled down idols, ordered the temples to be cleansed of crusted blood and human skeletal remains, all of these things representing the obvious hand of Satan and accordingly "crimes against both God and nature." Cortés had with him a generous supply of icons of Mary with the Christ Child in her arms and an even greater number of banners bearing the same image. By design these images were placed in native temples after they had been cleansed and marked with a great cross. The chain began on the Isle of Cozumel and gradually extended all the way to Tenochtitlán. Cortés did not just happen to have the images on hand; they were the paraphernalia of an earnest crusader.[12] Before he left Cuba, Cortés planned to make Mary the symbol of Spanish sovereignty as it should be extended in the West. At Cozumel he employed Jerónimo de Aguilar as an evangelist, a reasonable choice since he was a priest and knew the Mayan language.[13] The Indians proved receptive and accepted Mary, making her a prime goddess. Long after he had moved on toward Mexico, the Indians of Cozumel continued to revere her image; they even put it in a large canoe and rowed out to welcome visiting ships with cries of "Cortés! Cortés! Mary! Mary!"[14] Following victory over Tabasco, Cortés instructed many of the Indians, both nobles and plebeians, in the basic tenets of Christianity, ranging from Genesis to the accession of Charles V. During lessons, a large statue of Mary and the Christ Child was wheeled out, presumably as a visual aid. The Tabascans accepted Mary as Teuccihuatl, which meant "Great Lady." His troops had already rolled down the stone idol from the great *cue*, as the Spaniards now called all pagan temples.[15] A Christian altar was built in the chastened temple, and an image of Mary was enthroned beneath a huge cross. Tabasco was now renamed Holy Mary of Victory, even as lords and nobles pledged themselves to uphold the sovereignty of the Emperor Charles.[16] Ever the symbol of Spanish dominion, the Virgin never actually intervened in combat, but her champions gratefully acknowledged that on occasion she did cast dust into the Indians' eyes so that they could not see to fight.[17]

It is difficult to guess when Cortés first learned of Quetzalcóatl and his rumored return. It is possible that Doña Marina, one of the slaves given him by the lords of Tabasco and now his concubine and Nahuatl interpreter, might have provided some insights; he could have heard tales anywhere along the way, but they probably had little significance for him until he made contact with Montezuma's emissaries. As we have seen, this took place on Holy Thursday, April 20, just after he had led his fleet into San Juan de Ulloa. It was immediately obvious that the boarding party putting out from shore was comprised of emissaries of a major power; its members bore themselves imperiously and their attire and adornments were wondrously rich. Once aboard and conducted to the commander's presence, the emissaries treated him with divine reverence. Squatting abjectly before him they touched a dampened finger to the deck and then placed it to their lips, a gesture the Spaniards had seen at Tabasco and knew as "eating dirt." Rising, they called him "god" and "king" and dressed him in a peculiar royal costume and presented him with rich gifts. They made it clear that he had long been expected, that he was welcome in his own kingdom. Rising to the occasion, Cortés played the role by ear. After putting on a fearful display of what must have appeared to the emissaries to be supernatural power, and loosening their tongues with wine, he released them to flee to their master.[18] If the treasures given to Alvarado on the Papaloapán were the guide to what Cortés was seeking, there could be no doubt in his mind that he had found it.

The following day, which was Good Friday, Cortés determined to set up a base camp ashore, and was greeted by hundreds of laborers who had been sent at Montezuma's order. He put them to work at once; Montezuma would build the invader's defenses. On Easter Sunday Tendile arrived with a personal greeting from the Mexican emperor. He and the governor of Cuetlaxtlán and their aides approached Cortés and, after waving the plebeian tamemes back, squatted and ate dirt three times, then did the same before other Spaniards who stood close by. Obeisance was followed by incensing of the strangers. There could be no mistaking it, the Spaniards were being received as supernatural beings. Cortés was not flattered; he was shrewdly pragmatic. He saw to it that his guests witnessed Easter Mass, after which he put on another display of supernatural power. The cannons were overloaded to provide a thunderclap; bells were tied to prancing horses; steel and hardware were highly polished. Sound, sight, and smell were recorded faithfully by Tendile's artists on agave parchment, even to flying cannon balls and the sounds they made as they tore up trees and thudded to earth. Tendile noticed a helmet worn by a soldier and told Cortés that it looked exactly like one that had been left by an ancestor and now rested on the head of Huitzilopochtli, the god of the Mexica. In view of this, Cortés agreed to permit Tendile to carry the helmet to Montezuma for inspection. And so the emissary, burdened with the helmet, scores of sketches and pictographs of the strangers, and carrying Cortés' account of Christianity and the role of the Emperor Charles V, hastened to Tenochtitlán.[19] Cortés had now heard the name of the Hummingbird, of whom he and his followers were shortly to learn much more. But they never were able to pronounce his name, and from the very beginning chose to call him Huichilobos,* an untranslatable Spanish corruption of Huitzilopochtli.

* Wee-chee-lōbōs.

In the days that followed, the Spanish camp was abundantly supplied with every necessity by Indians whose numbers had swollen to over a thousand. The trade that Cortés requested grew in volume, but it did not occupy his thoughts. Seven or eight days after his departure, Tendile returned with a large train of carriers, all heavily burdened with rich gifts. Upon approaching Cortés, the emissaries again ate dirt and incensed the captain and those around him. This must have been somewhat puzzling to Cortés. Certainly by now the Indians realized that the Spaniards were mortal. They had fought and died along the way; their dogs and horses had been proved equally vulnerable; it was obvious that the soldiers were inveterate *donjuanistas,* as any of the camp women could testify; the Indians had experienced with the invaders every human appetite, had seen them involved with every human function. Why, then, did they continue to treat them like gods? Because Montezuma ordered it so, and his word was absolute law. He believed that the Spaniards represented divinity and must be treated accordingly. It should be remembered that although the lords around Montezuma may have considered divinity and mortality to be mutually exclusive, the emperor did not. He was himself the living Huitzilopochtli. And, as we already know, at this point he feared that Cortés might be the living Quetzalcóatl, or at least his emissary. This gesture of incensing the invaders has on occasion been explained away as a defensive maneuver on the part of the Indians: the Spaniards did not bathe and smelled badly, especially with festering wounds and unchanged dressings. Now, there is no doubt that one could smell a conqueror before he could be seen if the wind was right. But it is doubtful if he could have equaled the odor of the very priests who wielded the censers on these occasions. Their robes were usually crusted with gore from past sacrifices; their hair, which they never washed, hung heavily with blood clots beneath ears that were cauliflowered by years of penitential laceration. And they not infrequently wore human skins over their robes until they fell away. "They stank," declared Bernal Díaz, "like sulphur, and they had another very bad odor like decayed flesh." No, the Spaniards were fumigated because they were supermen, if not gods.

Upon his arrival Tendile presented Cortés with a staggering treasure trove: a fabulous golden disk, delicately carved and chased in representation of the sun, the size of a cartwheel; a matching moon disk of pure silver; beautifully worked gold pieces and jewelry; loads of brilliant feather work, gorgeous fabrics, and the soldier's helmet, now filled with fine gold. The emperor's message was brief. He said that he had been watching the movements of the strangers since their arrival and was pleased to hear of the great emperor of whom they spoke. But it would not be possible for them to advance further, and so with this gift they could feel free to return whence they came. Cortés instantly calculated his position: he was being treated as a deity; he had been given a huge bribe, obviously out of fear. Montezuma was afraid that he would come to the capital, but did not dare forbid it. Cortés' reply was that he would not leave without first seeing Tenochtitlán and the emperor.

When days later Tendile again returned with more gifts and another plea for the strangers to depart, Cortés, sensing his advantage without fully understanding it, began to probe. He explained carefully to Tendile that the Emperor Charles had sent him for the express purpose of abolishing human sacrifice and worship of idols and exercise of their evil rites. After prolix discussion of Christian theory, all the while warming to his own arguments, Cortés ended by suggesting that Montezuma erect a tall cross over the central temple, even going so far as to offer an image of the Virgin to replace Huitzilopochtli.

While Tendile was in the capital relieving himself of this burden before a frowning emperor, Cortés received emissaries sent from Texcoco by Ixtlilxochitl who, posing as an enemy of tyranny and a claimant to the throne, offered alliance with Texcoco's powerful anti-

Montezuma faction. The exact nature of their exchanges is unknown, but from Cortés' subsequent conduct it is apparent that the emissaries disclosed Montezuma's fears and laid bare the internal weakness of the empire. It was therefore no surprise to Cortés when Montezuma suddenly withdrew all support from the Spanish camp and forbade further trade or other association with the intruders. On the heels of Mexican withdrawal, five representatives of Totonacapán entered the camp in search of Cortés. They had been waiting several days to approach him without the knowledge of Montezuma, against whom they also sought military alliance. Cortés talked with them at length, learning still more about the Mexican empire. With presents for themselves and their lords and promise of a visit to their rulers in the very near future, Cortés sent them back to their capital at Cempoalla. This remarkable chain of events was genuine cause for elation. A grand design of conquest was rapidly taking shape in Cortés' mind, and it was now that he conspired with his trusted followers against Velásquez men in his company in founding a settlement, Villa Rica de la Vera Cruz, which provided him with the two things he needed most: the municipium of Vera Cruz, which authority he could usurp and use to challenge that of Governor Velásquez pending royal approval, and an operational base for the conquest of Tenochtitlán and Montezuma's throne.[20]

Following weeks saw the Spaniards rambling over the littoral, studying terrain and visiting prospective allies. Not unmindful of division within his own ranks, Cortés pacified Velásquez partisans with diplomatic finesse; for the most part, their greed was found to outweigh their loyalties. Near what is today Jalapa, a small group of Cholulans met with Cortés and offered more evidence of imperial unrest. Although inconclusive, the source suggests that they represented a group in opposition to Mexican hegemony and intrusion of Huitzilopochtli cult. Failing in their opposition, they had been forced to leave Cholula and subsequently settled in Cuauhtlantzinco. But it was in Cempoalla and neighboring towns that Cortés learned everything he needed to know about the Hummingbird and his imperial sway. Arriving as promised for negotiations with the lords, Cortés was met by the king, a ponderous mountain of flesh whom Bernal Díaz referred to as "the fat *cacique*." In presenting his credentials, Cortés identified himself as a special emissary of the Emperor Charles V whose mission it was "to redress grievances and punish evildoers." Cortés would maintain this pose until the last blow had been struck. Finding himself confronted by an avenging angel of sorts, the king hastened to enumerate his grievances against Montezuma's empire. He explained that his province had but recently been conquered by the Mexica. In the beginning they had gained entry through religious discussion, although this turned out to be a mere entering wedge for imperial forces; the whole province had been seized before anyone could defend what was his. Once under tribute levy, he went on, anyone who opposed it was sacrificed, and everyone lived in dread of being taken away for sacrifice to Huitzilopochtli or Tezcatlipoca. Mexican vengeance was described as swift and terrible. He further complained that gold, jewels, and valuables of all sorts were regularly carried off, and without recourse. What would the supermen do about this? Cortés listened patiently and then calmly announced that the Totonacs would soon be relieved of their oppression.

After extensive interviews with the fat cacique and his lords, the Spaniards moved north a few leagues to the town of Quiahuitztlán. Hardly had formal greeting and incensing been accomplished when porters arrived, groaning under the load of the fat cacique on his litter. Apparently enthusiastic over the prospect of being rid of Mexican exploitation, he had followed the Spaniards in order to act as their advocate. The lords of Quiahuitztlán confirmed all that the Spaniards had heard in Cempoalla, adding a general discourse on Montezuma and his imperial system. They were especially bitter in denouncing the annual levy of sacrificial victims for Huitzilopochtli, the forced service of their people on estates belonging to Mexican lords, and the ravishing of their daughters by Montezuma's tax collectors. No sooner had Cortés given his assurance that he would rectify these wrongs than it was announced that five of Montezuma's tax collectors were approaching the city. In panic the lords fell away from Cortés. As Montezuma's officials entered the gates and passed by the curious Spaniards, they presented a startling effect. Attired in richly worked robes, ornately colored, hair groomed and shining, they were closely attended by Totonac lords with fly whisks and a host of lackeys. With necks arched in arrogant pride, they looked through the Spaniards as though they were not aware of their presence. In a flower-bedecked pavilion they deigned to pick at a sumptuous banquet table hastily laid in their honor. The fat cacique and his peers cringed and bowed as they waited for them to make known their desires. They did not have to wait long. The superior of the collectors roundly castigated them for having received the Spaniards without express orders from Montezuma to do so. Furthermore, he continued, Montezuma intended to capture the Spaniards, and the Totonacs must immediately hand over twenty sacrificial victims for Huitzilopochtli, to the end that he will favor Mexican victory over the intruders. The fat cacique immediately informed Cortés of their demands.[21]

For most men this would have been a moment of decision, but by his response it is clear that Cortés had already reached a decision and was acting upon it. He ordered the fat cacique and his lords to arrest the tax collectors without delay. The Totonacs were astonished at the very idea; it was unheard of; Cortés bristled and insisted, at which they dared not refuse. One of the imperial officials haughtily resisted his bonds, but on Cortés' prompting he was flogged until he changed his mind. With Montezuma's officers in confinement Cortés now proclaimed that henceforth no one should pay tribute to the emperor, nor should his commands be obeyed. Montezuma's sovereignty was

ended forthwith, and a proclamation to that effect was sped by messengers to every town in Totonacapán.

Seeing that he had virtually swept the Totonacs off their feet in
authoring the revolt, Cortés now attempted to soften the blow for
Montezuma. Late that night he had two of the tax collectors brought
in secrecy to his quarters where he greeted them cordially, denying
that he had any part in the unfortunate events of the day. Restored to
freedom and escorted beyond the local frontier by Cortés' own men,
they were sent to Montezuma with assurances of Cortés' friendship
and a promise that he would try to gain the release of the others. The
following morning disclosed their apparent escape, at which the fat
cacique and his peers determined to slay the remaining three. But
Cortés forbade it, upbraiding them for being so careless as to permit
the escape. Ostensibly as a move to guard against possible repetition,
he had the remaining prisoners transferred to the brig of one of his
anchored ships. The lords of Totonacapán were now utterly dependent upon Cortés, who stood between them and Montezuma's vengeance. In return for his pledge to defend and protect them they swore
allegiance to Charles V and accepted everything that such an oath
implied. More than thirty towns joined in celebration of what was to
be a brief escape from tyranny. Cortés now had the nucleus of an
alliance.

At best his strategy involved calculated risk; he had openly dethroned Montezuma. What would the emperor's reaction be? Cortés
was betting that his fears would overcome his displeasure. But if they
did not, what then? He had been told that Montezuma could field
150,000 men. Using all available labor, including his own men,
Cortés hurriedly constructed a medieval fortress with church, arsenal,
and market place as functional members of a walled complex. This
was the first Villa Rica de la Vera Cruz, located about a half-mile from
Quiahuitztlán. Even as Cortés and his men put their backs into the

task, another embassy from Tenochtitlán arrived. Cortés had won his bet. The emissaries made it clear that Montezuma was grateful to him for having secured the release of his tax collectors, but he could not understand why Cortés, who was beyond doubt the one whose return his ancestors had foretold, should countenance—even encourage— rebellion against imperial authority. Cortés countered with a query of his own. Why had the Mexica deserted his camp and deprived him of food? It was on this account, he lied, that he had been forced to seek supplies in Cempoalla. Let Montezuma understand that the allegiance of Totonacapán had been but temporarily shifted to the Emperor Charles V; as soon as he and his men had arrived in Tenochtitlán and placed themselves at Montezuma's service, imperial unity would be restored. To emphasize his good will, Cortés now released the other three tax collectors. The local lords who witnessed the arrival of Montezuma's emissaries did so with misgivings. But when they saw them present Cortés with gifts of gold, they were astonished. How great was the power of the supermen, and how much the emperor must fear them! Cortés had dispossessed him of sovereignty and Montezuma had paid a handsome reward, or so it appeared. The impressions of the Totonacs were relayed to the capital where they were received as fact, and in that way the plebeian masses were confirmed in their belief that the strangers were indeed supermen.[22]

Cortés was now possessed of proof that Montezuma had him confused with a legendary deity and that he dared not attack him, whatever the provocation. He also understood more clearly the nature of the imperial system and the stature of Huitzilopochtli, or Huichilobos, as he and his followers called him. It had become apparent that Huichilobos was a prime demon—perhaps the devil himself—who stood behind the throne. In looking back, it all became clear: the Grijalva expedition had found freshly slaughtered sacrificial victims on an island off the coast that its members appropriately named the

Isla de los Sacrificios, and more were discovered at San Juan de Ulloa; in trying to answer the Spaniards' queries of why, the Indians attempted through signs and gestures to indicate Culhua-Mexica. Then had come the sacrifices before the Spaniards on the beach. Recent experiences and information received in Totonacapán had finally made everything plain. Huichilobos was responsible; it was he who demanded human sacrifice. Indeed, he was even now calling for the blood of the Spaniards if what the Cempoallans said was true. Did the tax collectors not say that he ordered their capture? Information was coming out of the capital in growing volume, providing Cortés and his men with food for thought. In nightly discussion around the campfire Huichilobos loomed ever larger in the Spanish mind as the principal enemy to be overcome, as Bernal Díaz so clearly reveals: Montezuma was said to be in communication with the Hummingbird and daily made sacrifices in order to find out what he should do about the Spaniards. The reply was that "he should not listen to Cortés nor to what he proposed about the cross, nor should the image of Our Lady be brought to the city." [23] It was obvious to the invaders—above all, to their leader—that Montezuma was relying upon Huichilobos for salvation. Religion and sovereignty being inseparable, it seems likely that Cortés was even now anticipating the ultimate confrontation of Huichilobos and the Virgin.

From Totonac lords who had been to Tenochtitlán as guests of Montezuma, Cortés doubtless learned of the Enemies-of-the-House and the perpetual war that was said to exist between them and the Mexica. Since Cempoalla and other Totonac towns had so easily fallen into his hands, why should not Tlaxcala and the other enemies join the growing alliance? It was not unreasonable to hope that his forces would grow to such proportions that the Mexica might not fight at all. And Montezuma did appear to be weak; if he dared not attack now, how could he do so later when the alliance included all his enemies? There was a distinct possibility that the conquest could be accomplished by diplomatic means; it might not be necessary to fire a shot. It seems evident that such thoughts weighed heavily in Cortés' decision to wreck his ships, wherein he forced all those of less faith to follow their leader.

At the same time, Cortés was learning that Indian allies could more easily be gained than managed. During a lull in his diplomatic offensive against the melancholy emperor, he permitted the Cempoallans to falsely incite him against their rivals of Cingapacinga. Arriving with a company of men at the scene of their fabled wrongdoings, he discovered that the Cempoallans were merely using him to screen what they intended to be a plundering expedition. Returning to Cempoalla in high dudgeon, he was determined to force a showdown. The fat cacique and his lords were summoned and castigated; more to the point, they were ordered to halt human sacrifice and cannibalism forthwith, and they were to take down the idols from their central temple. The priests made violent protest, and the nobles refused. Cortés gave them an ultimatum: either they or his own men would cleanse the temple. Peering down the throat of Cortés' cannon, the fat cacique threw up his hands and grudgingly yielded permission. About fifty Spaniards raced to the top of the pyramid and with iron bars levered the idols over the edge, watching as they rolled and crashed down the staircase and shattered in the courtyard below. The chapel walls were scraped and scoured with lime, then whitewashed. A cross was erected, and an image of Our Lady enshrined on a newly built altar. On the next Sunday, Mass was followed by the baptism of eight Indian girls who had been presented to the intruders as a peace offering by the nobles. If practicable, the Spaniard preferred his concubine to be Christian. "The niece of the fat cacique was named doña Catalina, and she was very ugly; Cortés was given her hand, which he accepted and tried to look pleased." [24]

With harmony restored and ships scuttled, there was nothing to hold the invaders on the coast. On August 16, just four months after their landing, Cortés and his men turned inland and began the long march to Tenochtitlán.

Eight days later Cortés marched into Xocotla, a large city of about 100,000 population. Strategically located in relation to Tlaxacala and the coastal provinces, it was a pivotal point in imperial defense and hosted a garrison of 5,000 imperial legionnaires. The lord of Xocotla, Olintetl by name, headed a delegation in extending welcome to the strangers, which was solemnized by the sacrifice of fifty unfortunates. On the basis of his previous experience, Cortés came straight to the point. Expecting to find another who would be happy to cast off allegiance to Montezuma, he inquired whether or not Olintetl recognized Montezuma as sovereign, in effect inviting him to say no. He was hardly prepared for the question Olintetl fired back. "Is there anyone who is neither a slave nor vassal of Montezuma?" At this, Cortés launched into a rather detailed description of his Holy Roman Emperor, concluding with a request that Olintetl accept him as sovereign and that he make the emperor a present of some gold. Olintetl refused to consider it, pointing out that Montezuma was the "Lord of the World," that he had thirty vassals who had over 100,000 troops each, that he sacrificed untold thousands each year in Tenochtitlán, which was the greatest city on earth. Montezuma's wealth was beyond belief, his sovereignty universal. No, Olintetl would not renounce his allegiance. Cortés could see that this man was hopeless. What he failed to realize, of course, was that Olintetl had been to the capital and had sat behind the rose screens, had seen everything the masters of the system wanted him to see. He obviously also thought what they wanted him to think. And he had 5,000 of Montezuma's best warriors at his back. In view of this, Cortés spent but five days in Xocotla. Bernal Díaz and the others counted thirteen religious temples, one of which had what they estimated to be thousands of skulls of sacrificial victims in a structure resembling a huge corn crib. Cortés had a mind to roll down the idols, and later in a letter to the emperor claimed that he had in fact done so; but Bernal Díaz said that Father Olmedo talked him out of it, pointing out that they would only desecrate the cross as soon as the Spaniards had moved on. And so Cortés had to satisfy himself with merely forbidding Olintetl and his peers further human sacrifice and cannibalism, which prohibitions were received in stony silence.[25]

After leaving Xocotla, the invaders marched on to the great Wall of Tlaxcala, a structure of stone and mortar nine feet high and twenty feet thick stretching for miles across the whole valley floor. Once inside, it became apparent that the Tlaxcalans would contest the Spanish advance. Thus was Cortés dealt another surprise: the Tlaxcalans refused to believe that the Spaniards were not in secret league with Montezuma, and, suspicious of treachery, they attacked with great force. Bernal Díaz brilliantly describes the action, which need not be repeated here. As in Tabasco, the Toledo blade, the cavalry, and superior tactical skills enabled the Spaniards to overcome the enormous numerical superiority of the Indians.

With victory, Cortés proclaimed the sovereignty of Charles V, which the Tlaxcalans readily accepted. But when he wheeled out the large image of Mary and ordered dethronement of the idols, the nobles faltered. They warned that the priesthood largely controlled the masses and the throne through their direct contact with the supreme deity. If ired, they could initiate a rebellion that would destroy them all. Cortés was not impressed and said so, apparently insistent on his course of action. At this juncture, according to Bernal Díaz, Father Olmedo again stepped in to offer counsel: "Sir, do not attempt to force this issue; it is not just that they be compelled to accept Christianity, neither should I like to see us do what we did in Cempoalla, that is, destroy their idols until they have some understanding of our Holy Faith." His judgment tempered by the sound advice of a religious whom he respected, Cortés agreed to moderate his demand. Merely one temple was cleansed and converted into a Christian church, complete with altar, cross, and an image of Mary. However much Cortés disliked it, this compromise proved to be the *modus vivendi* of the growing alliance. His usurpation of sovereignty could be tolerated if he did not immediately invite the further pressures of religious dislocation. To Cortés the dissociation of majesty and Christianity did violence to logic and reason, but he could also see that the Indian lords with whom he had to deal would react both violently and unreasonably if he pressed them too hard.

Once he had gained the confidence of Tlaxcala's rulers, Cortés learned most of what remained to be known about the imperial system, how it had developed and flourished and how it had finally begun to disintegrate; he understood the principle and function of the Flower Wars and was quick to perceive that Montezuma's excesses had triggered a reaction in which the Enemies-of-the-House became genuine. "I was not a little pleased to see this discord and want of conformity between the two parties," he wrote to the emperor, "because it appeared to me to strengthen my design. . . ." Montezuma was shocked by the Spanish victory over Tlaxcala and hastened to send another bribe. Grovelling before Cortés, the emissaries surrendered a load of gold, jewels, and fine cottons on behalf of their emperor, who volunteered his vassalage and unlimited tribute to Charles V provided the Spaniards would return to their own land without continuing on to the capital. Cortés put them off until he had concluded a treaty of alliance with Tlaxcala, which he especially desired them to report to Montezuma. A week later the emissaries returned with more gold, this time requesting Cortés, in Montezuma's name, to disregard everything the Tlaxcalans had told him and warning him against their treachery.[26]

Since the invaders ignored the emperor's warnings and took up residence in the Tlaxcalan capital, Montezuma's priests and counselors now argued that the Spaniards must be crushed before they could gain the rest of the Enemies-of-the-House in alliance, to which Montezuma apparently agreed. Consequently, four Mexican lords appeared before Cortés and in their emperor's name made a present of gold and invited him to come to Tenochtitlán at once; they offered themselves as guides, insisting that he was to go by way of Cholula. When the Tlaxcalans heard of this, they offered vehement protest, pointing out that Cholula was under Montezuma's domination and control. It would be much less dangerous, they argued, if Cortés went by way of Huexotzinco which, like Tlaxcala, was a genuine enemy of the Mexica. Cortés listened to the Tlaxcalans' arguments and thanked them for their good advice, but he was determined to go to Cholula. On the face of it, this would appear to be an unwise decision, especially since he already had inkling of an ambush. What apparently decided him was the fact that Cholula was the first locus of Huitzilopochtli cult he had encountered, and he wanted to beard the lion in his den. If he could win an impressive victory over Huichilobos in Cholula, might not entry into Tenochtitlán be made easier? It might force Montezuma to capitulate entirely. We can only guess at Cortés' thoughts, but Bernal Díaz states that the decision to go to Cholula was definitely part of a strategy to take Tenochtitlán without waging war. At this point Cortés apparently felt that such a psychological victory over Montezuma was worth more than alliance with Huexotzinco. At any rate, if the latter was really an Enemy-of-the-House it could be enlisted for military alliance if such need should materialize. Meanwhile, he would take the Virgin to Cholula. Arriving in that fabled city of temples, the invaders were met by a throng of lords and peasants. Cortés made a brief speech from the back of his horse, one in which he hurled unmistakable challenge: he and his followers had come at the order of their great emperor to put an end to human sacrifice and idolatry; the Cholulans had no recourse but to swear obedience and fealty to Charles V, whose sovereignty was absolute. Finis. Rankled lords in attendance muttered that while they *might* give allegiance they would not surrender their idols.[27] The issue was clearly defined.

The Spaniards were led into the city and lodged in a sumptuous palace whose courtyard was surrounded by a high wall. Their Tlaxcalan allies who had accompanied them were required to remain outside the city at the demand of Cholula's lords. The first two days passed without untoward event, although anxiety was mounting and tension hung over the city like a cloud. Cortés' scouts went out by night and watched the Cholulans prepare the city for battle, reporting that barricades were rising in the streets leading to the Spanish quarter, pitfalls were being dug and then camouflaged as a trap for the cavalry, and the roofs were all stocked with throwing stones. Other sources of intelligence, probably Tlaxcalan, revealed that women and children were being moved out of the city and that there was mounting sacrificial slaughter to Huichilobos in supplication for victory over the invaders. On the morning of the third day all service to the Spanish compound was discontinued, and the quarter was devoid of movement. Two emissaries arrived from Tenochtitlán, this time arrogant and defiant in manner. With all possible insolence they read a fresh decree from the emperor that commanded Cortés to quit the country. He smiled, chiding them because Montezuma was so vacillating, and announced his intention to depart for Tenochtitlán on the morrow. Using two priests as hostages, Cortés now commanded the ruling lords to appear before him. Once assembled, he warned that he would punish them for any treachery against the sovereignty of the Emperor Charles. Repeating his intention of leaving the following day, he demanded 2,000 Cholulan warriors to accompany him, to which the nobles readily agreed.

Meanwhile, Cortés had seized two more high priests who proved amenable to intimidation and bribery; they told all. According to them, Montezuma had been highly distraught and unable to reach a decision. One moment he ordered his regional lords to co-operate with Cortés, but in the next he reversed himself; in the same way he ordered that the Spaniards should be permitted to come to the capital, only to change his mind again and deny them. But now, the priests warned, Huichilobos and Tezcatlipoca had ended his indecision by deciding that the Spaniards should be captured in Cholula and taken to the capital as prisoners. To secure this end, Montezuma had sent 20,000 warriors, some of whom were already in the city, while more waited in reserve on the road to the capital. Once the invaders were captured, the Cholulans were to sacrifice twenty of them to Huichilobos immediately and send the rest to Tenochtitlán. This entire plot, it was related, was negotiated and financed by Huitzilopochtli's priests, acting through their confreres in Cholula who had influence with many of the great lords. Huitzilopochtli, they concluded, had guaranteed success. Cortés took this intelligence at face value, especially when his informants identified the twenty Spaniards who had already been selected by the Cholulans for their victory sacrifice.

The foremost problem was to discover when and how the trap was to be sprung. It was now that Doña Marina's espionage achieved crucial significance. She learned that the Spaniards were to be taken the following morning: as it appeared, the Cholulans would use the pre-dawn hours to smuggle warriors into the Spanish quarter so that when the 2,000 warriors Cortés had requested entered, there would already be as many, or more, on the inside. Thus as the invaders were preparing to leave, or perhaps before they had risen, they would be captured. Long before dawn of the fateful morning, Cortés had his men up and quietly dispersed for battle while a few of their comrades sleepily went through the motions of preparing to march, giving the impression that the others were still in their beds. The Cholulans arrived as predicted, and when they were within the walls of the courtyard the gate was slammed shut and locked behind them. And as suddenly, they found themselves outflanked by the Spanish cavalry, which seemed to materialize out of thin air. Now Cortés, facing them astride his horse, made another speech: in detail he reviewed the plot as he understood it, indicating every stage of the conspiracy and its chain of preparation, even down to the fact that cooking pots were at that very moment awaiting him and his men, pots already seasoned and dashed with peppers and tomatoes. He dwelt at length on the role and responsibility of Huichilobos, the "evil and false author of the plot" who could never overpower the Spaniards. Reminding them of the penalty for treason, he let his hand fall, which was the signal for attack. A shot rang out and the execution was on. There were so few Spanish casualties one must suspect that many of the Cholulans slain were servants and tamemes, rather than warriors. It was a frightful affair, as the principals testified. Said Cortés: ". . . We did such an execution that, in two hours, more than three thousand persons had perished." "And a blow was dealt them that they will remember forever," writes Bernal Díaz, "because we killed many of them and the promises of their false idols came to naught." "One could not move without stepping on a corpse," later wrote Gómara who listed over 6,000 dead. As the Spaniards attacked within the compound, their Tlaxcalan allies fought their way into that quarter of the city on Cortés' orders, apparently to provide an avenue of retreat should one prove necessary. Once within the city, the Tlaxcalans ran wild in murdering and plundering their ancient foes. Word of successful entry was relayed back to Tlaxcala, and even more legions were dispatched to get in on the sport. Only with great difficulty did Cortés finally prevail upon their leaders to restrain them and confine the butchery to the Spanish quarter of the city. As soon as Cortés had secured the compound, his forces were directed to Huitzilopochtli's nearby temple. The priests and soldiers manning its defenses were gradually slain and pushed back, the last defenders climbing to the very top of the Hummingbird's temple where, rather than surrender, they were burned alive as the superstructure was consumed in flames.

Until the end the priests were heard to lament their defeat and Huitzilopochtli's desertion of them and their cause. As the temple smoldered, an official delegation of priests and lords approached Cortés and disclaimed any complicity in the conspiracy, confirming that it had been the work of Huichilobos' priests and certain nobles who were in league with Mexico. In fact and effect, Cortés had wiped out Huitzilopochtli cult in Cholula, the very thing for which he had come. He now felt free to grant amnesty to survivors and to make peace with the rest of the city. Huichilobos' charred temple was cleared of rubble and ordered rebuilt at once, this time as a shrine for the Virgin. Word of Huitzilopochtli's defeat and enthronement of a successor goddess swept throughout the provinces as though borne on the wind.[28]

Cortés listened with interest as his spies told of Montezuma's reaction, how he had fled to Huichilobos' temple in desperation, how he accelerated the sacrificial schedules, and how Huichilobos now advised him to permit the Spaniards to enter Tenochtitlán so that they could more easily be taken. Summoning Montezuma's ambassadors, Cortés gave them a message. They were to repeat the account he gave them of the recent affair in Cholula, but Montezuma was to understand that he did not for one moment believe the charge made by Cholula that the emperor was implicated. He was also to realize that Cortés knew very well that Huichilobos was putting evil ideas into his head, but was equally certain that Montezuma, if he were to act on them, would attack in the open like the great prince that he was, and not from cowardly ambush. Let Montezuma be assured that the Spaniards would soon resume their march on the capital to carry out the commands of their great lord beyond the sea. So much for this gambit in his game of psychological war with Montezuma. What Cortés was really thinking was later revealed in a letter to the emperor: "I vowed to Your Royal Highness that I would have him prisoner, or dead, or subject to the Royal Crown of Your Majesty." [29]

Making good his word, Cortés and his troops again set themselves on the road to Mexico. At Amecameca lords representing the anti-Montezuma factions of Chalco, Tlalmanalco, Chimalhuacán, Acacingo, and other southern cities secretly approached Cortés with complaints against Montezuma and the imperial system. Thanking them for their offers of alliance and accepting their surrender of sovereignty, he cautioned that for the moment they must suffer continuance of the system, but that in good time he would put an end to Mexican dominium. Repeatedly they warned Cortés that Huichilobos had arranged a trap for him, to be wary of his wiles. Cortés invariably replied to the effect that only God could put an end to the Spaniards. Resuming the march, he assumed the sovereignty of each community through which he passed—Xochimilco, Cuitlahuac, Mizquic, Iztapalapán, Mexicatzinco, Huitzilopochco. If to the Indians the Spaniards appeared to comprise an invincible iron juggernaut, with their fearsome sounds of clanking armor, the strange odor and sight of horses, with slavering hounds in the van, the men inside the armor didn't appreciate it: "We set out for Mexico, and as the people of Huexotzinco and Chalco had told us that Montezuma had held consultations with his idols and priests, and that Huichilobos told him to allow us to enter so that we could be killed there, we dwelt upon it, being but mortal men in fear of death. We commended ourselves to God and to his blessed Mother, Our Lady, and talking about how and by what means we could enter [the capital] put hope in our hearts that since Our Lord Jesus Christ had seen us through past dangers, that he would likewise protect us from the power of Mexico."

At Ayotzingo the army was met by Cacama and a party of lords who had been sent out to greet Cortés and, if possible, persuade him to withdraw. Failing that, they were to accompany him the rest of the way. At Iztapalapán, Cacama, having failed in his mission, lodged the invaders in a spacious palace, luxurious in its baths and gardens and sweetly scented air. Well could the Spaniards look around in awe at its exquisite furnishings and compare the tales of Amadis of Gaul with what befell their eyes. And this was only the beginning! Early the next morning, which was the eighth day of November, they resumed their passage of the causeway, apprehensive, yet filled with wonder. The capital loomed ever larger, until, at last, they halted at Xoloco, a fortified section of the causeway just beyond the great gates of the city. There appeared to be thousands of lords awaiting their arrival, all dressed in brilliant costumes with rich personal adornments. For the great majority of soldiers who were afoot, the reception ceremonies must have seemed endless. At the head of their column Cortés sat astride his horse as each of the greater lords approached to pay him homage. Squatting before him, they touched the earth and then placed the finger in their mouths, as the soldiers had seen done so many times before. Cortés, anxious to meet Montezuma, himself grew weary of the seemingly endless procession and complained, "I was kept waiting almost an hour, until each had performed his ceremony."

Then a procession appeared through the gates with Montezuma's ornate litter in the lead. Carried by eight great lords, it was richly adorned with blue and green feathers and studded with gems mounted in finest gold. The litter stopped and Montezuma stepped down; immediately, attendants stepped in to shade him beneath a rich canopy of green plumes embroidered in silver and gold with pearl pendants; the golden soles of his sandals gleamed against the crimson carpet as he stepped forward. "Montezuma came in the middle of the street, with two lords, one on the right side, and the other on the left, one of whom was the same great lord, who, as I said, came in that litter to speak with me, and the other was the brother of Montezuma, lord of the city of Iztapalapán, whence I had come that day. Each supported him below his arms, and as we approached each other, I descended from my horse, and was about to embrace him, but the two lords in attendance prevented me with their hands, that I might not touch him, and they, and he also, made the ceremony of kissing the ground." Rising, Montezuma began to speak in haste, almost as though he could not govern his own tongue. As he spoke, Cortés searched him with his eyes: he saw a man of possibly forty years of age, of medium height, very slender, with an almost feminine air of delicacy about him; his complexion was lighter than that of his attendants, hair black and cut just below the ears, very shiny. His eyes were faintly almond-shaped, quite dark; he wore a beard, thin but well shaped, with small mustaches at the corners of his mouth that pointed down at the chin. His face was long and gave an impression of melancholy.

After Montezuma's speech had run its course, the two exchanged necklaces. Cortés placed around Montezuma's neck a chain of imitation pearls and glass diamonds strung on a scented cord, while the emperor adorned him with a double collar of colored sea shells with finely wrought golden shrimps as bangles. Now they and a few of Montezuma's lords led the entire procession into the city, slowly approaching Axayacatl's palace, which was to be the invaders' home. Montezuma himself showed Cortés into his apartments and seated him on a rich dais. "Malinche, you and your brothers are in your own house. Take your rest." Promising to return shortly, the emperor took his leave. Cortés promptly dispersed his troops and mounted the cannon, ordering constant alert until the future should reveal itself. Bernal Díaz was probably typical of the soldiers' frame of mind, overwhelmed by what he had seen but acutely aware of his peril. The impossibility of reconciliation was conducive to a literary aphasia concerning their arrival that Bernal Díaz still reflected many years later. "They had a very sumptuous meal ready for us, prepared according to their use and custom, which we ate at once. Such was our lucky and daring entrance into the great city of Tenochtitlán-Mexico on the eighth day of November the year of Our Savior Jesus Christ of 1519. For all of which thanks to our Lord Jesus Christ." [30]

Chapter IX

Confrontation

After the Spaniards had finished their sumptuous repast and briefly surveyed their surroundings, Montezuma returned at the head of a group of important lords. Each in turn squatted before Cortés and paid homage while he briefly took the hand of each one in his own and inclined his body in a faint bow. Servants placed a second dais beside Cortés' so that the two could sit closely for conversation. With deity and majesty seated, the lords and Cortés' captains took their places in a semicircle around the twin thrones. Cortés, flanked by his interpreters, Doña Marina and Aguilar, could see that the emperor desired to make a speech and invited him to do so. Montezuma began:

> We have known for a long time, from the chronicles of our forefathers, that neither I, nor those who inhabit this country, are descendants from the aborigines of it, but from strangers who came to it from very distant parts; and we also hold, that our race was brought to these parts by a lord whose vassals they all were, and who returned to his native country. After a long time he came back, but it was so long that those who remained here were married with the native women of the country, and had many descendants, and had built

towns where they were living; when, therefore, he wished to take
them away with him, they would not go, nor still less receive him as
their ruler, so he departed. And we have always held that those who
descended from him would come to subjugate this country and us, as
his vassals; and according to the direction from which you say you
came, which is where the sun rises, and from what you tell us of
your great lord, or king, who has sent you here, we believe, and hold
for certain, that he is our rightful sovereign, especially as you tell us
that since many days he has had news of us. Hence you may be sure
that we shall obey you and hold you as the representative of this
great lord of whom you speak. . . .

Cortés listened carefully as his interpreter translated Montezuma's
secularized version of the Quetzalcóatl prophecy; it was obvious that
he wished to avoid discussion of religion. In reply Cortés confirmed
the truth of all Montezuma had said, that indeed the Spaniards had
come at the bidding of their great lord across the sea. The principal
reason for their coming, he added, was to convert the Mexica to
Christianity so that their souls might be saved by the one True God.
As his remarks were being translated, Cortés studied Montezuma's
face intently. Already perspiring under his steady gaze, Montezuma
began to lose composure at mention of deity. With a gush of words, he
hastened to deny all the things that he knew the Tlaxcalans and
others had told about him: "I know they have told you also that I have
houses, with walls of gold, and that the furniture of my halls, and
other things of my service, were also of gold, and that I am, or make
myself, a god, and many other things. The houses you have seen are of
lime and stone and earth." Now in undisguised anguish, he leaped to
his feet and flung aside his robes, baring his entire body, nude but for
an ornate breech clout. "Look at me," he pleaded, "and see that I am
flesh and bones, the same as you, and everybody, and that I am mortal,
and tangible." With this he feverishly plucked and grasped the flesh
of his arms and breast. "Look how they have lied to you!" Cortés did
not answer him, but sat and stared. Calmer now, Montezuma gath-

ered his robes and swept an arm through the air. "It is true indeed that I have some things of gold which have been left to me by my forefathers. All that I possess, you may have whenever you wish." As though relieved, he now sank heavily into the embrace of his throne. Actually, he had pointed to Axayacatl's treasure that lay hidden behind a wall of the very room in which they were seated. "I answered to all he said," wrote Cortés, "certifying that which seemed to be suitable, especially in confirming his belief that it was Your Majesty whom they were expecting."

Having made his plea, Montezuma signaled for waiting servants to fetch his bribes. Loads of jewelry, mantles, precious feather robes, and concubines were distributed to the Spaniards, after which the emperor and his lords rose to leave. Cortés saw them out to the street. Once back within the privacy of his palace, the Conqueror gave vent to his surging elation and danced a lively step as he called for a victory fete. He had won it all! Late into the night wine flowed, and Montezuma's women were heard to laugh. At regular intervals cannon belched flame and thunder, their echoes rumbling and reverberating over the brooding stillness of the lake. The populace was terrified.[1]

Since Montezuma had stated his readiness to abdicate in favor of Charles V, the next step was to dethrone Huichilobos and replace him with Mary. Only then could sovereignty be truly won. And so, the following morning after breakfast Cortés took four captains and five soldiers and sought out Montezuma in his palace. The emperor already had several guests, nephews and partisans who were involved in imperial management and thus much concerned over Montezuma's reception of the Spaniards. The nephews were, in fact, Montezuma's political heirs. Although tradition forbade the presence of any but intimates in this part of the palace, Cortés and his men were ushered into the reception hall, where they found Montezuma in conversation with his lords. As Cortés took the place offered him by the emperor's right hand, the others were seated on low stools. Scarcely indulging in amenities and without preamble, Cortés went straight to the point. He began by saying that with the previous day's interview he and his men had fulfilled the emperor's command to visit Montezuma. Even so, there remained a still higher obligation to be met: the message of "Our Lord God." This message, he reminded, had been delivered to Montezuma through his ambassadors at Vera Cruz; therefore, Cortés now hoped that Montezuma would do what had been asked of him. Without actually saying so, he was requesting the emperor to replace Huichilobos with the Virgin, and in such a way that his nephews would not understand unless Montezuma had previously confided in them. But he was not yet finished. A long discourse followed in which Cortés explained the whole of Genesis and the later history of the world. The Emperor Charles, he concluded, was sick at heart over the loss of so many souls that were being led off to hell by the idols, all the more so because, as the children of Adam and Eve, all men were brothers. Therefore, it was as a deeply concerned elder brother that the emperor had sent Cortés to put down the idols, to end human sacrifice and cannibalism, sodomy, and imperial despoilment of lesser peoples.

Montezuma listened tensely to Cortés' long discourse; from time to time he glanced at his nephews as Doña Marina translated its veiled message. After a pause, he replied to the effect that he understood very well what Cortés had said about the "three gods" and the cross; but for as long as memory served, the Mexica had worshipped their own gods and thought them good. Therefore, Cortés need not speak further on that subject. On the other hand, Montezuma continued, the Mexica had long understood creation of the world, and it was precisely because Cortés' account of it to the Indians of Tabasco so closely followed their own that he became convinced that the Spaniards were those whose arrival his ancestors had foretold. In view of this, the emperor concluded, he would be most happy to give Cortés everything he possessed.[2]

Blunted in his thrust at the heart of the matter, which he now understood to have been premature, Cortés came away empty-handed. But he had learned something: his evangelical formula, practiced without deviation since the island of Cozumel, had saved the expedition. This he took without question to be evidence of the power of the Word, without suspecting the declension by which Montezuma really had made up his mind. Cortés spent the rest of that day and all of the next in pondering his future moves. How to get at Huichilobos? Indeed, the palace in which the invaders were lodged was no more than a bow shot from the Coatepantli and Huitzilopochtli's temple; around the clock they could hear blaring conch shell trumpets summon priests and penitents to service; neither through sleep nor diversion could they shut out the throbbing rhythm of the great snakeskin drums, giving assurance that human sacrifice to Huichilobos was going on unabated, that he still sought the Spaniards' blood and would, if possible, claim their beating hearts. No one was more cognizant than Cortés himself; he knew full well whom he was fighting and was determined to face the enemy.

So it was that on the morning of the fourth day, he sent Doña Marina and Aguilar to Montezuma to request permission for a visit to Huitzilopochtli's temple. Probably because he considered it inevitable, the emperor acceded to his request, but arranged it so that he would first have an opportunity to perform expiatory sacrifices. To do this, Montezuma sent Cortés and his party on a guided tour of the great market place of Tlatelolco, promising to meet them later at Huitzilopochtli's temple. The Spaniards went willingly and were astonished at what they saw: every kind of commodity and luxury, a daily trade of what appeared to be 60,000 people or more, innumerable shops and markets. Cortés and Bernal Díaz both wrote enthusiastic and detailed descriptions, although the latter maintained that it was of such magnitude that two days would not be time enough to take it all in. Leaving Tlatelolco, they bypassed its recently restored temple in order to meet

Montezuma atop the capital's great pyramid.[3] Approaching the Coatepantli from Tlatelolco, Bernal Díaz marveled that the plaza before the
wall was greater in size than Salamanca's. Once inside the Serpent
Wall they were conducted to the base of the pyramid where six priests
waited to escort them to its summit platform. As they cleared the last
of its 114 steps, they saw two slabs, red with fresh blood, a few idols
standing on pedestals, several ornamented snakeskin drums, and the
ubiquitous twin temples, or "towers," as the Spaniards called them.
Rising three stories, the lower was the temple proper, being constructed of stone with a stucco facade. The two upper tiers were of
intricately carved wood and served as burial vaults, containing the
ashes of cremated kings and high priests.

After his customary greeting, Montezuma voiced a fear that Cortés
was tired from his ascent of the pyramid. The Hawk stiffly replied
that he and his men were never tired by anything. It was an idle boast,
for many of his soldiers were pained by syphilitic lesions in the groin
and on their legs that climbing the great staircase in heavy armor only
made worse. But Cortés would not forego any opportunity to elaborate
the myth of his own invincibility. Looking over the island city from its
highest point, truly a pinnacle at dead center, the Spaniards were all
but overwhelmed, especially by the precision of the city's streets, its
causeways, and the connecting roads that disappeared in the distance
in uncurved lines; by the aqueducts from Chapultepec, the squadrons
of canoes on the lake; by the hum of activity rising from the market
place far below. From this height it could be seen that the four walls
of the Coatepantli could easily contain a Spanish village of 400
dwellings, and the invaders could now appreciate that the Serpent
Wall enclosed a city in itself that was the very heart of the empire.

However impressive, these were not the things Cortés had come to
see. Drawing Father Olmedo aside, he suggested that this might be a
good time to feel Montezuma out on the idea of converting the temple
into a Christian shrine. Olmedo vigorously dissented, but Cortés con-

tinued to hold the thought. Turning to the emperor, he requested Montezuma to reveal his gods. After brief consultation with hovering priests, Montezuma beckoned the Spaniards to follow. Entering one of the temples, they found themselves in a small antechamber that was separated from the sanctuary by a heavy veil. At a signal from Montezuma the curtain was drawn aside and the Spaniards entered to view what only the highest of priests and lords had ever seen. All eyes fell on two altars, each holding a huge stone idol the size of an ox. On the right was Huichilobos, his broad face and monstrous eyes partially hidden behind a golden mask. His polished body was crusted with mother of pearl and precious stones; thick golden serpents entwined his bloated belly. In his right hand he held a bow, golden arrows in the left; a necklace of faces and hearts, intricately fashioned of gold and silver and set with turquoise, fell in a wide loop around his neck. Tezcatlipoca squatted on the altar to the left; his face resembled that of a bear, with shining eyes set deeply in his head. Similarly covered with gold and precious stones, his thick middle was girdled by a string of little gargoyles. When they could tear their gaze from Huichilobos, the Spaniards saw that the walls were deeply sculpted and painted in the likeness of more idols, slightly larger than life. Their gaping mouths and grotesquely jutting chins were built up of dried blood. two or three fingers thick, by repeated "feedings" over the years, so that dimensional realism was greatly enhanced. Blood drooled from their maws formed scabby vests before dripping to the floor, there drying in large pools, some of them six inches thick. Before each of the idols a brazier containing freshly plucked hearts bore testimony to the sacrifices that had immediately preceded the visit of the Spaniards. The awful impact of sight and smell was too much for the visitors who, staying but moments, broke for cleaner air: " . . . There was on the walls such a crust of blood, and the whole floor bathed in it, that even in the slaughter houses of Castile there is not such a stench," wrote Bernal Díaz. Once outside, Cortés' anger welled and he could not restrain himself. Half-smiling, but deadly serious, he said to the emperor, "My Lord Montezuma, I do not understand how a great and wise lord like yourself could fail to perceive that your idols are not gods, but evil things called demons. . . . " After roundly denouncing Huichilobos, he proposed to erect a tall cross over the pyramid and to place an image of the Virgin in the sanctuary with the false gods so that Montezuma might see by the fear his idols would display that they were not genuine deities at all. When Cortés' words had been translated, Montezuma was seized with dismay, while the priests who flanked him became furious and made threatening gestures. Cortés' men already had their weapons partially drawn—the moment was tense. Montezuma spread his arms restraining the priests and bitterly declared that had he foreseen Cortés' insult, he would not have permitted him to enter the temple. Correctly reading the fury in the priests' faces, Cortés realized that he had gone too far. Beating a hasty retreat, he put on a smiling face and announced that it was time to be going. Montezuma readily agreed, but declared that he would have to remain behind to placate Huichilobos and expiate the insult paid the gods and his own error in permitting Cortés to see them. Cortés looked into his face and sneered: "If that be so my lord, I beg your pardon." And with that, he turned on his heel and left.[4]

The following two days afforded ample time for reflection. Cortés had confronted Huichilobos in his lair, but he had been premature in proposing his overthrow. To suggest it on the beach at Vera Cruz was one thing, but to do so in Huitzilopochtli's temple was quite another, especially in the face of the high priesthood. Since the incident, Montezuma's "guides" had vastly multiplied and now stuck like shadows, never allowing a Spaniard beyond their sight unless it was through the gates of Axayacatl's palace. And Montezuma himself now seemed to be growing more bold in his refusal to consider Cortés' religious proposals. As for the men, they were beginning to show fear; the novelty of arrival had worn thin, and it was obvious that the

Spanish takeover was not going to be as casual as it had first appeared. While Montezuma had repeatedly offered to turn everything over to Cortés as the representative of Charles V, he just as consistently refused to tamper with Huitzilopochtli, who was the real essence of sovereignty. If one considered the tactical disadvantages of the Spanish position, it became clear that Montezuma was merely temporizing and offering nothing at all. The Spaniards did not hold Mexico; it held them. This had in fact been true since the beginning of their adventure. All along the way Cortés had proclaimed the sovereignty of Charles V and the advent of Christ without stopping to effectuate either. As soon as he moved on, the scene reverted to *status quo ante*, and he and his men became more deeply buried in a hostile continent. But Tenochtitlán was the end of the line; if Spanish sovereignty and Christianity were to be made real, it would have to be done here and now. If successful, then the new law and the new god could be made to retrace their steps and force the provinces back into submission. In the event of failure the Spaniards and what they stood for would be washed away in the flow of their own blood. These were sobering reflections, but it seems quite evident that Cortés' supreme confidence in himself and his cause was not lessened by them. On the contrary, his determination to defeat and destroy Huichilobos was all the while growing to almost maniacal proportions. He had already risked the whole venture on this issue, and he would do it again.

The optimism of the first few days is reflected in the fact that no altar was constructed in the Spanish quarters, nor was one seriously considered. Cortés and his men apparently believed that the first Mass would be sung in Huichilobos' temple. But now they knew better, and without further delay set about building a chapel in their palace. In searching for a suitable site, they discovered a doorway that had been filled in with mortared stone. Suspicious over the fact that attempts had been made to age the masonry in appearance, they knocked a hole in it and crawled through into what proved to be Axayacatl's secret treasure room; caskets of jewels, pure gold and silver in slabs and plate, and exquisitely worked articles of endless variety comprised a fabulous treasure hoard. The discoverers gazed greedily, but kept their heads and resealed the chamber.

By the end of the first week in Tenochtitlán, nerves were growing taut; Cortés' Tlaxcalan allies continued to warn against Mexican treachery and insisted that just since the incident in Huitzilopochtli's temple they could sense a change in their hosts. And had not Huichilobos instructed Montezuma to permit them to enter the trap? Was he not even now advising the emperor? These thoughts and fears were frequently discussed by the Spaniards in their new chapel. Cortés apparently held open councils there in order to provide the men with a vent for their mounting tensions. How could they defend themselves against Montezuma's daily guard? What if he issued orders to deprive them of food and water? How could their allies help them in the event of siege? In spite of the treasure they had seen in Axayacatl's secret room, some were prepared to settle for nothing but their lives. According to Bernal Díaz, it was the captains and wittier soldiers who first thought of taking Montezuma prisoner and holding him as a hostage. In explaining it to Charles V, Cortés wrote, " . . . It appeared to me . . . that it would be conducive to your Royal Highness's service, and to our security, that Montezuma should be in my power, and not at his entire liberty, so that he might not relax his intention and disposition to serve Your Highness." The decision was obviously made on the grounds that however risky the strategy might be, to leave Montezuma free was infinitely more dangerous. And so it was planned that on the following day, November 16, Montezuma would be taken. Early the next morning, two Tlaxcalan scouts arrived with ominous news: Mexican forces had attacked villagers in the vicinity of Cempoalla, and when the Spanish garrison in Villa Rica had gone to their aid, a fight ensued in which six Spaniards had been slain. As a result, the Cempoallans were falling away from Cortés because they feared he could not protect them from Montezuma's wrath.

Cortés readily understood that the whole of Totonacapán might be lost if he did not act at once. Taking five captains, Bernal Díaz, and his interpreters, he went straight to the emperor's palace, acting as though nothing was amiss. Montezuma's greeting was still on his lips when Cortés accused him of treachery and duplicity. Relating the entire affair on the coast as he interpreted it, the emperor was made wholly responsible. This act, Cortés declared, was as infamous as the plot at Cholula, but this time Montezuma must pay: he would accompany the Spaniards without creating an incident or he would die on the spot. Montezuma paled and recoiled as though struck in the face. Denying any knowledge of the affair, he stripped the Huitzilopochtli seal from his wrist and sent it by courier to fetch the responsible officers in whose jurisdiction the incident had occurred. He would prove his innocence; but meanwhile, he refused to leave the palace. Cortés would not be put off, nor did the emperor seem ready to comply, however weak he appeared. There was no doubt of his complicity, although the strategy may have been forced on him by the priests and lords who were now determined to resist Huitzilopochtli's overthrow. The incident in the temple had made Cortés' motives and objectives transparent; what Montezuma had failed to tell his lords they now knew. As Montezuma and Cortés wrangled, Juan Velásquez de León, he of cavernous chest and hoarse voice interrupted: "What's the use of all this talking? Let's either take him or stab him; tell him once more that if he shouts or puts up a fight we'll kill him, because it is better that we should either save our lives or lose them right now." As this was translated, he made a move toward the emperor, who suddenly wilted and began to plead. Let Cortés take his son and daughters as hostages. "What will my lords say if they see me taken away as a prisoner?" His secret concern, probably, was that enemy factions would be sparked into action—he could easily be deposed under such circumstances. Cortés refused to answer him until he had submitted; in a flood of weakness he now did so.

How to get the emperor past his guards and out of the palace? Cortés' plan was simplicity itself: Montezuma was instructed to tell anyone who might ask that he was accompanying the Spaniards to their quarters because Huichilobos had told him to do so. The stratagem worked perfectly, and the emperor was whisked away before his nephews realized what had happened. In Axayacatl's palace he was placed under heavy guard but without personal restraints; his life was made as regular and comfortable as possible. He was permitted to receive visitors and enjoy the service of his own domestic staff; he was urged to hold court and administer the empire. To all outward appearances it was made to look as though he had simply moved back into his old palace, but under no circumstances could he leave its premises alive. His nephews and partisans were not deceived; they came at once and demanded to know of his seizure, offering to free him by force if he would but give the word. No, Montezuma lied, he was there because Huitzilopochtli had ordered it. This excuse was as good as any. How could they understand, as did he, that inexorable fate was following its prescribed course? And there he stayed, as Bernal Díaz said, with his women and his baths and twenty great lords, his counselors and captains. From now on he was to be Cortés' creature utterly. The Hawk had finally seized his prey.

About ten days later Quauhpopoca, the lord of Nauhtla and Tuxpan, his son, and fifteen officers arrived to answer for their attack on the Spaniards and their allies. Montezuma handed them over to Cortés, who gave them a mock trial and condemned them to death by burning. Under sentence they all pointed the finger of guilt at Montezuma, but it did not save them. They were burned alive in front of the palace, their pyre being made from weapons taken from Huitzilopochtli's temple armory at Montezuma's order. Thus did Cortés symbolize the significance of retribution, even as he broke the emperor to his will. While the guilty were being fired, Cortés clapped Montezuma in chains, which, for him, was the final step to complete degradation. After the burning, Cortés returned and freed Montezuma, offering him his complete freedom. But the fallen emperor was now tamed, and, weeping his gratitude, he refused to leave the Spanish compound. Using loving words, Cortés warmly embraced him: "It is not in vain, my lord Montezuma, that I care for you as I care for myself." Aguilar, at his instruction, had already warned Montezuma in strict confidence that although Cortés wanted to free him, his men would not permit it, so that to save his life he must refuse to leave.[5]

Although Cortés appears not to have fully realized it at the time, such a maneuver was unnecessary to hold Montezuma. His enemies had grown commensurately powerful with his decline, until now the greater peril to his survival lay with them. Only Cortés could save him, if he would. The proud emperor, the living god, had become a craven lamb, and it had happened before his enemies' eyes: the transition was told in his tragic failure to employ imperial might against the invaders when they were still on the beach; his sickening surrender to Cortés at the gates of the city; his cowardly failure to exact revenge for insult to Huitzilopochtli; in his betrayal of Quauhpopoca, whom he permitted to be burned in fire from the Hummingbird's own weapons! Even within his own party there was shifting of alignments. Cacama, whom he had enthroned in Texcoco, had remained fiercely loyal; even so, he was unable to comprehend his uncle's strange obsession and had been among those most urgently demanding forceful action. Now he emerged as a leader in resistance against the Spaniards who, in unerring perception, called him El Infante, "the pretender," and marked him down accordingly. Since the incident in the temple, most of the moderates had joined with the priesthood and military, whereupon Montezuma confided to Cortés that he could no longer be certain of his position, even within his own party. He was still emperor, but to what extent and for how long were open to question.

Cacama made his move when he learned of his uncle's captivity. Losing no time, he convened a junta of old political allies from Texcoco, his half-brother whom Montezuma had invested with Coyoacán, the lords of Tacuba, another of Montezuma's brothers, the lord of Iztapalapán, and the lord of Toluca, who was closely related to the emperor and held by some to be "the rightful heir" to the lordship of Mexico. The purpose of the junta was to create a united front against the usurpers, to map a course of direct action and to put it into effect. The first meeting was in session at the very moment in which Cortés burned Quauhpopoca, his son, and the fifteen captains who had accompanied them. The only reason that Cortés was able to hold this *auto* "without occasioning any commotion," as he put it, was because the junta had not yet completed its formulations. But they were working. Although he did not yet know what was afoot, Cortés sent to Villa Rica for all the things needed to build two stout ships for possible flight over the lake; he was guessing at the truth. Meanwhile, as Cacama and the others came daily to see Montezuma, they made no mention of the junta, nor did they even hint at its purpose. As if by script, they daily offered to free him, to which he replied in equally rote fashion that Huitzilopochtli's will was being done.[6]

If Montezuma's fiction of voluntary captivity was to be maintained, it was imperative that he go to the Hummingbird's temple for sacrifice and worship. Cortés could offer no alternative, however much he disliked the idea. On the other hand, if the emperor could be made to appear free, it might slow down the machinations of those who opposed him and his accomodation of the intruders. It was growing increasingly apparent that El Infante was developing dangerous momentum. Warned that he must not permit human sacrifice and that any suspicious act on his part, the merest change in demeanor, would occasion a knife in the ribs, Montezuma was sent off to the temple accompanied by his retainers and surrounded by a company of Spanish soldiers. Father Olmedo was sent along to put a stop to any human sacrifice that might be attempted. Once on the pyramid, however, Montezuma slipped beyond dagger thrust and thence to freedom. Going ahead with normal ritual, he had several men and boys sacrificed, later disappearing in Huitzilopochtli's sanctuary for secret conversations with his priests. The Spaniards were filled with disgust and anger: " . . . We could do nothing about it at the time but dissimulate because Mexico and the other great cities were at the point of rebellion under the leadership of Montezuma's nephews." The emperor had called their bluff and won the hand. But freedom was short-lived. The priests confirmed much of what Montezuma already suspected and feared. He reappeared and voluntarily returned with the Spaniards to their fortified compound, apparently because there was no other place for him to go.

The junta, meanwhile, had split when the ambitions of its leaders were disclosed. Some of the conspirators withdrew entirely when the idea of deposing Montezuma was formally introduced, not so much out of loyalty as from lack of confidence in the motives of the plotters. As his price for participation in war against the Spaniards, the lord of Toluca demanded the imperial throne. Cacama, who already fancied it his own, steadfastly refused. By promising rich rewards and high office when he should assume control of the imperial system, El Infante had put together a powerful faction that gradually dominated the junta. When he realized that he would not have his way, the lord of Toluca withdrew, and in spite sent a complete report of all the junta's proceedings to Montezuma. Now the emperor had his turn at vengeance; he passed on the intelligence to Cortés. Through diplomatic approach Cortés tried to reach some understanding with Cacama, but the latter would have none of it. He saw the issue as one involving practical sovereignty and naked military power, without a shred of fatalistic nonsense. In a powerful Mexican lord this was the kind of thinking Cortés had reason to fear. Acting through Montezuma, Cortés laid a trap and El Infante was taken by stealth. Facing his betrayer, Cacama rattled his chains and reviled Montezuma as a coward and traitorous wretch. Within the week his fellow conspirators had been rounded up and joined him in a dungeon; they were shortly followed by some of the others who had participated in the junta. At Cortés' direction, Montezuma placed Cacama's brother on the throne of Texcoco. As heir apparent, he had been a constant target for his brother's assassins, so that his hatred of the king made him a willing instrument in the fulfilment of Cortés' designs.

The invaders could now breathe easier; while not eliminated by any means, the prospect of armed revolt was much less immediate. Always ready to turn every opportunity to advantage, Cortés now moved in to tighten his hold on political control. He informed Montezuma that it was time for him and his lords to swear fealty and pay tribute to the Emperor Charles V and to acknowledge formal transfer of sovereignty. In preparation for such a momentous step, Montezuma suggested the need for a meeting with his principal lords. Cortés agreed, although it was understood that no Spaniard should be present. Orteguilla, the Conqueror's youthful Indian page, was sufficiently bilingual to listen in and make a full report. Many great lords of the Pipiltin refused to come; they would neither consider the proposal nor recognize Montezuma. To those who did appear, Montezuma presented his familiar argument, one which even he was now beginning to choke on: "I hold it to be certain, and you must also hold it thus, that his sovereign is the one we have been expecting. . . . " Everything that had come to pass, he explained, had been at Huitzilopochtli's behest, " . . . and if for the present our gods permit me to be held prisoner here, it would not have happened, unless, as I have told you many times, my great Huichilobos had commanded it." Upon their agreement to follow his example, Montezuma led them into Cortés' reception hall where each in turn took an oath of allegiance to Charles V, all of which was taken down and reproduced in triplicate by the royal notary.[7]

Cortés now assumed control of the levy and collection of imperial tribute. As a token of Montezuma's submission, he deigned to accept the whole of Axayacatl's treasure. With whetted appetite he sent collectors to gather provincial gold and to survey the sources whence it came. While the imprisonment of Cacama and the others tended to shore up Montezuma's position temporarily, Cortés realized that resistance would again polarize and offer threat from a new quarter, and so it would ever be so long as Huichilobos squatted atop the great pyramid. In spite of Montezuma's virtual abdication and confirmation of it by some of the lords, the essence of sovereignty eluded his grasp. And so it would until he had destroyed the Hummingbird. He knew that the rulers of the Pipiltin were waiting for Huichilobos to speak, just as Montezuma was patiently awaiting his words. When activity perceptively quickened in the temple and Huitzilopochtli's priests began to scurry back and forth between the sanctuary and Montezuma's quarters, Cortés put his forces on constant alert and strained every nerve to scent the wind, even to the extent of sending Andrés de Tapia over the Serpent Wall to furtively reconnoiter the marbled halls of the great pyramid. Unable to divine his enemy's next move, or from whence the blow would fall, Cortés decided to attack at once. Approaching Montezuma with several of his captains, he presented the following ultimatum: the Spaniards were prepared to remove Huichilobos and replace him with Our Lady, which could be done peacefully if Montezuma supported the act; if he did not concur they were determined to do it by force, and they promised to slaughter his priests in the process. Montezuma was aghast at the prospect and begged Cortés to reconsider, pleading that the entire city would be consumed in the violence that would surely ensue. Now Cortés sent his captains from the room and in feigned confidence told Montezuma that it was his men who were so insistent, but that he could control them if Montezuma would permit Our Lady to have a private sanctuary in Huichilobos' pyramid. Taken in by what appeared to be a compromise, the emperor summoned his priests and after hurried whisperings agreed to the settlement. A small apartment in the pyramid was made available in which daily Mass was subsequently sung by Father Olmedo, with a large force of armed soldiers in attendance. The presiding image of the Virgin was guarded around the clock by armed sentries. With Cortés' prompting, Our Lady had inched closer to the throne.

With this somewhat large foot in the door, Cortés again approached Montezuma a few days later: he had explained many times how a throne, any throne, was held from God rather than from false idols. Was it not then time for Montezuma to emerge from his deception? And how better could he do this than to command Cortés to roll down the vicious idols who would not be served except by the blood of the innocent? In their stead let him erect an image of Christ, the True God, and His Blessed Mother, so that from this time forth his subjects might know Him who created and redeemed them. And then let Montezuma become the first Christian; one so feared and obeyed by his people could single-handedly convert the masses, who would not dare oppose his wishes. And for those who would resist, Montezuma had Cortés and all his power upon which to draw! Montezuma listened thoughtfully to the impassioned plea and answered that he did not think ill of what Cortés had said, but the times were not auspicious for such a move. With utmost gravity he warned that the people—meaning the Pipiltin—would not desert their old cult; in the event of a showdown they would listen to Huitzilopochtli rather than himself. Indeed, let Cortés understand that Huitzilopochtli had already spoken to the priests and was demanding the death of the Spaniards because of what they had done. All the gods were reported wroth and threatening to leave the country because of the Christians' insults; they refused to remain in the presence of the cross and Our Lady; they were angered because their gold had been seized and melted down into ingots; because the Spaniards were holding Cacama and four other high lords hostage; because the aliens were taking over the country. Huitzilopochtli had issued final warning: Our Lady and the cross must be removed from his temple and the Spaniards driven from the land. Any further move against the idols, Montezuma predicted, would provoke an immediate uprising of the lords.

Cortés stiffened at this reply and angrily remarked that he and his men would handle any opposition with force. Montezuma repeated his warning; then, dropping his arms in a gesture of futility, he added, "Do what you will, but remember that I have warned you. You will all die." Now Cortés was furious. "Let them try me and you shall see their efforts come to naught because I have God on my side, for whose honor and glory I came here; I will not rest until I have rolled down those cursed idols and placed His image there. . . ." With this he stalked from the room. This was it. Cortés would brook no further delay. So Huichilobos had made demands, had he! He had guessed as much, seeing the priests in their frantic coming and going. Orteguilla, his most reliable source of information, had been purposely shut out of their conversations; and whenever he did get within earshot, Montezuma and the priests lapsed into a dialect he could not understand. But Cortés did not have to know the words they spoke; it was the devil that was behind them; it was he who spoke through Huichilobos and who whispered in Montezuma's ear. The Evil One could not suffer the daily Mass in Huichilobos' temple; and unless Cortés quickly stifled his principal mouthpiece, there was no telling what might happen.[8]

Sending four squads to take command of as many gates to the Coatepantli, Cortés selected eight or ten men, picked up a stout iron bar, and headed for the temple, leaving the balance of his troops and the cavalry deployed for ready action. Once inside the Serpent Wall, he sent Andrés de Tapia ahead as a scout. Accompanied by priests who intercepted him while making no attempt to halt his advance, he sped to the summit and Huichilobos' sanctuary. There he found the entrance barred by a curious alarm device consisting of hemp and bells strung in such a way that anyone trying to enter could not help but make his presence known. With Cortés and the others close behind, Tapia tried the alarm, finding that it "made such a racket that I thought the walls would fall in." Knowing Cortés' mind, the priests had installed the device as a precautionary measure. A few quick sword strokes disconnected the alarm just as Cortés and his men cleared the last step. Converging on the antechamber, they again found entry to the sanctuary barred by a heavy veil, now pulled tightly shut. As the curtain fell to slashing steel, their eyes were met by the nightmarish gargoyles on the walls, with their pointed, scaly chins and crusted mouths, just as their nostrils were assailed by an overpowering stench. Huichilobos sat glaring from behind his golden mask. Cortés slowly turned his head, his face and neck reddening, his voice choked with emotion. "Oh God! Why dost Thou permit the devil to be so grossly honored in this land?" The noise of the alarm set off by Tapia had brought the high priests and their aides. Turning to his interpreters, Cortés told them that he had come to place the images of God and His Blessed Mother in this very sanctuary; therefore, the priests could go and get water and brushes and start cleaning the walls while he and his men—now gesturing broadly toward the idols—would move the rest of the stuff out.

With comprehension of his words, the high priests sneered as though such a thing were ridiculously impossible. The whole land, they replied, held these to be their gods, and that one was Huitzilo-pochtli, ". . . whose creatures we are; the people hold their fathers and mothers and sons as nothing compared to him, for whom they are ready to die. Since seeing you climb up here they have [already] taken up their arms and are prepared to die for their gods." Quickly, Cortés ordered a soldier to return to their compound and warn the garrison to protect Montezuma against attack, and to send forty men to the summit of the pyramid at once. Then he turned to the priests, his voice rising in anger. "I shall take great pleasure in fighting for my God against yours, which are no gods at all." Huitzilopochtli's priests answered with insults directed at the Virgin. Beside himself with rage, Cortés seized the iron bar; and before anyone could move, he leaped at Huichilobos and brought it down in a crushing blow. "Upon my word as a gentleman," wrote Andrés de Tapia, "I can still see him as he leaped high in the air, hovering over us almost supernaturally as he smashed the iron bar down on the idol's head, tearing away the golden mask from one of its eyes." The priests were struck dumb, and at this moment a messenger from Montezuma arrived begging Cortés to do nothing further until he should arrive. Virtually flying up the pyramid steps, Montezuma came just in time to halt the priests who had recovered their wits and were calling for assistance. A single glance told him the full story. Anxious and fearful lest this incident provoke major conflict, Montezuma attempted compromise, suggesting that the Spaniards put their god on one altar and permit the Mexica to leave theirs on the other. Cortés snarled a refusal. At this Montezuma winced and gave assurance that Cortés should have his way, but he insisted that the Spaniards must leave at once without inflicting further injury on the idols. Seeing that he had won his objective, Cortés began to calm himself; he did not want to fight. Telling Montezuma to go ahead and see to removal of the idols, he fired a parting shot: "You can see that they are merely of stone. Believe in God, who made heaven and earth, and by the work shall ye know the Master." The confrontation was over.[9]

A few days later hundreds of laborers and priests were seen to scale the great pyramid. With an ingenious system of ropes, levers, and rollers they laid the idols with reverence on huge litters and slowly and gently lowered them to the pyramid's base. However delicately they were handled, the idols suffered slight chipping against the corners of the ledges during descent. The fragments were eagerly seized by workmen and priests as sacred relics. The lowering was accompanied by a procession of priests, all clad in hooded black robes. The whole operation was accomplished in deathly silence, an eerie performance that struck fear into the Spaniards who witnessed it. At the base the idols were quickly covered with reed mats and mantas to protect them from vulgar sight. Placed on bedlike carriers, they were borne away by great lords and priests, the train being followed by a multitude of armed nobles. The Spaniards watched until the idols and their bearers had disappeared from sight.

Cortés issued orders for immediate cleansing of the twin temples, including destruction of the idols on their walls. When all had been scoured and washed down with lime, he made an inspection and for the first time noticed that Huitzilopochtli's inner sanctuary was smaller than the external measurements of the temple indicated it should be. Searching for a hidden chamber, he found one in the front wall. Entering, he discovered a mass of dough made from amaranth seed and human blood that was used for quasi-sacramental rites and a jar of "holy water," both of which he destroyed. But the hidden sacrarium also contained a quantity of fine jewels set in gold. Like inquisitive monkeys, his men climbed up and rifled the temples' burial vaults. Poking through the ashes of Tlacaellel and the dead kings, they retrieved a considerable store of gold. A new altar was built in each of the temples, one for Our Lady, the other for Saint Christopher, whose image happened to be the only other one Cortés had on hand at the time. As soon as all was in readiness, the Spaniards, armed to the teeth, climbed the great staircase in solemn procession. First came the cross followed by the images of Our Lady and Saint Christopher; all who knew it sang a resounding *Te Deum laudamus*. The

Mexica watched in silence; to the Spaniards "it appeared as though God had tied their hands and struck them dumb." The Virgin was enthroned at dead center of the Mexican universe and the act was finalized by a solemn Mass.[10]

Chapter X

Revolt

Montezuma could no longer pretend, even to himself, that Huitzilopochtli had ordered his own desecration and overthrow. Deeply did he
now drink at the cup of bitterness with the awful realization that he
had been mistaken about Cortés' identity and mission from the very
beginning. No harbinger of deity this; he was a cunning and rapa-
cious preditor. Cacama and his own brother, Cuitlahuac, had realized
this and done their best to warn him. And where were they now?
Languishing in subterranean dungeons beneath the palace. And Montezuma, the once mighty emperor, was no less chained than they.
What a fool he had been! Come what may, Montezuma now resolved
to save Huitzilopochtli from further harm, for his was to be a resurrec-
tion the usurpers and their white goddess would not soon forget. Once
again freed from the paralyzing effects of his borrowed fears, the
emperor regained his old form: he ordered the arrest of 400 harlots
who performed in the largest of Tlatelolco's market place bawdy
houses. Because of their public crimes, he charged, the gods had been
offended and for this reason had permitted the Christians to enter the
capital and overpower its rightful ruler.

This disclaimer of responsibility did not deceive anyone, nor did the public execution of 400 pitiful scapegoats lend it substance. Those lords of the Pipiltin who had spurned Cacama now had cause to regret having done so; the priesthood was almost riotous in its clamor for vengeance. Watching the Spaniards pass by on daily pilgrimage to their goddess who now reigned in Huitzilopochtli's temple, they made no attempt to hide their hatred for the ones they knew to be responsible. Except for Montezuma's shrinking party, the lords and priests were united in their determination to kill Cortés for authoring Huitzilopochtli's dethronement and Montezuma for permitting it to be done. Neither they nor the emperor could suffer loss of the *sine qua non* of their structured world. Thus Cortés, in attempting to win sovereignty without warfare, had committed the very act that made war inevitable. As Montezuma now viewed the situation, there seemed to be but one way in which he might save himself, and that was to bring about Cortés' withdrawal together with restoration of the Hummingbird. And so he confided to Cortés that if the invaders fled the country at once, they might save themselves from the wrath and vengeance of the Pipiltin. Cortés listened and agreed, but stalled for time, citing lack of vessels for departure from Vera Cruz as an excuse. While the escape craft were being built, Montezuma agreed to temporize with the priests and nobles and through his partisans try to restrain them. From now on the Spaniards slept in armor, sword in hand, beside horses that remained saddled and caparisoned for instantaneous response.

What Cortés' real intent was we do not know, for he did not commit it to paper. But it seems certain that he had no intention of retreating at this time, however formidable and threatening the posture of the Pipiltin. He could not have been unprepared for the most obvious reactions to his enthronement of the Virgin. That the enraged nobles failed to retaliate at once nourished a false hope that violence might be avoided entirely, given time for cooler heads to prevail.

Weeks passed, and hope became conviction. Meanwhile, the Virgin did her part. When the peasants came to the temple and asked for rain, Cortés gave his word that they should have it. On the following day his troops took part in a special religious procession toward that end, all having prayed hard for rain as ordered by their leader. The large image of Mary led their procession from the pyramid's courtyard all the way to its summit. Before the Mass was ended, an unseasonable cloudburst let fall sheets of rain until it ran ankle-deep in the court-yard.[1]

The Spaniards had been in the capital nearly six months now, and time had passed almost unnoticed, so intense had been the quest for sovereignty and the process of "discovering mines, and learning and inquiring into many of the secrets of Montezuma's dominions." Cortés had prying agents everywhere. At the same time, the lords of the Pipiltin had settled on a plan of revolt, the nature of which remains obscured by the secrecy of its inception. Cortés appears to have known little more than we do about it beyond the fact of its existence. But it was obvious that the blow would fall during the coming ceremonial period of Toxcatl, May 9 through 19, the latter being one of the greatest of patriotic fete days and therefore one of Huitzilopochtli's most significant calendrical events.[2] How Cortés planned to cope with the pending crisis we can but surmise. We do know, however, that he ordered Montezuma to command every ruling lord of the empire to attend, and that those so invited numbered well over 8,000. Did he intend to deal with the problem in the manner of Cholula? This may well have been in his mind, for such a slaughter would without question have brought about collapse of the Pipiltin and their religious system.

This problem, however grave, was overshadowed by more imminent peril: a courier from Vera Cruz announced the sudden arrival of

Pánfilo de Narvaez with nineteen ships and an army bent on Cortés' destruction. The governor of Cuba appeared determined to reclaim control of the expedition at any cost. Velásquez' forces could not have arrived at a more unseasonable moment, much to Cortés' chagrin. If he withdrew from Tenochtitlán, his action would doubtless invite immediate attack by the lords. But neither could he permit Narvaez to close in on him like the second jaw of a vise. It happened that Montezuma learned of the unexpected arrival before Cortés did and immediately made contact with Narvaez who, acting on the advice of three Velásquez men in Cortés' camp, offered to free the emperor and slay Cortés. While plying Narvaez with bribes, Montezuma sent runners to the coastal provinces instructing the ruling lords to support the newly arrived Spaniards against Cortés. In the long run his strategy was certain to fail because the provincials clearly understood that if Cortés fell, they would be exposed to Montezuma's retaliation. And so they silently refused; and instead, warned Cortés of the emperor's secret diplomacy, which, for the moment, he pretended to ignore. At the same time, the nobles temporarily halted their plans until the newly risen issue between the Spaniards should be resolved. If Narvaez should do them the favor of removing Cortés, they could then deal with Montezuma at leisure. There must have been something gratifying in the prospect of the Spaniards eliminating each other. Engaging in his own style of diplomacy, Cortés ascertained that he could swing the major part of his opponent's forces to his own banner, and with this knowledge formulated a strategy: he would leave a skeleton force with the Tlaxcalans to maintain the capital garrison while he led the balance of his forces against Narvaez. If all went well, he could be back in the capital within a short time, and heavily reinforced. In preparation for this maneuver he had Tlaxcala's rulers send in a generous supply of maize, and strengthened the palace barricades. Leaving Alvarado in command of eighty men, old Velásquez hands for the most part, he marched out and headed for the coast, hopeful of taking Narvaez before he could generate any more mischief.[3]

At best it was a difficult situation for Alvarado. Cortés' departure could not be delayed until after Toxcatl, hence for the Spaniards and Tlaxcalans who remained behind the immediate future was much to be feared. Alvarado was a capable officer and a good leader of men. A handsome man and a splendid physical specimen, the Mexica called him Tonatiuh, which meant "Child-of-the-Sun," a pretty compliment indeed. But he did not possess the genius of his commander. As the climax of Toxcatl approached, anxiety and hysteria threatened the compound from within. If the nobles attacked, could the garrison hold out until Cortés should return? The seeming impossibility of their position made inaction unbearable for the invaders. Yet they could do nothing but wait. Apparently speaking for their emperor, two of Montezuma's partisans now approached Alvarado and warned that attack was imminent, but could be forestalled by his prompt dethronement of the Virgin in favor of Huitzilopochtli. Alvarado quickly seized a pair of priests who, under torture, confirmed what the others had volunteered. Armed with this intelligence, he went straight to Montezuma and demanded that he call off the attack, which Montezuma refused to do. As far as the emperor was concerned, Tonatiuh must choose between the Virgin and his life.

Meanwhile, May 19 and the climax of Toxcatl arrived. The capital was packed with reigning nobles from all quarters of the empire. The Tlaxcalans, who hated Toxcatl passionately for its traditional sacrifice of their countrymen, were eager to fight, whatever the odds, and so were constantly found at Alvarado's ear with rumors of plots and imminent attack. As Alvarado understood it, the lords would be roused to religious frenzy by the speakers and ceremonies to be held in the Coatepantli, after which they would take up arms and restore Huichilobos. Alvarado apparently determined to do what he felt certain Cortés would have done had he been in command: he ordered Montezuma to invite the Spaniards as guests. The lords saw no objection to this, and may even have thought it amusing that the victims should witness the warmup for their own execution. But unlike the celebrants within the Coatepantli, the Spaniards would be armed to the teeth.[4]

The fete went off as scheduled, with speeches and festivities. Huichilobos was the central attraction, his body wrought of amaranth seeds pasted with blood and honey. Royal raiment clothed his limbs, and his head was covered by a green hummingbird crest. A thousand or so imperial lords alternately danced and rested as the Spaniards watched their every move. Noticeably the tempo quickened, and the dancers began a frenetic whirl. The crescendo of rhythm was joined by a chant that grew ominously in emotional volume. Alvarado had the four gates quietly closed, and at this his men drew their weapons: ". . . The first thing they did was to cut off the hands and heads of the drummers, and then without any mercy they turned among the people and began to slash off arms and legs and ripped open their bellies. . . ." Some attempting to flee the swinging steel fell, tripping over their own intestines; others were speared as they tried to climb the walls; blood formed pools in low spots of the flagstone pavement, and piles of flesh mounted as the slaughter progressed. Only those who feigned death survived.[5] When the armed warriors who waited nearby discovered that their surprise appearance had been foiled by Alvarado's closing of the gates, they launched a screaming attack on the Serpent Wall. But it was too late to save most of those on the inside. Alvarado's men had done their job and were hurriedly stripping the corpses of valuables when the blow fell. Under clouds of javelins and arrows, the Spaniards were forced to yield the Coatepantli, leaving the temple and Mary to the attackers.

At the same time Alvarado had struck, the few Spaniards who remained in the palace led their Tlaxcalan allies in co-ordinated attack on Montezuma's honor guard. It was shattered, and so a corridor of retreat was provided for the major force in flight from the Coatepantli. Safe for the moment behind his barricades, Alvarado confronted Montezuma. Bleeding from a head wound and stained from the carnage he had wrought, he angrily demanded, "See what your vassals have done to me!" To which Montezuma replied, "Alvarado, if you had not attacked my vassals would not have done this. You have ruined yourselves and me also." Alvarado clapped him in irons and sent to the dungeon for Itzquauhtzin, the nominal lord of Tlatelolco, who had been Cacama's ally. Leading him to the palace roof where he could address the besieging lords, Alvarado forced the prisoner to plead for cessation of hostilities in the name of Montezuma, who was in chains. The lords listened briefly, then responded with rude noises and a heavy shower of arrows. Seeing Itzquauhtzin howled down as "el puto de Montezuma," the Spaniards covered him with their shields and dragged him back to safety. Dissatisfied with this result, Alvarado returned the prisoner to his dungeon and tried again, this time with Montezuma himself. Pushing the emperor before him, both stepped out on the roof to confront the mob. This time the riotous lords refused to listen. Alvarado drew his dagger from its sheath and put it to Montezuma's heart. The emperor pleaded for silence and attention, but to no avail. He was no longer their sovereign lord. His bluff called, Alvarado retreated from the roof and sent Montezuma back to share the dungeon with Cacama and his fellow conspirators.

The Spanish compound was now deprived of food and water; the streets were blocked off, and bridges in the causeways were raised; the siege was complete and there was to be no escape. At the same time, Montezuma's servants and friends were slain on sight, presumably so that neither word nor aid might be received by the beleaguered garrison. These precautionary measures were swiftly followed by a studied purge of persons known to sympathize with Montezuma or the Christians.[6]

For a week the rebels daily stormed the barricades, but on the eighth day their attacks ceased, although they continued to sustain the blockade. Cessation resulted from news that Cortés had beaten Narvaez. Confident that they could defeat the invaders in the capital more easily than elsewhere, the lords decided to avoid any further action that might keep Cortés from returning to Tenochtitlán. Their intelligence told them everything about Cortés' victory, that he had enlisted the bulk of his opponent's forces, and of his forced march at the head of 1,300 soldiers to raise the siege. Let them come, and welcome to the trap.[7] Within the compound Alvarado incorrectly assumed that Montezuma's continued efforts to influence the rebellious lords had succeeded and on that account released him from his chains.

Cortés first learned of the revolt in the capital from two Tlaxcalan scouts who escaped from the compound during a moonless night and swam for it. A letter from Alvarado, smuggled out in the same manner, followed shortly: the palace had been under daily attack and was presently afire; seven Spaniards had been killed and scores were wounded; the situation was desperate. Bitterly disgusted, the commander prepared to march on Tenochtitlán. Just as the columns were setting forth, a messenger from Montezuma arrived with the emperor's explanation, one which laid responsibility squarely on Alvarado's shoulders. When the army reached Tlaxcala, Cortés received a comprehensive report in which, as would be expected, Montezuma played the villian. Adding 2,000 Tlaxcalan warriors to his force, Cortés resumed the march as quickly as possible. On nearing the capital, he and his men encountered a strange and foreboding silence. All avenues of approach as well as the surface of the lake were devoid of any sign of life. Pausing in hesitation, he fired a field piece, anxiously waiting for the beleaguered garrison to reply. When the answering cannon thundered its message over the lake, he moved forward. The garrison still held out.

The invaders reached Axayacatl's palace without incident; the city appeared to be deserted. Going straight to Alvarado, Cortés requested explanation. He listened to what his lieutenant had to say, nodding in understanding as Alvarado told of Huichilobos' wrath over the cross and the Virgin in his temple, of the planned revolt, and of Montezuma's refusal to intervene. But when the last word had been spoken, he frowned and shaking his head replied that the whole affair was ill done and an error of tragic proportion. As he turned and stalked away, Montezuma approached to give greeting, but Cortés refused to acknowledge his presence and rudely brushed him aside. Correctly reading the implications of what had happened in his absence, he had no further need for Montezuma, who was sent back to the dungeon. Taking stock of the compound's resources, he failed to find encouragement in the tally: after a month of siege, the maize was almost gone; the well his men had dug after their water was shut off could not long fill the needs of the men and horses who had come in relief. Their position was untenable. From the compound Cortés could hear the drums on Huichilobos' temple. What had happened to the Virgin? Becoming moody, an unusual state for the Conqueror, Bernal Díaz described him as "easily irritated, very sad and fretful." He plainly realized that he had led the men into a trap. How long would it be until the Mexica renewed their attack on the barricades?

Seeing that Cortés persisted in his rejection of Montezuma, two of the latter's partisans attempted to intercede in the emperor's behalf. "Let the dog go to hell," snapped Cortés, "he neither keeps the market open nor feeds us." Some of his captains heard the exchange and offered a rebuke, pointing out that Montezuma had been most useful in the past and had even given Cortés his daughters as concubines. "What civility should I show a dog who treated with Narvaez behind my back and even now tries to starve us to death?" Turning to the nobles, he angrily warned them that Montezuma had better open the market quickly or be prepared to pay the consequences. The emperor's faithful retainers delivered the message, then returned to Cortés with an answer: Montezuma pleaded that he no longer had the authority to comply with Cortés' wishes, but that one of his fellow prisoners could readily calm the rebels, open the market place and supply food, if he were freed. Cortés accepted forthwith, whereupon Montezuma sent out his brother Cuitlahuac. Evidently convinced that he had more to gain than lose by freeing the prisoner, Cortés permitted him to leave the compound. Within twenty-four hours the Spanish garrison again fell under heavy attack, this time under the generalship of Cuitlahuac, who now wore the imperial crown. Cortés had been tricked into freeing Montezuma's successor.

Screaming warriors stormed the palace barricades day and night without pause; from time to time the walls were breached, only to be closed again by the bodies of the attackers as they fell under the onslaught of Toledo steel. Fire-arrows rained down on the palace roof; in desperate conservation of their water supply, the Spaniards extinguished them with dirt. In addition to taunts and insults hurled over the walls, the besiegers constantly reminded the defenders that Huitzilopochtli's slab awaited them. So numerous was the enemy and so high his spirits that Bernal Díaz declared 10,000 Trojan Hectors and as many more Roldans could not have tipped the scales in the Spaniards' favor. A breakthrough appeared utterly impossible. In what apparently was a bold attempt to bolster the morale of his own forces and shatter that of the enemy, Cortés led an incredible sortie from the palace; storming the Coatepantli and fighting like a man possessed, he recaptured Huichilobos' temple. As the Christians met its defenders in hand to hand combat, bodies literally rained from its ledges, until the Spaniards had gained the summit and hurled the last priest from its high terrace. The victors searched everywhere for Mary, but failing to find any trace, gave her up as lost. Hurriedly they set fire to the temple's wooden superstructures and an amaranth image of Huichilobos and other idols that were found. Fighting their way back to the palace, they surrendered the Coatepantli for the last time.[8]

By the following day it had become apparent that the enemy's morale was not lessened by temporary discomfiture; his legions were reinforced by the arrival of fresh squadrons, of which there seemed an infinite number. Time was running out for the garrison, and Cortés knew it. Determining to use Montezuma to the very last, he proposed to have him again mount the roof and plead for cessation of hostilities so that the Spaniards might withdraw. Sitting morosely in the dungeon when his aides arrived with Cortés' command he replied, "What does Malinche want of me now? I have been brought to this ruinous state [by acting] on his behalf. I want neither to go on living nor to see him again." Apprised of his refusal, Cortés sent Father Olmedo and Cristóbal de Olid to reason with him. "I will not be able to do anything to end this war," he told them, "they have already chosen another Lord and have made up their minds that you shall not leave this place alive, and so I am afraid that all of you must die." But Cortés had the whip hand and forced Montezuma to comply. As he was pushed out onto the roof, all action stopped and silence fell over the scene. With neither strength nor conviction in his voice, Montezuma offered a bargain: if the lords would stop their attack, the intruders would leave the city. A youthful officer named Cuauhtemoc now stepped out from the command group, his face flushed with anger. "What is he saying, this villainous Montezuma, this effeminate tool of the Spaniards who delivered himself and the country into their hands out of pure fright and in so doing placed us all in such straits? We will not obey him because he is no longer our king, but we shall see that he is paid for his infamy." With an ugly roar the mob loosed a shower of stones and arrows on Montezuma and the Spaniards who flanked him. Struck in the head and on the arm and leg, Montezuma would have fallen had not his guards pulled him back to safety. Refusing to accept treatment of his injuries, he was returned to the dungeon and the company of Cacama and Itzquauhtzin.[9]

The attack resumed with greater fury than ever, but now the

gunpowder began to dwindle and the food was nearly gone. In spite of the brutal punishment and staggering casualties inflicted on the attackers, they continued to come on in ever greater volume. Cortés and his captains saw that they must fight their way out or perish, and so they planned to make the attempt that very night of July 10. The shortest route to the lakeshore was the Tacuba causeway, being slightly over three miles to land and five miles from Axayacatl's palace to the plaza of Tacuba. Hurriedly they constructed a heavy wooden platform with which to bridge the gaps in the causeway. Heavy rain fell steadily through afternoon and into evening, forcing Cuitlahuac to suspend the attack, a not unwelcome respite for his warrior lords. It also provided the Spaniards with the opportunity they needed to get out of the palace undetected. Just before midnight they filed out; the night was dark and still, and hushed by a gentle fall of rain. The enemy's sentries were either asleep or eliminated by Cortés' scouts; the sources do not say. Slowly the column moved out over the causeway; the Tlaxcalans put the portable bridge in place and the infantry crossed without incident. But as the cavalry passed over the planking, there was a great hollow noise from the horses' hoofs that carried afar on the heavy night air. Sentries cried the alarm, and in a matter of minutes the column was under attack on all sides. The Spaniards and their allies could do little to defend themselves, especially against the hordes of warriors who swarmed their flanks from thousands of canoes. The only escape was to push ahead; gaps in the causeway quickly became filled with the bodies of the fallen, forming bridges over which the survivors could flee. For those lucky enough to reach it, Tacuba gave little more than a chance to get second wind. Pursuing warriors flushed the quarry, which now struck out cross-country for the safety of Tlaxcala. So ended what was forever to be remembered by the survivors and those who came after them as the fabled Night of Sorrow.

Back in the capital the cold gray of dawn permitted the victors to go about the tasks of removing the dead from the canals and streets and reclaiming some of the treasure that had been abandoned by the Spaniards in their flight. Searchers combing Axayacatl's scarred palace went to the dungeon and found Montezuma's lifeless body still chained to the wall with five dagger wounds in his breast. With him were Cacama and Itzquauhtzin and two unidentified lords, probably Montezuma's aides; all had been stabbed to death. While the others were borne off for resplendent heroes' funerals, Montezuma and Itzquauhtzin were dumped into a nearby canal like carrion. When subsequently rediscovered and fished out, the Tlatelolcan was claimed and mourned by his peers, but Montezuma was cast on a heap of faggots and reviled as he burned.[10] Nezahualpilli's prophecy was fulfilled.

Chapter XI

Victory and Defeat

The death of Montezuma created a vacuum, a void that could not be filled. As the first and last living god, he represented the end of an evolutionary process that had begun with formation of the empire. If one is to mark the apogee of the imperial system in its trajectory, it must be the colossal sacrifice of 1487 that elevated Huitzilopochtli to empyrean heights and proclaimed the awful lengths to which the Mexica would go to maintain their system and its symbol. Up to this point Tlacaellel, essentially through his control of Mexican eclecticism, had preserved a working balance between destructive and creative forces within the system, even as he crushed every threat from without. But after he had passed from the scene, the stronger elements of the complex began to move of their own volition, this as a prelude to a period in which the entire system would seek its ultimate fulfilment and conclusion. From the zenith, that moment of terrible splendor in which all parts were held in balance, the imperial course was a declining one and increasingly erratic through the shifting weight of its parts. The lords became divided in loyalties and interest and could no longer control their appetites; the priestly caste lusted for power beyond its capacity for restraint. Montezuma mounted the throne just in time to reap the harvest. Caught up by a fate that he believed inexorable, he became a tragic figure in the classic Greek sense. Just as a poet said of Oedipus:

> 'Twas pride that bred the tryant;
> Drunken deep with perilous things was he.
> Which brought not peace.
> Up, reeling, steep on steep
> He climbs, 'till lo, the rock-edge and the leap
> To that which needs must be.

When Montezuma permitted Huitzilopochtli to be overthrown, the system lost its momentum; as he fell against the dungeon wall with a dagger in his heart, its motion, like his life, was ended.

Montezuma could be succeeded, but he could not be replaced. There would never be another living god because a new age had dawned. The emperor was no longer monarch of the world, nor was Anahuac, the tropical empire, any longer a reality. A whole new world beyond the sea had been revealed to the Mexica, one that lived by superior technology and was said to possess a universal emperor. As recent history had shown, his claims and power had substance, and his minions were possessed of a religious faith and zeal that was frightening. Between king and pope what position remained to Huitzilopochtli? No ruler could again clothe himself in the Hummingbird's sanctity and power, for the day of the living god has passed.

In addition to the wrenching shock of Huitzilopochtli's overthrow and Montezuma's death, there were other complicating factors. The Pipiltin had suffered irreparable losses in recent years. During the emperor's siege of terror and indecision prior to the Spanish arrival, he had ruthlessly executed the best men of Mexican science without reckoning the cost; now the loss was keenly felt as the managers of the system sought to shore up its foundations and restore its identity. The cream of the Pipiltin, the ruling plateau, was largely lost in the Toxcatl massacre and the rebellion that it set off. Not without cost was the intruder driven from the city.[1] Higher levels of the religious hierarchy perished in defense of Huitzilopochtli's temple when it was stormed by Cortés just prior to the Night of Sorrow. And yet another factor may be added, the onslaught of an invisible enemy that was by far the most deadly killer: smallpox. An infected Negro had come to New Spain with Narvaez; within two weeks epidemic was ravaging the coastal area from Vera Cruz to Cempoalla, with local mortality ranging from 50 to 100 per cent. The very air itself was contaminated by nasopharyngeal secretions, dried scales from the lesions of infected persons, and by unburied bodies and excreta, so that the plague was borne on the wind; wherever it passed, the streets became cluttered with dead and dying.[2] Before long the killer was stalking the capital:

> It was [the month of] Tepeilhuitl when it began, and it spread over the people as great destruction. Some it quite covered [with pustules] on all parts—their faces, their heads, their breasts, etc. There was great havoc. Very many died of it. They could not walk; they only lay in their resting places and beds. They could not move; they could not stir; they could not change position, nor lie on one side, nor face down, nor on their backs. And if they stirred, much did they cry out. . . . And very many starved, there was death from hunger, [for] none could take care of [the sick]; nothing could be done for them. And on some the pustules were widely separated; they suffered not greatly, neither did many [of them] die. Yet many people were marred by them on their faces; one's face or nose was pitted. Some lost their eyes; they were blinded.[3]

The horror persisted for sixty days. Staggering under shock and loss and suffering the effects of plague, the Pipiltin needed time for regeneration and regrouping, time in which to shuffle their human resources, to alter the system to fit the changing times. All the yesterdays had died with Montezuma; tomorrow must be different.

Those who ruled the Pipiltin had no intention of changing Huitzilopochtli or his symbolic significance. But there was no longer any confusion over his being, or that of the enemy, now that Montezuma had joined Nezahualpilli in the peace of the grave. Without religious and philosophical anxiety to restrain them, the lords beat their propaganda drums more loudly than ever for Huitzilo-pochtli as the god and savior of the Mexica. Since the slaughter of the priesthood and Montezuma's downfall had weakened and discredited the priestly caste, the military lords now moved in to possess them-selves of the entire religious structure, which in the new age became increasingly secularized. The purge of Montezuma's partisans that began after Toxcatl was renewed with vigor. Although many of his daughters survived, his sons were generally less fortunate. His legiti-mate son was slain during the Night of Sorrow, as was Doña Ana, one of the daughters whom he had given to Cortés and who was carrying the Conqueror's child. Another son was a helpless alcoholic, another insane, another a paralytic. Even as others were slain, two of his sons joined the anti-Montezuma party and thereby saved themselves. Cui-tlahuac, Montezuma's half-brother who had spoken out against the Spaniards from the very beginning, was chosen to succeed in the customary collateral line of succession. Superficially, the new rulers attempted to maintain a fiction of continuity; they even had Cuitla-huac take one of Montezuma's daughters as his bride. His coronation was fashioned after the old style, with captive Spaniards being sacri-ficed to the Hummingbird. But the anguish of the victims was the only genuine feature of a ceremony that, without the presence of quaking spectators, was quite empty of significance. There were no Enemies-of-the-House in attendance, no guests, nor could the fete realistically proclaim the glory and power of Huitzilopochtli. The coronation was paled by the indifference that surrounded it.

Cuitlahuac's first assignment was to restore the fabric of practical sovereignty. He called upon all the states and provinces to join in alliance against the Spaniards. Only his immediate neighbors felt themselves sufficiently intimidated to heed the call. The majority stoically continued to sit on the sidelines, waiting to see what the Spaniards would do. Sending an embassy to Tlaxcala, the emperor tried to revoke the past, pleading with the Tlaxacalans to unite for survival. They spurned him, knowing full well that should the Spanish peril be eliminated, the Mexica would again seek to impose the old imperial system. In the failure of his diplomacy Cuitlahuac was forced to reveal the depths to which the imperial image had fallen by offering remission of tribute to all who would join the alliance. He still had no takers, nor did many of the old tributaries resume payment of their regular dues. The Hummingbird could no longer evoke his old degree of terror. His first assignment yet unfinished, Cuitlahuac died of smallpox after a brief and futile reign of eighty days. The dead king was succeeded by Cuauhtemoc, one of his own and Montezuma's nephews who had risen to leadership in the struggle to oust the intruders. A fanatical supporter of Huitzilopochtli cult, he would suffer no compromise with Christianity. Cuauhtemoc despised Montezuma for his weakness and had led the throng in its final show of contempt for him as he pleaded the Spanish cause from the battlement. Like his predecessor, he married one of Montezuma's younger daughters, Tecuichpo, who was destined to later become a Christian and outlive him and four Spanish husbands.[4] But however anxious the new emperor was to close with the foe, neither he nor his lords could obviate the ultimate need: the Mexica had to have time in which to reorganize the state and its imperial system.

Cortés had escaped to Tlaxcala with 440 men, losing nearly 1,000 Spaniards and untold thousands of Indian allies. Granted the military miracle of his victory at Otumba, he could never have won it had not the imperial system already been smitten and falling of its own weight. The lords who massed on the plain at Otumba to cut off his retreat to Tlaxcala were neither organized nor prepared for such an action, however numerous their ranks. It was their own disorder and Spanish desperation that tipped the scale in Cortés' favor.

After a scant three weeks of rest and recuperation in Tlaxcala, Cortés mustered 420 able-bodied soldiers and his remaining seventeen mounts in what was proclaimed to be the beginning of the reconquest of Mexico. First step on the strategic road back consisted in securing communications with the gulf coast. Leading his own men and some 2,000 Tlaxcalan allies, he fell on Tepeaca and destroyed the Mexican garrison. This being the crossroads to Mixteca and the south, Cortés here founded Segura de la Frontera as one of his primary strategic positions. Such proved to be a timely move, for almost at once word was received from Vera Cruz that a ship had put in, its holds laden with gunpowder, arms, and a number of horses. Reaching into substantial gold reserves from Axayacatl's treasure that he had managed to preserve, Cortés acquired the entire cargo.[5]

Leaving a garrison at Segura de la Frontera, he now returned to Tlaxcala and the second step in reconquest of the island capital. On the basis of his past experience Cortés now planned to force a surrender by means of blockade. Ordering construction of thirteen sailed brigantines, he recruited over 10,000 Tlaxcalan warriors for a strike against Texcoco, obviously the best strategic base from which to operate on the lake system and its peripheries. The Conqueror and his legions marched the day after Christmas, 1520. By New Year's Eve they had entered the city without firing a shot; from the summit of Huichilobos' temple they observed Texcoco's loyalists streaming out across the lake to Tenochtitlán, led by their king. In looking over contenders for the now vacant throne, Cortés settled on Ixtlilxochitl who, with his brother Coanacochtzin, led the pro-Spanish party. It had been they who betrayed Cacama into Montezuma's hands.[6] Some of Texcoco's subject towns now came in to accept Spanish sovereignty; the provincials seemed eager to join what for the moment appeared to be the winning side. Before the assembled lords Cortés delivered his old lecture on Genesis and the Emperor Charles V with seemingly wondrous effect. Ixtlilxochitl rose to his feet and showed that he perfectly understood the nature of sovereignty by demanding baptism. By merest chance Cortés had the chaplain and his baptismal font at hand, and he himself sponsored the candidate and gave him his name. Pedro de Alvarado then stepped forth to sponsor brother Coanacochtzin, and so the lords followed in order of precedence. It was a grand spectacle and successful in pulling several important lords off the fence of indecision. Going to his ancestral palace, Ixtlilxochitl approached his dowager mother, Yacotzin, and suggested that she offer herself for baptism. In calm rejoinder she averred that he must be out of his mind to have allowed himself to be so quickly converted by a handful of barbarians. Seeing her obstinate in refusal, Ixtlilxochitl set fire to the palace as a hint of his displeasure. She took it and hastened to comply. Cortés sponsored her and gave her the name of Mary "for being the first Christian woman." [7] With this much accomplished. Cortés ordered a large canal dug from the lakeshore to a point about a mile inland where he intended to assemble the brigantines after their portage from Tlaxcala.[8]

Using Texcoco as a base, Cortés now proceeded to reduce the surrounding lakeshore cities to his control. In Iztapalapán he first matched military wits with Cuauhtemoc and found him a worthy adversary. Striking deeper into enemy territory, he probed Chalco and Tlamanalco. Routing Cuauhtemoc's imperial forces there, he found many Chalcan nobles ready to come over. The lord of Chalco, dying of smallpox, enjoined his peers to seek out Cortés and have his sons installed and confirmed in their legacies by the Conqueror's own hand. Cortés made an impressive show of it as he accepted their pledges of fealty to the Emperor Charles. After witnessing the ceremony, eight of Cuauhtemoc's lords who had been captured were released with messages for their leader: let him remember the might of the Christian God and accept Spanish sovereignty. Cuauhtemoc

did not deign to answer, except to send word to Chalco that all
Spaniards who might be captured were to be forwarded to Mexico for
sacrifice to Huitzilopochtli.

With Chalco secured, the road to Tlaxcala was made safe enough
for transport of the brigantines, which were now finished. Sending a
large force to accompany and defend the "brigantine column," made
up of 15,000 tamemes carrying the thirteen dismantled ships on their
backs, passage was safely made. As the column, six miles long, wound
into Texcoco, it encountered a gay holiday mood. For their part the
Tlaxcalans were dressed in their finest array; amidst a sea of colorful
banners and the sound of drums and trumpets the marchers chanted
"Long live our lord the emperor, Castile! Castile! Tlaxcala! Tlaxcala!"

Cuauhtemoc could not afford to countenance the disaffection of
Chalco. Many neighboring towns and territories that had been traditionally held by the ruling clergy and nobility were refusing to pay
customary tributes. With Cortés' aid, their independence could be
sustained. In anticipation of the coming blockade Cuauhtemoc was
feverishly seeking provisions; but now his demands for maize were
being refused. He retaliated with heavy attack on Chalco, which,
since the days of Axayacatl, had been an appanage of the Mexican
throne. Fully appreciating the profound economic and psychological
implications coloring the issue at Chalco, Cortés sent Sandoval with
an expedition to raise the siege. After hard and bitter fighting, the
Mexica were defeated and routed from Chalco, and then from Oaxtepec and Yecapixtla. With intelligence that the Spaniards had returned
to Texcoco laden with plunder and a horde of pretty girls, Cuauhtemoc dispatched another force 20,000 strong to reclaim the sovereignty of Chalco, and with it control of the Mexican breadbasket. The
Chalca sped another call for help to Texcoco and supplicated Huexotzinco for immediate aid. The ancient Enemies-of-the-House responded and together they fielded a force of some 20,000 men. So it
was that a major engagement was fought between equal forces, one in

which the Mexica were soundly thrashed. Cuauhtemoc and his lords were painfully disgraced in the eyes of the lake world. The emperor could not even defeat his own appanage! [9]

Toward the end of May Cortés was ready to initiate the blockade of Tenochtitlán. His forces occupied the three main causeway towns; the brigantines held command of the lake. On May 26 he severed the water lines from Chapultepec and the siege was on. As Cortés saw it, the defenders would have no alternative to surrender. Surely Cuauhtemoc would listen to reason and thereby save life and property. But it did not turn out that way; reason was not to Cuauhtemoc and his lords what it was to the Conqueror. The siege was to drag on for seventy-nine days, encompassing almost unbelievable suffering and hardship for both sides. One cannot improve upon Bernal Díaz, Cortés, Sahagún's informants, and other Mexican chroniclers in their telling of the titanic struggle. [10] But within and between their accounts there are interstitial dramas that need to be seen.

As Cortés brigantines swept the enemy from the lake and his ring of steel tightened around the capital, domestic crisis threatened Cuauhtemoc and his party. Influential segments of the Pipiltin began to join in a demand for negotiated settlement of the conflict. Two of Montezuma's sons, Axayaca and Xoxopeualoc, emerged as spokesmen of the group, which to some suggested a restoration of the old and discredited Montezuma party with its "soft line" on Christianity. In spite of their political connections Cuauhtemoc had them executed, along with some of their backers, as a memorial of sorts to those who perished in the Toxcatl massacre. In retaliation their partisans murdered the high priests of Huitzilopochtli and Tezcatlipoca cult. And so there began a quiet but deadly struggle within the ruling plateau that seriously impaired the resistance effort. The Tlatelolca and provincial lords who had come to the capital in its defense found that they were frequently fighting alone while the feuding Tenochca ripped each other. For the most part Cuauhtemoc maintained the upper hand; and as long as he did so, Montezuma was constantly held up to the Pipiltin as the arch-traitor of Mexico and the empire.

As the Tenochca fought each other, Cortés made steady advances on the city. Alvarado's forces attacked over the Tacuba causeway as the commander's company forced the southern approach. Relentless pressure gradually exhausted the defenders until, in mid-June, Cortés forced his way into the city and held the Coatepantli long enough to once again fire the Hummingbird's temple. Slashing the curtains that darkened the inner sanctuary, he and Ixtlilxochitl struck down the wooden Huichilobos they found before retreating from the flames. The entire lake world saw the pall of smoke hanging over Huitzilopochtli's temple and knew what had transpired. In desperation Cuauhtemoc turned to his relatives in Tlatelolco; the Tenochca could or would no longer defend themselves or the things in which they were supposed to believe. Thus far the power of Tlatelolco was intact. While the Tenochca had suffered catastrophic losses of effective population through Montezuma's purges and the ensuing struggle against the Spaniards, the Tlatelolca had suffered much less; the merchant aristocracy was as powerful as ever, and now had a better grasp of the imperial scene than did the rulers. And it had a good reservoir of manpower.

The lords of Tlatelolco had a price for their intervention: the Tenochca must surrender the throne and control of the imperial system. Not since the days of Moquiuix and his abortive uprising against Axayacatl and Tlacaellel had the Tlatelolca dared so much, but this time they could do so with impunity: the Tenochca had simply to choose between them and Cortés. Cuauhtemoc and his party apparently encountered little opposition to their intended move. Going to Huitzilopochtli's temple, they retrieved the charred and broken idol and carried it to the temple in Tlatelolco, which now became the center of resistance. By nightfall the Tenochca were streaming into Tlatelolco. In solemn ceremony witnessed by loyalist

213

lords of Texcoco, Tacuba, Atzcapotzalco, Coyoacán, Tenanyuca, Quauhtitlán, Teotitlán, and other important powers, the Tenochca formally transferred sovereignty: "Here is your dominium, the warriors' insignia kept by the sovereign, the shields, the bracelets, the quetzal headdress, the golden ear plugs, the jewels; [take them] for now they all are your possessions, your property." [11] Many Tenochcan lords now retired from the war in humiliation and disgrace; the Hummingbird and his system were no longer theirs.

Abdication of the Tenochca was known throughout the world of the lake within forty-eight hours. The lords of Iztapalapán, Huitzilopochco, Mixquic, Mexicatzingo, and Culhuacán heard the news and, doubting the longevity of the new regime, made overtures to Cortés. If the old regime was to collapse, they wished to have standing with its successor. Ixtlilxochitl was also enabled to deliver powerful Texcocan lords who previously had refused to commit themselves to the alliance against Mexico. Everywhere around the lake there was a shifting and adjustment of position. Cortés took full diplomatic advantage and sent the lord of Culhuacán, now his staunch adherent, to speak with the Tlatelolca. His message was brief and pointed: The Tenochca were ruined, finished; their cowardice had made orphans of the Tlatelolca. Let them and their system fall, that war might end. Cortés even sought and obtained a meeting with influential Tlatelolcan lords, whom he pressed with the same arguments. "Why seek the greater misery of perishing with them," he asked, "which will only happen because they have made such great fools of you?" [12] Beneath Cortés' appeal to reason lay his own fear of Tlatelolco's power, especially under the guidance of Huichilobos and Cuauhtemoc. If the latter was successful in his designs, the war could go on to extreme lengths, necessitating the utter destruction of Tenochtitlán.

Cortés did not understand the thinking that lay behind the Tlatelolcan strategy. The Pochteca now had control of sovereignty and believed that they could win the struggle. Although the Christians

had them encircled, they could draw Cortés in while the Tolucan
legions came up behind him, so that the besieger would suddenly
become the besieged. Such, in miniature had been Cuauhtemoc's
basic strategy from the beginning. And it had yet to fail. Every time
Cortés needed to be checked, Cuauhtemoc drew him into the capital
by feigning retreat until his forces could be cut off and besieged. That
is why the Spaniards could burn the temple without being able to
occupy the site; Cortés could never guarantee his own retreat. Taking
a long view of the struggle, the Tlatelolca apparently believed it to be
just another in the historical rising and falling of powers in the lake
world. The Tenochca had had their day and were finished, while
theirs had just begun. The Tlatelolca would rise to new heights as the
true successors to ancient Tula.

And so Cortés was rebuffed after five days of fruitless negotiation.
Reacting as expected, he now determined to occupy the Tenochcan
part of the capital. With Alvarado moving in from Tacuba and his
own force from the south, they would meet in the southwestern
corner, from which they could then advance in a line on Tlatelolco.
Mustering over 100,000 allies he set the plan in motion. But Cuauhtemoc guessed his objective and stalled the offensive by smashing
Alvarado's forces on the causeway. Heavy fighting for two weeks
failed to revive the strategy, and Cortés was forced to adopt another.
The Tlatelolca now had their best squadrons on the line, and the
leadership was determined to show its right of possession.

There was much discussion in the allied camp. The siege had
begun on May 26, yet a month had since passed without yielding any
visible evidence that it might soon achieve its objective. Most sentiment therefore favored a massive assault on Tlatelolco, since it was
now the seat and center of resistance. Poring over his maps, Cortés
decided to split the force into thirds, each attacking along one of the
main streets that converged on Tlatelolco. On the morning of June 30
he signaled the attack, spearheaded by 60,000 men and supported by

the brigantines and countless allied canoes. Although his three divisions made good progress early in the day, resistance rose with the sun, until by noon he was under ferocious counterattack on all sides. Fighting like demons, the enemy overwhelmed the invader at the Calle de Tacuba and all but wiped him out. Under this impetus they came on with greater force until the allies broke and fled in shameless retreat. Over seventy Spaniards were taken alive, and a good part of the cavalry was destroyed. Wounded and spent, the allies retreated to their causeway camps. Even as they fled, they could hear the throbbing of the great snakeskin drums on Huichilobos' pyramid as it sounded tidings of victory. Those who cared to stop and look back saw naked Spanish soldiers, their faces dark with beard and sun against the white of their bodies, now wearing feathered headdress as they were made to dance for Huichilobos. But not for long. The priests flopped them on their backs and tore out their hearts before the horrified gaze of their comrades. The victims were cooked and eaten, except for their heads, feet, and hands, which were sent to the lords of those cities and towns that had recently joined the Spanish alliance as warning to quit their treachery. The lords received their tokens with dismay and began once again to nervously eye the fence. Cuauhtemoc and his associates issued a specific ultimatum: Huitzilopochtli had turned the tide of battle and promised victory to Tlatelolco. Unqualified victory was to be won within eight days, therefore let all who wished to be on the winning side make their decision before the end of that time.

Cuauhtemoc was not as secure as his posture indicated. His food and water were in short supply, and suffering was intense among the macehualtin. His warriors had been harangued and worked to fever pitch with the biggest show of Hummingbird pageantry seen in many years. But propaganda could not long serve in place of food and arms. His negotiations with Toluca had been successful, and within the week he expected their legions to cut off Spanish retreat from the south, then close in from behind to form the final trap. That was why he gave Cortés' allies eight days in which to return to the fold. Cuauhtemoc was successful in his maneuvers; knowing their former masters, the allied lords could not risk being found among the enemies of the victorious Tlatelolca. Wavering, then breaking under the pressure of indecision, they withdrew by thousands to await the outcome of Huitzilopochtli's promise. Cortés had no alternative but to fort up in his camps, still in command of the causeways and the lake, to wait out the eight days. Had he been as strong as his boasts implied, Cuauhtemoc could have ended the siege then and there. But without the Tolucan legions, he could not hope to break out. Doing the next best thing, he made repeated raids on the Spanish camps, carefully keeping beyond range for the most part, but hurling magnificent insults at the Spaniards and their dwindling allies. Even the Tlaxcalans and Texcocans had doubts and removed most of their forces while they met in council at home and debated future policy. Every night the great temple claimed the Spaniards' attention. Called by trumpet blasts and throbbing drums, they watched fires being lit on the summit, like floodlights, so that they could see the sacrifice of their comrades. Each night a quota was slain, after which Huichilobos' priests harangued the crowds and promised victory to Tlatelolco. Approaching the breastworks of Cortés' camps, the enemy heaved in roasted thighs of Spaniards, inviting the soldiers to dine.

It was quite by accident and just in time that Cortés learned of the Tolucan threat and consequently the full dimension of Cuauhtemoc's strategy. Allies in Chalco called for help against the lords of Malinalco and Cuixco who, convinced by Cuauhtemoc's restoration of Huitzilopochtli, were threatening them with war. Although he could spare neither man nor horse, Cortés realized that failure on his part to go to their relief would substantiate Cuauhtemoc's propaganda. Accordingly, he sent Andrés de Tapia and a small force accompanied by cavalry to Chalco. In the meantime July 10 turned on the calendar, and the eighth day had passed. The Tlaxcalans and Texcocans, seeing that the Spaniards still held their ground, now returned en masse, profuse in apology for having doubted the ability of the Christians to withstand Huitzilopochtli's wrath. In formal harangue Cortés made a point and then drove it into the ground: it was Jesus Christ and not Huichilobos who would hand out final victory, and let none forget it. The allies had just returned when Cortés received an urgent message from Andrés de Tapia: he had caught the Malinalca napping and dealt severly with them, but he had then discovered the existence of a massive army that was gathering at Toluca for an attack on the Spanish flank and rear; its vanguard was already threatening pro-Spanish cities in the south. In a flash Cortés comprehended the whole of Cuauhtemoc's design and moved to thwart it, realizing that the fate of the conquest now turned on victory or defeat in Toluca. Mounting a force of 60,000 allies, led by Sandoval and the cavalry, he hurled it against the Tolucans, hoping to stop them before they could build momentum. His blow caught the enemy as anticipated, and Sandoval won a stunning victory. Just as he received this good news, word from Vera Cruz proclaimed the arrival of a cargo of arms and gunpowder that had been unladen and was already on its way to his camp. Nothing could save Cuauhtemoc now.

Assuming that the emperor and his peers knew as well as he the consequences of their defeat in Toluca, Cortés sent an embassy of captive nobles with a plea for surrender. The emissaries were instructed to impress upon Cuauhtemoc the fact that Cortés understood the role of the priests and idols and their guilt in what had taken place. But let him also understand that responsibility for refusal and its consequences would be his. Cuauhtemoc was, as Cortés knew, bitterly disappointed in defeat, understanding too well that nothing could save the city or its defenders. The Tolucans, upon whom so much had rested, were even now coming to terms with the invader and taking part in the siege. But Cuauhtemoc and his associates refused to surrender; they would keep faith with Huitzilopochtli to the end; for even though the city should be destroyed, the end of Huitzilopochtli was not yet.

Grimly accepting Cuauhtemoc's refusal, Cortés now gave up his long cherished dream of taking the capital without its total destruction. Delegations from cities and towns daily appeared to accept Spanish sovereignty and offer assistance. Labor battalions were formed from their ranks, a growing pool hundreds of thousands strong. Increasing the brigantine patrol to prevent smuggling of food and water by night, Cortés severed the last bond between Tlatelolco and the outside world. At his order the rest of the city was systematically razed, its canals filled in and the whole reduced to a flat surface. Throughout the siege the defenders had used buildings and ruins as tactical cover in their guerilla actions. They would use them no more. The Spanish line advanced with demolition, but never beyond it. Thus did Tenochtitlán disappear from sight, as though devoured by a swarm of locusts. Within two weeks seventy-five per cent of the city had vanished.

As the Spanish line advanced, Huitzilopochtli's temple loomed high against what could now be called the Plain of Cortés. Although vigorously defended, it fell after the fourth day, its defenders slain to a man. From the summit Cortés could see that he held seven-eighths of the city, the enemy being confined to a quarter of about 1,000 buildings, all surrounded and interlaced by canals. Again he offered terms of surrender, which were taken under "consideration" by Cuauhtemoc and his lords, consideration being more Huitzilopochtli hocus-pocus. The high priest claimed a visitation that promised that within four days the "Founder of the Empire" would come to save it. Dressing a lord in one of King Ahuitzotl's ceremonial robes, now reputed to bestow Huitzilopochtli's power on him that wore it, he was given a magic arrow to shoot at the Spaniards. If he scored a hit, Huitzilopochtli would save them. Mounting the barricade he fired away and started a skirmish in which three Spaniards were taken prisoner. Cuauhtemoc personally sacrificed them to the Hummingbird with thanks. While Cuauhtemoc and his fellow fanatics desperately sought to bring the official history to life, to invoke the power of the past, the suffering of those within the bulwarks was terrible. Even though some ravening women and children had been permitted to leave, there were still many thousands of noncombatants whom Cuauhtemoc would not release. While he and his warring nobles fed generously on the bodies of their foe, the macehualtin were disallowed.

> And all the common folk suffered torments of famine. Many died of hunger. No more did they drink pure, clean water—only brackish water did they drink. Of it many people died, and many people therefore [suffered from] a bloody flux, of which they died. And all was eaten—lizards and swallows; and maize straw, and salt grass. And they ate *colorin* wood, and they ate the glue orchid, and the frilled flower; and tanned hides, and buckskin, which they roasted, baked, toasted, or burned, so that they could eat them; and they gnawed sedum, and mud bricks. Never had there been such suffering.[18]

As the Spaniards awaited Cuauhtemoc's reply, the besieged continued to shout imprecations over the barricades. They urged the allies on in their demolition of the city, pointing out that it would also be their task to rebuild it, whoever won the final victory. Others asked Cortés to come in and kill them quickly so that Huitzilopochtli would grant them reward and rest. One of Ixtlilxochitl's uncles who had remained loyal to the system, but who had been wounded and captured in the struggle for the temple, was persuaded to carry a last appeal for surrender to Cuauhtemoc. He was passed through the barricade and delivered the message from Cortés. He was sacrificed to Huitzilopochtli as a traitor, and Cortés had his answer.

The Conqueror now unleashed the final assault. His allies, know-

ing full well that this was to be the final act in their revenge upon the
Mexica, were beyond restraint. "Our friends accompanied us, armed
with swords and shields," Cortés wrote, "and such was the slaughter
done that day on water and on land, that with prisoners taken they
numbered in all more than forty thousand men; and such were the
shrieks and the weeping of the women and children that there was
none whose heart did not break; and we had more trouble in prevent-
ing our allies from killing and inflicting tortures than we had in
fighting with the Indians, for no such inhuman cruelty as the natives
of these parts practice was ever seen amongst any people. . . ." The
canals ran red with blood; the roofs of the houses, the walls, the
courtyards were littered with limbs and bodies, splashed with gore.
Maggots swarmed in the streets. Cuauhtemoc and his captains were
captured as they sought to escape by boat and returned to the scene of
disaster where the Conqueror waited. But the smell was unbearable;
Cortés was ill from it as were the others, and so the victors retreated to
safer ground. For three days survivors streamed from Tlatelolco,
mostly noncombatants who had escaped slaughter and starvation.
At the periphery of the great stench they were "processed" by the
victors:

> And everywhere the Spaniards were seizing and robbing the people.
> They sought gold; as nothing did they value the green stone, quetzal
> feathers, and turquoise. [The gold] was everywhere in the bosoms or
> in the skirts of the wretched women. And as for the men, it was
> everywhere in their breech clouts and in their mouths.
> And [the Spaniards] seized and set apart the pretty women—those
> of light bodies, the fair [skinned] ones. And some women, when they
> were [to be] assaulted, covered their faces with mud and put on old
> mended skirts and rags. . . . And also some men were singled
> out—those who were strong, grown to manhood, and next the young
> boys, of whom they would make messengers, who would be their
> servants, and who were known as their runners. And on some they
> burned [brand marks] on their cheeks. . . .

221

Elsewhere on the lake, Spaniards in their boats sacked those palaces and buildings accessible only by water. Diving parties were already at work on the Tacuba causeway trying to recover the treasure that was drowned during the Night of Sorrow. At the same time, other squads were rounding up certain individuals. Huitzilopochtli's high priest was captured in Coyoacán, as was the priest of Xipe Totec. Both were interrogated and hanged when they failed to disclose their idol's treasure horde. The lords of Huitzilopochco and Culhuacán, among others, were hung, ostensibly for secreting treasure, while still others were torn to pieces by the conquerors' savage mastiffs; Cuauhtemoc was tortured. The treasure hunt was on.

Cortés moved his headquarters to Coyoacán as the remaining quarter of Tlatelolco was being razed. One was still overcome by its stench. A ship with a cargo of Spanish wine had put in at Vera Cruz, just in time for a grand victory fete. A drove of pigs from Cuba provided fresh meat; native turkey, maize, and other provender there was in abundance. But the wine was the thing. A frightful bacchanal ensued, with dancing on the tables and drunken orators who outdid each other in extravagant squandering of shares yet to be divided, or treasure discovered for that matter. Even Bernal Díaz, who was no stranger to the revelry of soldiers, was shocked, and reflected that it would have been better if the banquet had not been given, so disgusting were some of the things that took place.[14]

The morning after came early as Cortés routed his men for a Mass of thanksgiving. Dousing their aching heads with cold water, the revelers put on their best attire. In solemn procession they followed the cross and an image of the Virgin to a prominence overlooking the lake where Mary was enthroned with a *Te Deum*. In looking toward the capital, however, there was nothing to be seen but a six mile radius of rubble from which not a stick protruded upright and whence issued not a sound.[15]

Chapter XII

The New Pipiltin

That Huichilobos subsequently arose from the presumed dead to offer what some of the conquerors imagined to be a challenge to imposition of Spanish sovereignty is historical fact. But to fully understand how this happened and to comprehend its many implications, one must have a sound grasp of the nature of Mexican society as it reassembled after the physical disappearance of Tenochtitlán. This chapter is intended to supply the latter need and to introduce a final chapter in the history of Huitzilopochtli as idea.

The final collapse of the Mexican system may be seen as the last reverberation of Montezuma's fall. It all seemed to follow the whim of a malevolent fate, or, from the Christian point of view, the design of a beneficent deity. The statistics of defeat told a grim tale: some 60,000 survived the siege, while over 240,000 perished. Cortés estimated that about 100,000 were military casualties, the balance dying of disease and privation.[1] It is impossible to reckon the grand total if one begins at the beginning, which was the onset of Montezuma's emotional and philosophical disintegration. Gone were most of the Tlatoque, or highest lords, the priests, the administrators, the merchants.

224

But many of the provincial towns emerged unscathed if one does not count the omnivorous appetite of the plague. There nobles and priests continued to maintain the system while they waited to see what the victors would command. The physical disappearance of Tenochtitlán, even more than its defeat, was deeply traumatic. And yet, in the presence of death and the void, there was almost immediate activity as indigenous society sought to restore itself. Several movements occured simultaneously: surviving nobles took full charge of religious cult; local and provincial lesser lords stepped up to fill now vacant positions in higher ranks; adventurous tenants and mayeques declared themselves independent and claimed the lands to which they had been bound; the macehualtin generally began to seek a way out of their subordination. All along the spectrum of Indian society, there was movement, essentially upward, each level moving and reacting against the next.

Cortés ordered immediate rebuilding of central Tenochtitlán, the area where the Coatepantli and royal palaces had stood, as the new command and residential center of the victors. Desirous of creating an illusion of continuity, he insisted that the entire project be completed within sixty days. He also called a convention of lords in his headquarters at Coyoacán in order to implement the laws of the new regime. Tributes, it was learned, would be paid as usual but to the Emperor Charles, in whose name Cortés would receive them. The macehualtin would be given in custody to certain Spaniards whom Cortés would designate as encomenderos. It was made clear that the victors would respect the rights and privileges of the Indian nobility. Most surviving lords of the old regime failed to respond favorably; bitter in defeat, they hoped to free Cuauhtemoc and other leaders whom the Spaniards had imprisoned. They were also resentful over the treasure hunt and execution of un-co-operative lords who, like themselves, were trying to keep alive the spirit and substance of revolt. And so they refused to order the macehualtin to work. In view of this Cortés was

once again compelled to turn to Texcoco. Ixtlilxochitl, so instrumental
in the final victory, had just died of smallpox; but his brother Carlos,
whom Cortés had chosen to succeed, responded by sending thousands
of laborers to begin the project. Going over the heads of recalcitrant
nobles, Cortés next made a direct appeal to the more ambitious members of the petty gentry and administrative functionaries of the lakeshore communities and nearby towns. To all who would assume
leadership in getting the capital rebuilt he promised choice city lots,
tax exemptions, and full status as nobles, all to be held in perpetuity
by themselves and their heirs. He further created barrio "lordships"
and street "captaincies" as inducements and rewards for incentive.
Holders of the titles were also to exercise control over the granting of
home sites within their jurisdictions. For all plebeians who would
follow their leaders in construction and settlement of the capital he
held out the promise of full exemption from tribute. Response was
overwhelming; the lure of noble status and control of land was one
that few who did not already have them could resist, and the macehualtin, seeing the tribute scales that were being set, gladly accepted
the offer. Almost overnight 100,000 houses were erected in the Indian
barrios, with as many more families trying to crowd in. The city
rapidly acquired more population than it could handle, a problem that
has remained to plague Mexico to the present.

Cortés' promises were fulfilled, and formation of a new nobility was
begun. The individual noble was commonly given the Carib designa-
tion of *cacique*,* or "boss," which was hispanicized into the generic
term *"cacicazgo."* † For Mexico it was a new word and a new class.[2] In
towns of the central valley, then in the provinces as the wave of
Spanish sovereignty reached them, those who volunteered for service
were rewarded by admission to the new nobility as caciques or *princi-*

* Kah-see-kay.
† Kah-see-kahz-go.

pales, literally, "principal persons" of the community. Early in October, 1521, after little more than a brief rest, Sandoval led a Spanish and Indian force on a punitive expedition against the local lords of Huatuxco and Tuxtepec for having slain snooping Spaniards when they heard about the Night of Sorrow. Alvarado led a similar expedition against the provinces of Coaztlauac and Tochquianco. Cortés himself put up some 70,000 pesos to equip and finance an expedition of 40,000 Indians that he led in conquest of Pánuco. In these and similar expeditions that fanned out from the capital in all directions, the Indian leaders received certain privileges: the right to ride horses and use Spanish arms and dress, the rank of captain, the use of coat armor; and they were all *endonado,* that is, given the gentlemanly distinction of bearing "Don" before their names. In secondary conquest the Indians were of vital significance, and, from their point of view, well rewarded by the privileges and social status that membership in the cacicazgo bestowed.[3]

Even as the new nobility was forming, those surviving Pipiltin who would come were welcomed into Spanish ranks almost without reservation. And even more readily did the conquerors seek to join the Pipiltin. Matrimony was the most immediate and obvious means of entry, although relatively few conquerors married into Indian society. It was not necessary to go that far. If one sets aside the quest for gold and treasure, no amount of which could survive a drumhead once it was cut up to make a deck of playing cards (as had been proved time and again during the conquest), it becomes clear that the conqueror was really seeking a way of life. In the Pipiltin he thought he had found it. The Spanish conqueror was rather like what most Europeans would be when they went on adventure to the New World, that is, essentially conservative in their desire to reproduce the culture that had produced them; they could not fail to be a link in the cultural continuum. But if the conqueror was disposed to look over his shoulder to Spain for the ultimate blueprint of colonial construction, which

Spain would he choose to reproduce? Would it be the Spain of Charles V, with its voracious bureaucracy, its mounting tax burdens, its bludgeoned communes, its suppression of feudal *fueros,* its loss of private jurisdictions to a relentless royal authority? Or would he look to the more distant Spain of the *gran Reconquista,* with its private rights of justice and possession of feudal prerogatives? Even as they were ushering in the modern age, Spain's conquistadores were in headlong flight from its portents.

Cortés himself provided perfect example. Choosing a princely domain, he persuaded the crown to give him full criminal and civil jurisdictions, in addition to which he sought and obtained absolute patronal rights over the church in his lands from the papacy. With Spanish and Indian nobles as his vassals and the macehualtin as his servants and serfs, he was in fact a sovereign feudal lord, armed with supreme authority in both secular and ecclesiastical spheres.[4] This kind of thinking was even more evident in his institution of the encomienda and what he and his fellows made of it. Theoretically, all free Indians became vassals of the Spanish crown with the fall of Tenochtitlán, and like freemen in Spain and elsewhere in the empire, they now owed taxes. As a reward for services rendered, the crown transferred to qualified conquerors a privilege of sovereignty: they might collect and keep for their own use the tribute of a specified number of Indians that would normally be due the crown. The Indians so held were also made liable to personal service as part of the tribute that was owed. In return the encomendero was obliged to maintain a good mount, weapons, and armor, and stand ready to defend the emperor's sovereignty. And at his own expense he was to provide for Christianization of the Indians assigned to him. All of this was spelled out in detail by Cortés in his *Ordenanzas de buen gobierno* of 1524, so that there can be little likelihood that anyone failed to understand precisely what was involved. Nevertheless, the conquerors almost immediately decided that the crown had actually surrendered to them a portion of its "immediate sovereignty" over the Indians, which meant full and private jurisdiction. In arguments for perpetuity of the encomienda, Cortés stated the case succinctly: he granted that "supreme jurisdiction" would rest with the crown, but "each [encomendero] would look upon the Indians as his personal property and would thus care for them as he would any property that is to be inherited by his nearest [heir]." [5] By such casuistry was the free Indian converted into chattel.

Granted the conqueror's sentimental attachment to the Spain of the Cid, it appears doubtful that he sought more than a vague semblance of that milieu. While we recognize the relationship he established between encomendero and Indian as a feudal one in the European sense, it was only through ironic coincidence that it turned out that way. What Cortés and the encomenderos actually did was to employ the Caribbean encomienda to describe and justify the status of the mayeque as they found him. They were not looking backward; they sought to secure the present and project the future. Recognizing the possibilities of the Mexican labor system as it had been developed and enjoyed by the Pipiltin, the conquerors moved in, applying Castilian juridical sanction to a Mexican institution. [6] It remained to be seen whether or not the crown would countenance their design.

Even before the fall of the empire, the Spaniards had begun to emulate the lords of the Pipiltin in quite another way. While lodged in Axayacatl's palace during their first stay in the capital, they were attended by female servants who did their every bidding; for six months Montezuma took pains to see that his visitors were plied with attractive women, much as he would his peers and other lords of the Pipiltin. For their part the Spaniards were in their masculine prime; the oldest was not much over forty, the vast majority being somewhere between eighteen and twenty-five years of age. And they were *donjuanistas* in the best Spanish tradition. Beginning at Vera Cruz, they had undertaken amorous conquest of the continent and continued to pursue it to the very gates of Tenochtitlán. Along the way they became expert in preparing a soothing balm for the *mal de mujeres* that was widespread among them. In the capital and at their leisure they abandoned themselves to studied emulation of the Pipiltin.

After the Night of Sorrow and recuperation in Tlaxcala, the sexual conquest was resumed with full force. Besides the women made available through the alliance, thousands of female slaves were taken and possessed utterly. In relating the struggle to win control of the countryside around the lake, Bernal Díaz frequently remarks on the many women that were taken, and frankly admits that he and his companions were more interested in finding pretty girls than in fighting the enemy.[7] Not infrequently were the officers accused of taking all the best looking ones for themselves. From the beginning Cortés appeared ready to compete with the best of the Pipiltin. Besides Doña Marina and other women given to him by various rulers en route to the capital, he accepted one of Montezuma's daughters as a "legitimate" wife, that is, by Pipiltin standards. Baptized and named Doña Ana, she went to live with him in his apartments. Accompanying her were two sisters, Inez and Elvira, and a sister of Cacama whom the Spaniards called Doña Francesca. It was a pregnant Doña Ana who was slain on the causeway during the Night of Sorrow. Still another daughter of Montezuma, Isabel, subsequently bore Cortés a daughter, which suggests that almost upon arrival he installed his own harem in Axayacatl's palace, quite in the mode of the Pipiltin.[8]

The primary conquest of Mexico was really more biological than military. However strenuous the fighting was at times, love-making was just as intense, certainly more frequent, and of infinitely greater consequence. Although it cannot be statistically proved or disproved, I would guess that the Spaniards commonly left more pregnancies in their camps than they did casualties on the field of battle. Biologically speaking, it was neither microbe nor sword nor mailed fist that conquered Mexico. It was the *membrum febrilis*.

After the fall of Tenochtitlán the amorous conquest continued, but now at a more accelerated pace. The encomienda served as a procuring device for the encomendero, who, if married to a woman in Spain, frequently found ready excuse to delay sending for her while he sinfully enjoyed his harem. This early became one of the crown's and the local clergy's thorniest social problems. The stature of the conqueror was immense: he walked the earth as a demigod; no plebeian dared look into his face, or contradict him, or overtake him on the street; as he passed all prostrated themselves and ate dirt; he could go anywhere without fear, certain in the knowledge that his merest whim would be obeyed; that which appealed to him was his. His was the overlordship of the new Pipiltin. This is not to imply that the conqueror was necessarily a rapist: She sought that exquisite pain as avidly as He, and beneath the enveloping Christian heaven She also found guilt, but with it the understanding of another woman, the Virgin, who would be her eternal intercessor; there gradually formed an identity and relationship between them that has never changed. Simultaneously, He spurned guilt and expiation and made *donjuanismo* a Mexican *raison d'être*. The black veil has fought temptation in Mexico ever since.

This phenomenon of extramarital relationships has oftentimes been identified and discussed as institutionalization of the *barraganía*, the ancient Spanish form of common-law matrimony. Although it did eventually become such, it was quite a different thing in the early years. Though the conquerors might have used the term in reference to their many concubines, they steered clear of any of the barraganía's legal restraints and responsibilities. What they insisted upon was the carefree sexual libertarianism so long enjoyed by the lords of the Pipiltin, and to which they had become accustomed during the conquest. What they seemed not to realize, or perhaps chose to ignore, was that the Pipiltin as a group bore joint responsibility for the children whom they produced; they were given excellent care and granted status and position by birth alone. Illegitimacy, in the European sense, was unknown to them. For that matter, the barraganía as it existed in Spain also had protective devices for the women and children born of such unions; the *Siete Partidas* clearly took them into account, providing legal definition. But the conquerors steadfastly refused to recognize or assume responsibility for most of the children they sired. During the conquest, of course, such was largely impossible; but even after they had hung up their swords and moved in with the Pipiltin, the conquerors continued to deny them, so that most of their offspring were relegated to the hated abyss of illegitimacy and all that it implied. For fifty years the word *mestizo* was synonymous with bastardy.

The problem of illegitimate mestizos reacting in violence against a society that spawned and rejected them grew to grave proportions for Bishop Zumárraga and other churchmen and officials who were responsible for social welfare and maintenance of public order. The camp children who were conceived and born during the conquest were just reaching their teens in 1532. Roaming in packs like wolves, they did whatever they had to do in order to survive. The crown urged its representatives to use a firm hand, suggesting that the older children be entered in forced apprenticeship, the younger to be put in the charge of an encomendero to work for his keep until he or she too could be apprenticed.[9] Such was the tragic origin of *mestizaje** in Mexico. Born to a callous world, its members for the most part lacked familial ties and had no juridical status, no identity, no legal existence. They and their children became known and feared for their depredations against organized society and were instrumental in making necessary organization of the *Santa Hermandad* in 1554 as a rural constabulary. Indian society was equally hostile, and not a few mestizos were taken by the caciques, "some of whom they sell amongst themselves

* Mes-tee-zah-hay.

in the manner of a business, much as the Christians do animals." [10]

The new cacicazgo was at the same time rapidly finding its own identity in post-conquest society. Through intermarriage and other channels of co-operation, the caciques lived with the conquerors in relative equality, forming growing bonds of mutual interest.[11] For the most part administration of heavily populated regions, like Michoacán, Texcoco, Meztitlán, Tlaxcala, Tepeaca, Cholula, Huexotzinco, and Acatepec, was carried on by provincial lords who merely acknowledged suzerainty to the Spanish emperor in the capital. Working closely with local encomenderos, they ruled their towns with iron discipline. Encomenderos were forbidden by law to reside in the towns they held in encomienda; for this reason they retained the calpixques who had previously served the Pipiltin in the same capacity. Since most of these overseers sprang from plebeian ranks, they were anxious to rise in the new order and exploited their charges mercilessly in order to show large profits and thus ingratiate themselves with their masters. In course of time they stood a good chance of becoming both wealthy and endonado themselves. Land division continued to be controlled by the caciques, as demonstrated by the land register of Santiago Guevea, the greatest change being a transfer from oral to written legal procedures as introduced by the conquerors.[12] Everywhere the caciques set tribute scales themselves and supervised collection; they regulated communal agriculture, corvées, and *tandas;* they were the eyes, ears, mouth, and oftentimes the brain of the system that was forming, and they were securing for themselves a powerful position within it.

If by their garish dress, tapestried and ornamented homes—usually quite without taste—and their exaggerated punctilio the conquerors proclaimed their plebeian origins, the cacique did no less. Having risen, his image grew huge in his own sight; he was the lord. An early act of the cacicazgo was to increase the old tribute scale of one-third of all production. As in days of old, tributes varied from place to place,

although upward revision tended to be constant. The crown insisted
that tributes be scaled according to the levels maintained by Montezuma II; but since the caciques were in full command of tribute levy
and collection, they exacted what the traffic would bear, and not
infrequently a little more. In the same manner ancient regulations
that governed the weights and distances of tameme transport were
abandoned in favor of unrestrained exploitation of the carriers. In
1531 the Audiencia complained that it had to labor ten or twelve
hours a day, seven days per week, in order to keep up with the
machinations of the conquerors and caciques. In spite of the Audiencia's direct command that they hold a census of tributaries, the caciques refused, obviously because they did not wish anyone to know
how many commoners they taxed; the cacicazgo was making the Spanish system of indirect rule serve its own ends. Since the encomenderos
were sharing in the spoils, most of them supported the caciques. Try
as they might, the *oidores* of the Audiencia could do nothing. They
were not even permitted to know what Montezuma's old tribute rolls
called for; without that information they were powerless to challenge
the obviously ruthless exploitation of the macehualtin. Nor, taking the
problem from a different angle, could they always determine which
Indians were genuine lords by lineage and which were upstarts and
poseurs. The commoners were so fearful of retaliation that no threat
of punishment or promise of reward would make them talk.[13]

The newly risen cacicazgo was impressive in its constructions. As
former plebeians, landless for the most part, the caciques well knew
how important land was. The remnants of the Pipiltin already appre-
ciated this; with the advent of Spanish dominium and the conquerors'
veneration for latifundia, the fact was confirmed absolutely, and the
rush was on. Lands, goods, and produce previously claimed by the
state church and Huitzilopochtli's priesthood were seized by the
cacicazgo. Although an enormous quantity of choice agricultural land
was thus engrossed, it did not suffice. The lords now began to move in

234

on plebeian lands, both privately and communally held. The most convenient way to gain control was to raise tributes until the owner was forced to sell; some obstinate owners went to prison or were made slaves by the caciques. And then the lords confiscated their lands. The caciques also lined up at the land office with Spanish colonists and received grants of land large enough for cattle ranches, whereupon they went into the beef business. They also got into silk as soon as the conquerors proved the industry profitable. More often than not, their silk houses and auxiliary labor needs were filled through coercion of the macehualtin. Most of the land that entered their hands went into formation of large estates that were passed on to heirs through direct or collateral inheritance, so that during the early post-conquest period the cacicazgo acquired control over vast amounts of land and water. In all of this they, like the conquerors, were exempted from taxation and freed of other dues.[14]

When, in 1530, the crown ordered that every Indian town be given a Spanish-type municipality, complete with officers holding the traditional perquisites of each office, the caciques hastened to apply. They now became governors, councilmen, judges, jailers, prosecutors, and bailiffs, with full royal authority as manifested in the *vara de justicia,* or wand of royal justice, which they were permitted to wield. In the crown's view this was enlightened tutelage in civics, the source of not a little pride on the part of its theoreticians and idealists. But in reality it made the caciques impregnable because they now had control of the wheels of justice, which they converted into a rack upon which to stretch all who opposed them. While the cacicazgo thus maintained its ancient coercive power over the macehualtin, it now did so behind a screen of Castilian juridical sanction. Indeed, all that remained for the caciques was to get privileged exemption from arrest of themselves by public officers, which they eventually did. One of the most significant of their *fueros,* therefore, protected them from arrest by any authority save that of the Audiencia, and then only after formal presentation of charges before that body, followed by weighing and sifting of evidence. All of which meant that the cacique was freed from fear of retribution except under extraordinary circumstances. The encomenderos and caciques consequently became great lords who largely set their own laws and did what they pleased with subject populations, except for interference by the friars, which grew meaningful in the second half of the century. But in 1545 Tello de Sandoval, the crown's special investigator of this phenomenon, was shocked to find that thirty miles from the capital there was no royal law, and hastened to report the same to the emperor, describing "areas where the Indians hold their caciques and encomenderos to be kings and are ignorant of any other crown." [15]

Given the backgrounds and desires of the conquerors and new caciques, their alliance resulted from a case of hunger meeting appetite, the greatest evidence of which is borne by the official regulations governing treatment of the macehualtin issued between 1524 and 1528: the Indians might not be robbed of their possessions nor used as beasts of burden; they might not be forced to prepare and carry foodstuffs to the mines for resale; they might not be used to supplement labor in the mines, nor might they be assigned slaves' duties so as to free the slaves for labor in the mines; encomienda Indians might not be rented out, nor could families be broken; none might be enslaved or so branded under guise of being captives of war. It was in the last respect that the caciques worked most closely with the conquerors. The *rescate,* or indigenous slave trade, was monopolized by the caciques, and they virtually fed upon the macehualtin in meeting the demand for slave labor, which demand increased as the crown successfully disputed the conquerors' interpretation of the status of Indians held in encomienda.[16] As it worked out, exploitation of the macehualtin continued to be the basis of an arbitrary and lasting system. Through monopoly of town and village political structures, the caciques achieved their objectives and silenced opposition, even as they gradually consumed the property of the towns. In 1567 they still had not permitted a census of tributaries. Effecting a double swindle, they collected bloated tributes from undeclared tributaries, in addition to which they pocketed all of the king's taxes that were imposed in the local market place. Under such conditions many plebians deserted their homes and towns and moved north beyond the Chichimeca frontier. Others fled to the Marquesado del Valle, Cortés' vast principality where the cacicazgo did not enjoy so free a hand. Generally speaking, however, the caciques were aided and abetted by the encomenderos, who effectively influenced dominion in the towns. It was difficult for a cacique to get into office without the approval of the local encomendero. Having reached an understanding, their collusion was made effective by the fact that they were beyond effective range of royal authority. Free Indians were enslaved; others were dragged to court on trumped up charges and sentenced to penal servitude in factories, or perhaps in the mines, where only death could effect their release. Officials of the Audiencia seldom if ever inspected such places or questioned the legal procedures that kept them filled.[17]

If in the post-conquest world the plebians found themselves just as bad off, if not worse, than they had been under the old regime, there was substantial change in one area of existence that greatly influenced all the others: they were no longer forced to see their children sacrificed or to fear their own demise on the slab; in the stead of Huitzilopochtli and his male-dominated regimen of terror, they found a compassionate Mother Goddess who blessed and saved. Everywhere they were free to do so, the macehualtin crowded around the sign of the cross. The Christian evangel got underway officially in 1524 with the arrival of twelve Franciscan apostles who met with success far beyond expectations. Indians came in thousands, then by tens of thousands, to demand baptism, far in excess of the friars' ability to comply. In seemingly endless queues the plebeians besieged the monasteries until they got what they wanted. With no real alternative, and under an imperative of their own, the Franciscans began to baptize wholesale. Sacramental words were uttered over the throng, then each individual was briefly sprinkled with holy water; there was no instruction. It became common for a lone priest to baptize five or six thousand a day; the record for one friar was 10,000; some actually developed heavily muscled arms and calloused hands from hefting the baptismal pitcher. The same awesome response was experienced in town and country. "My companion and I," wrote Pedro de Gante, "have baptized over 200,000 Indians, often as many as 14,000 in a single day, [but] I have long since lost count." By 1530 a mere handful of Franciscans had baptized over one million persons; by 1540 over six million. Now there can be no doubt that the macehualtin, much like the Roman masses in the earliest days of Christianity, yearned for a redeemer and found a salvation cult almost irresistible. In so far as they could understand Christianity—and never forget that the Franciscans were specialists at reaching the illiterate masses—the plebeians recognized it for what it was, however superficially. But even so, the friars were utterly mistaken in their belief that the Indians were so avidly seeking Christianity for itself; the astounding phenomenon of Indian response rather commented upon the religious system from which the plebeians were in flight. They were not seekers, they were refugees—a distinction of which the friars would become painfully aware in due time.[18]

Although the commoners were virtually unanimous in their flight from the old imperial orthodoxy, the remnants of the Pipiltin were not. A few of the lords became lasting converts, but most remained bitter in defeat and determined to see Huitzilopochtli rise to power again, and they along with him. The new caciques, who soon became the patrician majority, tended to take a different view: it was through close co-operation with the Christians that they achieved their status and wealth and so were amenable to conversion, although time would prove them less willing to accept most of the restraints that Christianity demanded. But they would find good tutelage in obviat-

ing those restraints by the Old Christians themselves. Like the conquerors, the caciques settled down to create for themselves an ideal
world. Since most plebeians dared not act without the approval of
their lords, their massive response to Christianity measured and documented the rise of the new cacicazgo.[19] In the friars' view, these
became the "good" caciques who facilitated evangelization of the
masses and themselves readily ate pork instead of human flesh and
otherwise adopted a European veneer. At the same time the old lords
were the "bad" caciques because they carried on the old cult and
plotted revolution. As subsequent investigations would show, the old
lords continued to do with Huitzilopochtli cult what the new caciques
were doing with Christianity and the power gained from co-operation
with the conquerors: they both oppressed the helpless macehualtin for
their own ends. The conquerors and caciques, in seeking to enjoy the
best of both worlds, joined the worst elements of either in a new
system of tyranny from which first a physical and much later a
cultural mestizaje would gradually emerge.

Chapter XIII

Huichilobos and the Bishop

To most of the caciques Christian conversion and baptism meant little more than taking a Christian name, especially during the early years of the evangel. There were not enough friars to provide preliminary instruction, and all too often in rural areas there was little or no catechism following baptism, so that the first contact was not infrequently the last. Conversion was therefore primarily a political act for those who sought to rule. But as a functional focus of sovereignty, Christianity could not immediately succeed; it was not adequately understood or established to support the appeals that must be made to it under the Mexican way of life. While the caciques attempted to use the new cult as they believed the old one had been employed, they soon found that such was impossible, essentially because Christianity failed to evoke popular terror. And so, why should not the cacicazgo, after a brief period of experimentation, tend to lapse back into older politico-religious patterns of thought and behavior? Although Christianity served as a pole of sovereignty in the capital, it generally failed to do so in the country, for the convent was not yet an adequate substitute for Huitzilopochtli's temples. Among the caciques, therefore, the friars detected a shifting of position and posture that they interpreted as backsliding and even outright apostasy.

On the other hand the macehualtin remained much more stable in conversion, largely, one suspects, because the plebeians sought peace of mind rather than political power. In this respect Christianity proved more than adequate. They had known grinding poverty under the old regime, and were finding it perpetuated and sometimes increased under the new one; but it seemed less painful now because the Franciscans, after their gentle founder, made of poverty a virtue. This consecration of poverty was no less effective in Mexico than it had been on the European continent; it was a sublimation of harsh reality that the masses could understand quite without comprehension. Who needed to know more than he could feel?

At the same time the friars were horrified at the plethora of old religious ideas the Indians were carrying over. The plebeians possessed a rich folk cult in contrast to orthodox state cult as it had been dispensed by Huitzilopochtli's imperial center. As far as the commoners were concerned, the Hummingbird's orthodoxy was to be shunned and feared because it oppressed them and fed on their very bodies. Rulers of the Mexican state had incorporated much folk cult, especially in the early days of the empire when the system was being formulated. Tlacaellel and his mythologians wished to make orthodoxy as widely appealing as possible. But once the system was enthroned, they no longer cared because their power to impose it was greater than the plebeians' was to resist. At the same time the commoners were ruthlessly dehumanized until the masters of the system no longer considered them in need of cult and shut them out completely. There was, therefore, an intensified growth of folk cult in opposition to the orthodox state religion, especially during the later years of the empire. Food in the belly and avoidance of pain were its primary concerns. Would the plebeians desert their cult, however seductively the Virgin might beckon? The commoners were precise and filled with purpose as they carried over this "practical" cult to Christianity. And then a process was joined that involved conscious eclecticism and uncontrolled accretion, culminating after centuries of maturation in a distinctly Mexican Catholicism.[1] It is abundantly clear that the only religious trade that was made by the plebeians was one of rather remote orthodoxies; they exchanged an obnoxious one for a seemingly beneficent one. But beyond that they brought over their time-tested solutions to the problems posed by rain, planting and harvest, and life's daily challenge. It could not have been otherwise, for how in so short a time could the friars supply a new *Volksgeist*? It was indeed the friars' difficult task to make clear the fact that Christianity was not merely a canopy; it was a living faith, one in which the believer became a communicant and hence a part of a continuing tradition. But how to get over the idea that the Virgin and the saints were living ideas and not stone idols?

These problems all came into the purview of Don Juan de Zumárraga, the bishop of New Spain and the man responsible for spiritual and doctrinal oversight of Mexico during these momentous times. Himself a Franciscan, Zumárraga was deeply sympathetic with his confreres' plans to establish in New Spain a pristine church that might be a model for humanistic reform everywhere. The bishop himself initiated much of their program after his arrival in 1528. During this early period, the Mexican evangel was dominated by a radical wing of the Franciscan Order, ultra-observants for the most part who were steeped in both Cisnerian reform and the heady atmosphere of the northern Renaissance and Christian humanism. Zumárraga stood very close to the Erasmian *Philosophia Christi*, taking a subjectivist attitude that in some doctrinal positions placed him on the very edge of orthodoxy. In fact, a few years after his death, when the religious dispute over reform had polarized Europe into two contending power blocks and Erasmus had become suspect, Zumárraga's *Doctrina christiana* was to be challenged and carefully examined by the

Holy Office for heresy. Although his writings were found blameless by their examiners, Erasmus' influence should not be minimized, for Zumárraga was fairly steeped in the Erasmian school. And he read other humanists; his well-thumbed copy of More's *Utopia* may have been the only one in Mexico at the time. In addition to his intellectual humanism, the bishop periodically experienced ineffable moments of mystical union with his God. But he was one of those rare mystics who could also grapple with temporal problems most effectively. He was serving as Guardian of the convent at Abrojo, one of Spain's great mendicant reform centers, when the Emperor Charles V went there for Holy Week meditations in 1527. So impressed was he that he presented Zumárraga to the pope for bishop of Mexico, protests of the candidate notwithstanding.[2]

Bishop Zumárraga found apostasy among the caciques and principales a most vexatious and serious problem, essentially because they held such influence over the commoners. To combat it, he employed twenty missionary centers, each with a small staff of Indian constables who rooted out secret idolatry and otherwise acted as assistants to the resident friars. Most of these constables were sons of nobles who had been educated in the local monastery and had emerged fanatical Christians. In spying on their parents and the errant nobility, they became hated and were not uncommonly assassinated by disgruntled caciques. Gradually, there developed a horizontal cleavage in which the sons of the nobles were given aid and comfort by the macehualtin against their old lords. Although many points of conflict between friars and caciques were not religious in themselves, they served to make reconciliation difficult because almost every position the friars took had ultimate religious significance. The friars forbade the wearing of ear and nose plugs, which were a traditional badge of status. They demanded the caciques return excessive tributes and all properties illegally acquired—and this included manumission of their slaves—before they would grant temporal remission of sin. And the caciques were required to give up all their women except the one wife they married in the church.[3] This extremely sore point was commented on in a letter of Andrés de Olmos to Zumárraga from his outpost in Hueytlalpa: "I tell them that they can have as many women in their service as may be necessary, provided they do not [also] have carnal access. But it seems that no woman is to be admitted to their service whom they do not first try out, including mothers-in-law and other relatives."[4] Unlike the conquerors, the friars could not reconcile themselves to the mores of the Pipiltin.

The hard core of resistance was founded in a powerful minority of old lords who maintained the Mexican calendar and its pagan rites. In absolute control of the old cult, they hid their idols and manufactured copies faster than the friars could find and break them; at the same time they intimidated the macehualtin and continued to force them to pay regular tributes to their hidden gods. In every possible way they obstructed the Christian evangel and made life unbearable for the Indians who accepted it.[5] Zumárraga retaliated with frontal assault: by June of 1530 he had dismantled 500 hidden temples and smashed over 20,000 idols by count, and had also destroyed an unknown quantity of codices and manuscripts, some of which could probably have shed much light on the Mesoamerican past.[6] In spite of his efforts the Audiencia could still without exaggeration complain to the crown that the old cult was a continuing force in Indian life, and one through which the caciques held practical sovereignty. As for the nobles themselves, the oidores concluded that genuine and sincere conversions among them were rare, most of them merely using Christianity as a sham to make more respectable their exploitation of the macehualtin. To which the bishop could add that many encomenderos refused to co-operate in his struggle against apostasy, even going to the extreme of protecting the slayers of his constables.[7]

What to do? Zumárraga thought he knew the identity of the ultimate foe, as had the soldiery from the beginning of the conquest.

Pious folk still recalled the devil's reaction to the evangel: so hard was he hit, so discomfited, that Popocatepetl had ceased to smoke and had remained quiescent until the recent past when Satan again stoked the fires of hell, causing the volcano to awaken from its slumber. The Evil One was back in business at the invitation of the conquerors, some of whom affronted God by their sinful way of living, by their shameless exploitation of the Indians, by their lust for power and riches; the bishop could go on and on. Reports from all quarters of the missionary field read the same nowadays: as interpreted by the religious, Satan and his agents were assuming human and diverse forms in their urging of apostasy among Christianized Indians. The old cult was daily growing stronger rather than weaker; the future seemed gravely in doubt.[8] Whenever the press of episcopal business permitted, Zumárraga went out on visitation to confirm the most discouraging reports. Seldom did he consider them unfounded. His men were laboring beyond capacity. Typically, the friar walking circuit arrived in town just after the break of day. He found numerous sick people to confess, scores of couples to marry, hundreds or perhaps thousands of plebeians from the back country who had come in search of baptism, many burials, especially in time of plagues, sermons to preach. He was still working long past midnight.[9] When this regimen was multiplied by the friars in the field and the huge number of such towns they visited each day, the bishop could not but feel inadequate to the task. The demands of the evangel had what it took to cure a man of ambition. Who needed the calculated opposition of Satan?

Confrontation with the Evil One was nothing new for Zumárraga; they had met in contest before. In 1527 some Basques in Navarre succumbed to his blandishments and embraced a pact in which they renounced Christ and worshiped Satan in the form of a black billy goat. Wallowing in sensuous revelry solemnized by the Black Mass, followers of the cloven hoof bore witness to the popular heresy of their time. The Inquisition got on their trail and requested provincials of the Franciscans and Dominicans to send in Basque friars to clean up the infection. Zumárraga had been one of those chosen to treat the disease. As bishop of Mexico, he already wielded inquisitorial authority; all episcopal prelates were charged with discharge of the royal conscience and prosecution of war against the devil, in either of which the bishop might act as *Inquisidor ordinario*. But under usual circumstances such a role was reserved for only the gravest cases because none of the inquisitorial machinery was at hand. Nevertheless, Zumárraga considered the problem of such moment that he wrote to the emperor and Supremo of the Inquisition requesting authority to establish a tribunal of the Holy Office. Meanwhile, he used his episcopal authority to initiate cases against the Christians who were offending God and thus inviting the resurgence of Satan. Late in the summer of 1535 he received his answer from home: the Inquisitor General of Spain bestowed upon him the title of "Apostolic Inquisitor General Against Heretical Depravity and Apostasy," and included full authority to appoint a staff, establish and house a tribunal, maintain a prison, confiscate personal and real properties, and all other powers necessary to his holy task. The newly created tribunal was inaugurated June 6, 1536, with full pomp and ceremony, and Zumárraga immediately went after the many European blasphemers, heretics, apostatizers, and lechers who so flagrantly sinned. He had tried over seventy-three by the end of 1537.[10]

The Indians presented a more difficult and complex problem. As newcomers to the faith, they were to be treated with much less rigor along the entire spectrum of possible punishments than were Europeans, and there were some authorities who held that they should not be subject at all. Clearly, none but baptized Indians could be held liable to inquisitorial jurisdiction. The only crimes of which they could legally be charged, apostasy and idolatry, were the ones that lay at the very heart of the problem. And it was only through the agency of the Holy Office that Zumárraga could penetrate the caciques' principal defenses, their possession of the royal wand of justice and their privileged immunities. Just as in Spain, no immunity could stand before the prerogative of the Holy Office. There was no way in which the bishop could omit the Indians, however precarious pursuit of them might become.

Beyond the matter of apostate caciques, the plebeians were inadvertently guilty of idolatry, for broadly conceived it included belief in all superstitions that were contrary to teachings of the church; an idolater was one who read "signs" in bird calls, or who did things only on certain days as though God was favorable at just that precise moment, or one who kept unapproved relics and lucky pieces. And then, of course, there was the matter of determinism. All forms of astrological forecast and practices rooted in fatalism were idolatrous because they denied operation of the free will. The whole of folk cult relating to agriculture was considered to be idolatrous superstition because it was designed to obviate God's just wrath, of which lack of rain or blight was evidence. Theoretically, then, the remedy must be to expiate sin and do good works, rather than to cast a spell or charm an idol.

While his staff was busily prosecuting European sinners, Zumárraga initiated his first big Indian case against Taclatetle and Tacuxtetl, two baptized caciques of Tanacopán. Assisted by seven subordinate priests, they were revealed at the head of an extensive cult with full complement of ritual and sacrificial paraphernalia. Their temple was located in the depths of a hidden ravine and was regularly attended by a large group of nobles from Tula and surrounding towns. Plebeians were threatened with death for betraying the presence and activities of the religious community. As high priests, Taclatetle and Tacuxtetl maintained the old calendar and sacrificed commoners to their idols; at the time of arrest they had several youths in training for the priesthood. They kept accurate tribute lists and forced the macehualtin to pay every twenty days rather than the old schedule, probably because

247

of the need to hold them securely against the incursions of the friars. Tributes were high, and since they were added to those already borne in public by the straining plebeians, maintenance of ancient cult was not without economic implications. As typical members of the new Pipiltin, the high priests were exaggerated caricatures of the ancient priesthood. Both sired many children by different women, and Taclatetle had two children by his own daughter. One of his sons, on the other hand, was a fanatical Christian and therein the blight of his life. In the course of the trial the Guardian of the convent in Tula told of their successful opposition to the evangel. According to his testimony, they withheld needed labor and even sent crews to tear down a Christian chapel that had been completed in spite of them; when friars came to preach to the Indians, the accused plied them with alcohol, so that the friars frequently addressed themselves to a drunken audience. Facing what came to be a sheer mountain of testimony against them, Taclatetle and Tacuxtetl threw themselves on the mercy of the court and in so doing waived defense counsel. Zumárraga found them guilty of apostasy and imposed what was to become a routine sentence: bound together by a rope around their necks and placed on the back of an ass, the guilty pair were to be stripped to the waist and flogged from their prison cell to the capital's plaza, now the Zócalo, as Indian criers proclaimed their offenses. At the cathedral the flogging was to continue as they begged forgiveness and watched the executioner smash and burn their idols. Kneeling outside through the Mass, they were to be taken to the market place where their heads would be shorn, thence back to the cathedral for formal abjuration. Confinement in the Franciscan monastery at Tula at Zumárraga's discretion and permanent banishment from Tanacopán concluded the sentence.[11] A European Christian, under the same charges and circumstances, would have been relaxed to the secular arm and burned.

This case was followed almost at once by that of Martín Ucelo

(Ocelotl), who had been baptized in 1526. A wealthy noble, he was accused of preaching against Christianity, practicing sorcery, extorting tributes, entering pacts with demons, inciting rebellion, and many other crimes. In the course of investigation he was identified as one of the seers who had been condemned to death by Montezuma just prior to Cortés' arrival, but whose escape had lent him additional prestige. Traveling widely since that time, he had apparently accumulated a fortune through swindle and extortion. Once his case was begun, denunciations mounted as past victims sought revenge. His widespread activities as a seer, prophet, and inciter of rebellion made him a threat to both state and evangel, especially when his aristocratic connections were taken into account. Zumárraga alerted the Audiencia to the nature of the evidence that mounted against him, and it was determined that he should be banished from New Spain forthwith. Sentenced to life imprisonment, he was placed aboard a vessel bound for Spain in March, 1537. While he was thus destined to languish in the dungeons of the Holy Office in distant Spain, fate took a hand and issued a reprieve. His ship went down with all hands aboard.[12]

Ucelo's case led to another against Mixcoatl and Papalatl, two sometime associates who dealt in practical sorcery. Purveyors of spells and incantations, they also posed as rainmakers and claimed to have special arrangements with Tlaloc, the god of rain. The semi-arid north was their best territory, over which they traveled widely, preaching against the friars and Christianity much as any businessmen might inveigh against their close competitors. Both confessed and received the usual burro ride through the city, with public flogging, shearing, and abjuration of sin. In addition they were made to follow their old circuit, abjuring in the towns and villages where they had formally dogmatized, after which they were sentenced to one year in the Franciscan monastery at Tulancingo and loss of all possessions.[13]

As he proceeded against the caciques, the bishop discovered that they were also using the Inquisition against him. In areas beyond the direct authority of the capital the Pipiltin were getting their own men into rural political systems. Whenever the friars put one of their monastery youths in office, so many charges were filed against him with the Audiencia that his reputation and usefulness were ruined. On the other hand, when their own candidates moved in the caciques used public office to lodge serious charges against Indians who were trying to become hispanicized Christians. The real heretics were thus the accusers, and the genuine Christians found themselves being denounced as heretics and dragged off to answer before the Tribunal. When Zumárraga and his confreres realized what was happening, they took countermeasures. Whenever possible, they used coercion to prevent the inheritance of entailed estates by non-Christians and apostates. And as village lordship and higher offices tended to become vested in certain families, they applied the same coercive pressures to succession in office.

Before many cases had come and gone, the friars also began to understand the extraordinary sexual profligacy of the new Pipiltin. The caciques, running quite like barnyard fowl, indiscriminately seized the daughters of the commoners for sexual purposes, claiming them as tribute; they also ravished each others' daughters. Zumárraga became convinced that the only remedy, however drastic, was to take female children away from their parents at an early age, thus to foil the caciques. On an experimental basis he established several homes for girls in the larger cities. Orphans and small girls whose parents agreed were admitted at five years of age and kept until the age of twelve when they could be married off. By autumn of 1538 he had six such houses in operation with over 1,000 girls resident. Catechized and trained in domestic arts, they not infrequently married monastery trained youths; in any light it was a novel experiment in social manipulation. On the basis of his experience Zumárraga petitioned the Council of the Indies to lend financial aid and to make the foundations permanent. This solution, he argued, was the only alternative to simply hanging the greater part of the cacicazgo as incorrigible rapists.[14]

In June, 1537, Zumárraga paused to mark the first anniversary of his offensive against Satan and his works. The balance sheet was generally indicative of failure. His policy of leniency and mild punishment had seemingly done little but invite more delinquency on the part of the caciques. Spurning his "fraternal correction," they seemed to be reverting to their old ways. Everywhere the bishop looked, he saw heinous practices, at one time suppressed, coming back stronger than ever; human sacrifice and cannibalism were almost common again. Alcoholism was epidemic, as were concubinage and idolatry. The caciques had an organized training program under way for the priesthood that a resurgent paganism demanded. He was troubled, too, over the fact that some of the encomenderos found it more profitable to wink at idolatry than participate in its suppression. Not infrequently, his friars were forcibly opposed by caciques who so acted with full knowledge and support of local encomenderos. His missionaries and catechists in the field were growing insistent in their questioning: how long could they dissimulate public sin? How much did it take to bring scorn upon baptism and doctrine? How far could they permit caciques and encomenderos to go, pretending not to see what everyone knew they did in fact see? The bishop had no ready answer. He had tried calling down the curse of Rome during his violent struggle with the first Audiencia, but with small effect. There was, however, another Roman office that would not be so ignored. A tribunal of the Papal Inquisition, entirely independent of Spanish interference, could summarily deal with offenders of whatever category, and definitively. Foreseeing the problems that lay ahead and shrinking from the vision, Zumárraga first dreamed, then dared to suggest such an institution. From the crown's point of view, this idea in itself was a proper heresy. A Papal Inquisitor indeed! The crown had yet to permit even a nuncio to set foot on its overseas empire.

Probably with small hope of success, the bishop instructed his emissaries at the Council of Trent to seek an appointment.[15]

It was not merely the weight of the Indian problem that was draining the bishop's energy. He was deeply concerned with the trials of the Europeans; he was directing the evangel; he had to conduct episcopal business; oversight of the entire welfare program was his responsibility, including administration of hospitals and orphanages, schools, and economic assistance to the poor and infirm. His was, as he confided to an old and intimate friend, Suero de Aguila, an incredible burden. In spite of a robust physical constitution, he suffered perpetual exhaustion.[16] Zumárraga was perhaps the only man in New Spain who at this time could see the developing colonial scene as a panorama. His many responsibilities and innate humanism would permit no less. But it was a frightening scene: an exploding and antisocial mestizaje without identity or legal existence; the conquerors going their own way, pursuing what were to him the most selfish ends; he helplessly witnessed the catastrophic decline of the Indian masses, who grew increasingly reliant upon him as their protector against the ravages of exploitation and disease. Since 1531, measles had joined smallpox in stalking the land with terrible consequences. Around the mines of Oaxaca one could not help but tread on the bleached bones of tamemes and slaves; fat vultures feasted and blotted out the sun at sudden fright. The besieged Indians appealed to Zumárraga, but neither he nor Christianity could save them. The tropical regions of both coasts were grimmer still. In Colima over 80 per cent of the population would have vanished by 1550. We have no figure for the Caribbean coast, but it was probably much the same. Who besides Zumárraga comprehended the terrible dimensions of conquest's aftermath and of the new society he was expected to cradle in his church? He was a man lonely in despair. "Every day I see more clearly that what I have begun to build can never be finished, and that where the wisdom of Paul and the charity of Peter are required, I find in myself nothing but imperfections and faults. I . . . am filled with doubts, [and] facing the great difficulties which are daily offered in this new Church I stand before them naked of all that is necessary for their resolution." [17]

The prosecution of backsliding caciques continued, their cases being sandwiched in among those of errant Europeans. The Holy Office labored under the burden of a crowded calendar. The Indian cases were routine, that is, until arrest of certain caciques of Atzcapotzalco exposed a complete restoration of Tezcatlipoca cult. Zumárraga's investigation was thorough and relentless; before he was finished, his constables had ferreted out heaps of idols and sacrificial gear, most of which bore stains of fresh blood. Among the idols was a small representation of Huichilobos, all covered with jadeite and precious stones, his mouth crusted with traces of his favorite liquid repast.[18] Zumárraga was shaken by the discovery. Could it have deeper meaning? But no! His temple had been razed, broken into fragments with which the canals had been filled. And people still told of the time Cortés slew Huichilobos with an iron bar. Father Motolinía himself had investigated the story and found it true. Cortés had gone to the devil's own sanctuary and there, before Montezuma and the priests, he demolished Huichilobos. Invoking divine aid for what he was about to do, Cortés leaped high in the air and swung his deadly mace. The idol stood a full fifteen feet tall, but that meant nothing, for angels supported Cortés in mid-air as he crashed blow after blow on the idol's head.[19] Or so the current version went; and Cortés himself had since claimed personal credit for the slaying.[20] How, then, could this sudden appearance of a tiny Huichilobos be taken as portent?

What Zumárraga did not know, but was soon to learn, was that Huichilobos had not so perished, that he had survived both Cortés and the siege, and was even now held as the author of a government in exile that plotted the overthrow of the Spaniards. We must at this point go back seventeen years to the day on which Cortés attacked

Huichilobos. Montezuma had at the same time achieved a realistic appreciation of Cortés and his motives. At Cortés' insistence he had Huichilobos and the other idols removed from their twin sanctuaries atop the great pyramid, which act the Spaniards had observed closely. They never saw the idols again.[21] Montezuma was perfectly willing for them to think that the Virgin reigned in triumph, but he was secretly arranging for Huitzilopochtli's eventual restoration. Turning to a loyal confidant in whom he had absolute trust, Montezuma placed the Hummingbird in his care. Tlatolatl, as was his name, followed his instructions perfectly. Huichilobos was installed in a hidden shrine in his palace and kept tightly bundled and roped except during rites. Very few of the ruling stratum were even aware that such an arrangement had been made, and those who did know were silent under pain of death. So remained Huichilobos during the balance of Montezuma's captivity. During the later days of his imprisonment, Montezuma and Cuitlahuac had ample time in which to complete the design, sharing as they did the same chains. In the days approaching Spanish withdrawal and the Night of Sorrow, it was plainly to be seen that Montezuma was finished as emperor. The rulers of the Pipiltin made known their intent to elect Cuitlahuac to the throne, provided he could be freed. It was Montezuma who found a way. By withholding food and water, the rebellious lords were forcing Cortés to forage for supplies. By suggesting to Cortés at the proper time that Cuitlahuac could provide needed provisions, Montezuma effected his brother's release. Meanwhile, the two of them had completed their plans, and Montezuma could now rest more easily in the knowledge that his Huitzilopochtli would rise again and that he had made it so.

But fate intervened. Cuitlahuac died of smallpox within a few weeks. Tlatolatl, apparently instructed for such an eventuality, had Huichilobos carried in secrecy to the palace of Boquicin, a great lord of Atzcapotzalco. Boquicin and one of his peers, Tlalonca, provided a suitable shrine and added four more idols, one of whom was

Tezcatlipoca. The same security and ritual schedules obtained, and the idols remained there undisturbed all through the siege of Mexico. Cortés, had he known, could have reached out from his camp in Tacuba and touched Huichilobos all that time.[22]

As the capital fell to the besiegers, Cuauhtemoc and his intimates were captured in flight over the lake, presumably making for Atzcapotzalco where they would take Huitzilopochtli with them in founding an underground regime. The capture of Cuauhtemoc, of course, put an end to the venture, at least until such time as he could be freed and spirited away from the capital. Meanwhile, Huitzilopochtli's future, like Cuauhtemoc's, was in jeopardy. Cortés heard many rumors and took precautionary measures, hanging suspected nobles and hunting down high priests who had survived the siege. But he failed to learn the truth, even though many of the old lords fell into his hands because they were betrayed by others who were ambitious. Huitzilopochtli's secret was kept only because it was shared by so few. Striking at shadows without guessing at the substance behind them, Cortés was further pulled off the scent by rebellion in his own camp. Partisan struggle over the granting of encomiendas was taking ominous cast, much to the delight of the Pipiltin whose potential forces had the conquerors outnumbered by at least 5,000 to one. The lord of Yacapichtla, who was Tlacaellel's grandson, was showing the way in his vicious defense of Tepoztlán against late-blooming conquerors.

It was at this juncture that Cristóbal de Olid shook off Cortés' authority and sought to set himself up as lord of Hibueras (Honduras). Cortés dispatched a force to put him down, but when he failed to hear from its commander within a reasonable time, it seemed apparent that he must go himself. He apparently weighed the matter carefully: civil war might break out if he left the capital; on the other hand, if he permitted Olid to succeed in his ambitious venture, there would be no end to the anarchy that must surely follow. A dog fight in Mexico, albeit a large one, was the lesser evil. As for the threat of Indian rebellion, he knew that something was afoot but could not make it out. Always the strategist, he decided to take Cuauhtemoc and the most conspicuously dangerous lords with him on the march to Honduras. Appointing Alonso de Estrada, the royal treasurer, and Rodrigo de Albornoz as his lieutenants in command, he left on his incredible overland march to Honduras in late October, 1524. In the course of the march, as Cortés later told it, one of the nobles, Mexicalcinco, fell out with the others and revealed to him a carefully laid plot in which he and the other Spaniards were to be slain. After leading a makeshift force against Olid in Honduras, the plotters would enlist a huge Indian army as they marched on the capital. By simultaneously seizing the coastal bases, no Spaniard would get out of the country alive. The plotters had the provinces divided among themselves in what was to be a New Order. Cortés hanged Cuauhtemoc and two others forthwith, but not one of the hostage lords survived the expedition, all finding death in one way or another.[23]

Zumárraga might never have learned this later history of Huitzilopochtli had it not been for the fact that one day early in June of 1539 two brothers, Mateos and Pedro, both recent converts, came forward to tell what they knew about hidden idols. Almost a year before, Mateos had gone to the Franciscan convent at Toluca for confirmation. Hearing the friar preach what had by now become a routine admonition to report any knowledge of hidden idols and idolatry, he was moved by it and suggested to his brother that they should divulge their secret. After discussing the matter for the greater part of a year, they decided to come forward and make a clean breast of it. Mateos and Pedro were, of course, the sons of Tlatolatl, in whose keeping Montezuma had originally placed Huichilobos. When their father first brought the heavily wrapped object into their home, they didn't know what was going on; but they soon learned everything, being pressed into service as acolytes by their father and the few lords who came to worship and make sacrifices. When Huichilobos was transferred to Atzcapotzalco after the Night of Sorrow, they went along; and there they remained in attendance upon Huitzilopochtli until Cortés marched to Honduras, taking with him Boquicin, Tlalonca, and their father as part of that select number he unerringly judged to be "very powerful men for any revolution afoot." [24] Again, Cortés had been within touching distance of his mortal foe without knowing. When word of the death of Cuauhtemoc and the others stirred the capital, the underground Prince-of-the-House assumed control of the revolutionary movement, being successor to Cuauhtemoc's now empty throne. Quickly, the new king, Anahuacaca, and his adviser, the lord of Tula, sent deputies with a crew to secretly remove the idols to the capital. Again, Pedro and Mateos went along, this time accompanying Huichilobos to the home of Puxtecatl Tlayotla, more commonly known as Don Miguel since his conversion. Lodged as guests of Coyoca, the chief deputy under whose direction the transfer had been made, they awaited further developments. After a few days they were taken before the new Prince-of-the-House, who gave them a security test that they apparently failed. Coyoca abruptly informed them that the idols were to be taken elsewhere and that their services would no longer be required. Thus after nearly five years of playing nursemaid to Huitzilopochtli, the two brothers were discharged summarily. As though to prove the Tlacochcalcatl correct in his denial of security clearance, both subsequently converted and became Christians. This, they told Zumárraga, was all that they knew.[25]

Which was almost too much for the bishop. Huichilobos abroad! Suddenly, the vast problem of apostasy was made comprehensible to Zumárraga; he now saw Huichilobos as the instrument of Satan himself, whose strategy was finally revealed. As long as Huichilobos was free in the land, the evangel would know no peace, nor would the Spaniards hold sovereignty. On June 20, 1539, Zumárraga convened the first formal hearing of what was to be a sensational case. The hearing chamber of the episcopal palace was crowded that Friday morning as the court met to hear presentation of evidence. The bishop, with solemn mien, sat as judge and jury. Flanking him were secretary and notary, before whom at slightly less elevation sat the official interpreters of the court, the prosecutor, and several commissaries of the Holy Office from neighboring towns who were connected with the case. Bailiffs stood by to maintain order and respond to the calling of witnesses. In an opening statement to the court, Zumárraga briefly reviewed the testimony given privately by the two preliminary witnesses, after which Mateos and Pedro were called upon to tell how, contrary to previous belief, Huichilobos and other idols had been spirited out of the capital after the Night of Sorrow and were eventually taken to the home of Don Miguel, who was presently a vecino of Mexico. These idols must be found, declared Zumárraga, for "so long as they exist it may be presumed that the Indians will have them in their hearts rather than our Holy Faith. . . ." The preliminary testimony being more than sufficient to warrant an accusation, Don Miguel was bound over for trial. Ordinarily, the accused would have been free until after the initial hearings were concluded. But this case was of such moment that Zumárraga had had Miguel arrested and incarcerated at once. From this point on the court would become the scene of a struggle between prosecutor and defense counsel, with the bishop acting as final arbiter. The accompanying investigation and search for Huichilobos would also mushroom into the greatest manhunt in Mexican history.

On July 18 Don Miguel was made to appear before the court. In response to questions put to him, he established that he was a resident of Mexico, his home being located in the barrio of San Juan. He was a baptized Christian of almost twenty years standing. The prosecutor now rose and began. Did he now know, or did he ever know, an Indian named Tlatolatl? He answered that he did not. Did the accused know that Tlatolatl had been ordered to carry certain idols, all carefully concealed under heavy wraps, from the capital at the time the Spaniards were forced to withdraw, and that the said idols were taken to Atzcapotzalco and lodged in the palace of one Boquicin? He answered that he did not. Did Miguel not know that the Tlacoch-calcatl of Mexico had himself ordered the idols taken from Atzcapotzalco and placed in the home of the accused, and that the five idols were in fact delivered to him by one Coyoca and one Calnahu-acatl? Miguel now admitted that one night the two aforementioned persons did bring tamemes bearing five heavily wrapped objects to his home, although it was not until the Tlacochcalcatl himself came to pay reverence that he realized what was inside. To which he hastily added that they were in his house only ten days before being taken away, he knew not where. Was the accused absolutely certain that he did not know where they were taken, or where they were now? He answered that he did not know. Why did the accused deny these things when first asked? Miguel replied that he had forgotten, but that it all now "comes to mind." [26] The accused was excused from court and returned to his cell while formal charges were drawn against him.

Just as he was initiating these proceedings against Miguel, Zumár-raga got wind of an exceptionally significant denunciation. It seems that Don Carlos Chichimecatecuhtli, the cacique of Texcoco, had been denounced by a nephew for inveighing against Christianity. Don Carlos was one of the younger of the 145 children sired by Nezahualpilli, and had but recently risen to lordship of the old state of Texcoco. He was, therefore, an extremely important and influential noble.[27] Don Carlos had also enjoyed the best that Spanish dominion could offer: he had been raised in Cortés' own household and edu-cated by Franciscan tutors. At the same time, the Franciscan College of Santa Cruz in Tlatelolco was a significant part of a brilliant experi-ment in applied Humanism that Zumárraga and his confreres were conducting. After mastering Latin and the trivium, students went on to philosophy and scholastic theology and critical study of their own arts and languages. As one of its cofounders, the bishop was vitally concerned with the college's aim, which was to produce a Latinized Indian aristocracy from whose ranks new leaders would emerge in full possession of the best in the Spanish and Nahuatl traditions. The most radical Franciscans at this time envisioned an Indian priesthood. Zumárraga was not yet prepared to go that far, but he was staunch in defense of the college and its purpose against the criticism and opposition of more conservative Spaniards, especially those whose own children were being denied higher education of any kind. Since when were the children of the vanquished to be given preference over the sons of the victors? But Zumárraga and his partisans would not be deterred from their purpose, even though by 1539 opposition to the college was forming among more conservative groups within the Franciscan Order itself. The denunciation of Don Carlos was consequently of extreme importance, both to the college and its critics. Although there was no direct relationship, the case against Don Carlos was to be tried simultaneously with that against Miguel, usually one being heard in the morning hours, the other in the afternoon. In dealing with Don Carlos, Zumárraga was to be powerfully swayed by what unfolded in the case against Miguel, for in his mind the two cases came to represent separate aspects of a single problem. One cannot understand Zumárraga's disposition of either case without reference to the other.

In view of the stakes involved, Zumárraga convened his court in the central hall of the Franciscan convent at Tlatelolco on June 22. Bernardino de Sahagún, Alonso de Molina, and Antonio Ciudad Rodrigo, all of whom had interest in the experiment and were currently teaching at the college, were appointed as official interpreters. Before the court duly assembled, Francisco Maldonaldo stepped forth and denounced his uncle. Followed by a host of witnesses called in order, the accumulated testimony read as follows. About three weeks ago, Don Carlos had gone to visit his sister and her family in

Chiconautla. Upon arrival he met with a religious procession led by the local friar and which included some of the towns leading citizens, all in penitential garb and flagellating themselves in supplication for rain, New Style. Don Carlos broke in and ridiculed them, asking pointedly what good they hoped to accomplish, such nonsense being all right for plebeians but hardly suitable for the cacicazgo. Later that night, and apparently every night during his stay, Don Carlos bought drinks for the house as he held forth in the local tavern. Among other things, he urged the caciques to desert Christianity because it posed ultimate threat to their position; paganism, he argued, was just as good as Christianity, there being little difference between them, and it much better supported the claims of the nobility. The College of Santa Cruz and its teachings were described as worthless. The friars, he charged, cynically urged the caciques to shun women and liquor, even as they failed to stem the Spaniards' thirst for wine and lust for girls. The friars themselves were not above lechery, he concluded. What the caciques must do if they would save themselves was flee from the influence of the friars and go back to the ways of their fathers: what good was it to be a noble if one had to suffer even the lightest restraint? "Who are they that undo us," he demanded, "forbid us, live on us, suppress us? Hear me! Here am I, and there is the lord of Mexico, Yoanizi, and over there is my nephew Tezapili, the lord of Tacuba, and yet there is Tlacahuepantli, the lord of Tula. We are all one in our positions and agreed that this is our land, our possession, our jewel wherein no one shall equal us. Sovereignty is ours and belongs to us alone." [28] The court was rocked: this was pure treason and sedition. Don Carlos' arrest was ordered forthwith.

So gross were the implications of this case that Zumárraga adjourned the court and journeyed with his staff to Chiconautla and Texcoco to conduct further investigations and hear witnesses on the scene. A relentless procession of witnesses established or suggested more of the same: Don Carlos often ridiculed those who ate fish on

261

Friday, or who fasted or took part in processions or indulged in self-denial. All those things he claimed to be mere deceptions that the friars devised for the macehualtin. He was also accused of keeping idols and altars in his home, and of indulging in sexual irregularities; at the moment he was living with a niece who had borne him two children. His son was marched before the bishop, and it became apparent that Don Carlos had isolated him from Christianity. He was ten years old but ignorant of the most rudimentary doctrine. Called as a witness, Don Carlos' wife, Doña María, appeared and tearfully told how their marriage had broken up when, two years ago, Don Carlos suddenly changed and began to court evil. Wandering by night, she said that he created public disturbance and had many affairs with other women and made repeated attempts to seduce his brother's widow, who was thereupon called in to confirm the charge. As was customary, all of Don Carlos' properties and assets were seized and frozen by the Holy Office at the time of his arrest. In preparing inventories, it was discovered that he owned a palace that had not been declared with the others. Upon careful search the mansion was found to contain a gallery of idols and much ritualistic paraphernalia. Some of the idols were hidden in thick walls, all of which were apparently pulled down in subsequent search.

Taking the scent, Zumárraga now began to call a wider range of witnesses. Don Lorenzana de Luna, Don Carlos' half-brother and presently governor of the city of Texcoco, testified that during the early evangel many idols had been hidden, and that for several months he had been aware that persons unknown were invoking the devil and restoring the hidden idols along with their secret rites. His own investigations had disclosed sacrificial objects buried at the foot of crosses and Christian monuments, and he discovered while pushing the search intense pagan activity in the sierras around Texcoco. But so many important people were involved that he dared take no action. From his testimony and that of many others it appeared that worship of Tlaloc in the sierras of Chiautla and Guatinchan, and particularly Tlalocatepetl ("Sierra of Tlaloc"), which was the site of rain cult origin according to myth, was of pre-conquest intensity. Tlalocatepetl was in fact the center of Tlaloc's cult for the entire central plateau, and it was now apparent to the bishop that people still made pilgrimages there in time of drouth. Zumárraga was here stumbling on a primordial assocation. Lofty peaks all snowy and shrouded in clouds were considered divine by virtue of their close relationship with water, that element so essential to agriculture and life itself. Just as in Egypt where the mighty Nile was touched by divinity, Mexico's mountains were ageless sources of water and high pulpits from which one could supplicate the godhead itself. Every sierra held a thousand shrines. Now calling most of the principales and sages of Texcoco as witnesses, Zumárraga learned that during the reign of Axayacatl soldiers from Huexotzinco, vindictive over the Flower Wars, attacked and fractured the great stone image of Tlaloc that stood in Tlalocatepetl. Axayacatl had it restored, for it was the old and venerated original, but in recent years it had disappeared and was presumed lost. Delving into what was now a mass of testimony, Zumárraga plotted a map that, when followed, led investigators to a precise spot in the sierra where they ordered accompanying workmen to begin excavation. They dug up Tlaloc, his fractures still bound with golden wire and his body encrusted with gold and jewels. The bishop had come to catch a rebel and had found the god of rain instead.[29] Sovereignty was that close to religion. On July 12, after eight hectic days of hearings and widespread digging, many other idols being unearthed and smashed, Zumárraga returned to the capital with Tlaloc in tow and resumption of the cases against Miguel and Don Carlos.

On July 15 Don Carlos was made to appear before the court. Identifying himself as a descendant of the royal house, he stated that he had been a good Christian for fifteen years and had often served as a catechist. When questioned about the idols in his palace, he answered that all of his properties had been inherited from his father, and that an uncle had put idols in the walls of one of them, but he did not know which one. He denied any guilt of idolatry and emphatically denied the whole of testimony given against him. But he did admit to an incestuous relationship with his niece. The court noted his plea and adjourned until the first of August, when both his and Miguel's cases were formally given to the prosecution. On that day Cristóbal de Cañego took his oath as prosecutor, pledging to prosecute the defendants to the best of his ability within the bounds of office. At the same time Vicencio de Riverol was sworn as defense counsel, promising to loyally defend his clients to the best of his ability and giving assurance that he would obtain the services of other legal specialists if proper defense so required. On August 5 both Don Carlos and Miguel were formally accused, the former of idolatry, heresy, maintaining oratories, impeding the teaching of Christian doctrine, urging apostasy, and commission of incest. Lese majesty, his most palpable offense, was not mentioned. Charged as a "diabolical hider of the most principal and ancient idol," Miguel was further accused of obstructing and impeding investigation of idolatry.

Seventeen days later, Riverol was prepared to answer both accusations. The brief that he posted in Miguel's defense was specific. The accusation, he contended, was notably lacking in specific facts and dates that were essential to substantiate such a charge. It also appeared that Miguel was being held responsible for acts he might have committed prior to becoming a Christian, since he could not have been baptized prior to 1521. Therefore, when the idols were brought to his home he was still a pagan and could not now be held or charged on that account. Since baptism, he concluded, Miguel had lived a model Christian life. Riverol's opening defense of Don Carlos was much less strong. Largely following the testimony of the accused, he attacked the nebulous quality of the accusation and made counterclaims as to Don Carlos' virtues and manner of living. He was, according to

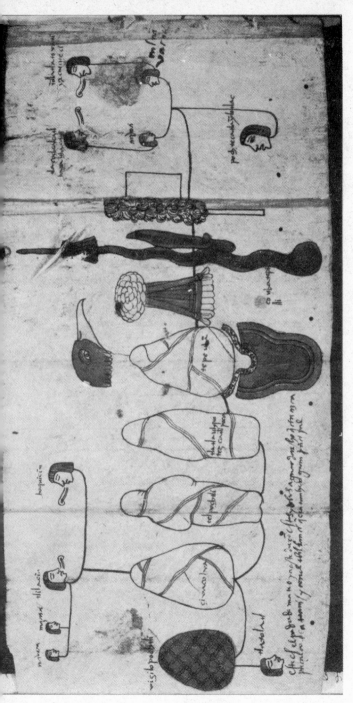

EVIDENCE ON MAGUEY FIBER PARCHMENT INTRODUCED AGAINST MIGUEL
INDICATING RELATIONSHIPS BETWEEN THE IDOLS
AND PERSONS INVOLVED

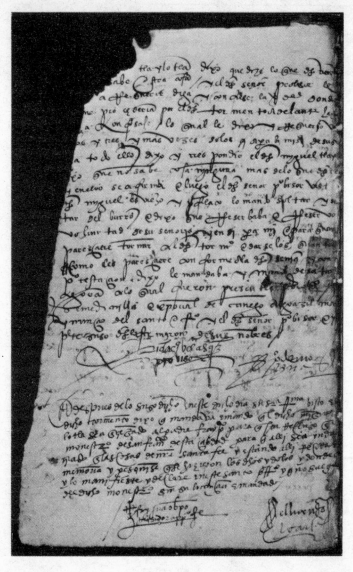

MIGUEL'S SENTENCE OF IMPRISONMENT
AS SIGNED BY ZUMÁRRAGA

Riverol, a victim of false witnesses who were taking revenge upon him for his past punishment of them for loose living and by others who were envious of his position. The struggle was now joined, with alternating parries and thrusts by either side; neither case moved very far until late autumn.

While prosecution and defense argued and heard witnesses called up by either side, investigations continued, oftentimes spurred on by revelations heard from the witness box. One of the prosecution's witnesses against Miguel, for example, hinted that an ancient idol could be found in Ocuituco. Zumárraga bolted upright at this, for *he* was the encomendero of Ocuituco. A team of investigators descended upon the town and quickly established that the cacique, aided by his wife and brother, were hiding images of Tezcatlipoca and Tlaloc and using them to extort heavy tributes from the macehualtin.[30] The bishop failed to find Huichilobos, but he could now understand how easy it was for the Indians to idolatrize under an encomendero's very nose, even if it happened to be the Inquisitor himself.

The court's calendar was glutted until October 14, at which time Miguel's case was resumed. The prosecution produced a witness who named one Culoa Tlapisque and five others as "old prophets" who knew the whereabouts of the idols in question, all of which, according to the witness, was public and notorious. A second witness confirmed the testimony and identified the prophets as known residents of the capital. A third witness, one of Zumárraga's constables named Martín, corroborated the foregoing and added that he had heard Culoa Tlapisque boast that he knew precisely where the idols were, and that in the old days the prophets' power was such that Montezuma could not run the empire without them. Delays in locating Culoa Tlapisque, apparently the only prophet who could be traced, and intervention of other cases caused continuance until October 24, when Culoa finally appeared as a witness. Identifying himself as a pagan priest of about fifty-seven years of age, he volunteered the following testimony: Tomolo, a fellow priest who was now dead, told him several years ago that Huichilobos and the idols in question had been in the possession of one Don Diego, a great lord of Mexico and four sons of the nobles who had assumed control of religion after the fall of Tenochtitlán. The sons, Palacatl, Cuzcasuchatl, Yzcuen, and Cocacal, spirited the idols out of the capital, apparently in 1525 after Cortés' march to Honduras; and to the best of his knowledge, they still had possession and were hiding them somewhere near Tula. In 1527, or maybe 1529, the witness elaborated, he and Don Diego happened to be in the town of Ecatepeque. In the presence of Achicatl, one of the local lords, and a group of principales who were discussing the Franciscan evangel and pleas of the friars to surrender hidden idols, Don Diego offered the suggestion that Huichilobos should be turned in. Achicatl took issue and a debate ensued, with the others following Achicatl's argument, agreeing that Huichilobos should not be surrendered. Later, in what was apparently private conversation, Achicatl confided to the witness that he had not laid eyes upon Huitzilopochtli for seven years, but that he was in a temple in Temazcaltitlán and very well cared for. Huitzilopochtli's robes and jewels, Achicatl said, were in the possession of Tomecao and Coatlayantl, two principales of Mexico, to whom the witness subsequently paid a visit and was shown the relics. This, Culoa Tlapisque concluded, was the extent of his knowledge.[31]

Achicatl, who loomed so large in Culoa's testimony, was now Don Pedro, one of the capital's leading caciques. He had been baptized only last year. Appearing as a witness, he denied that he knew or ever did know the whereabouts of Huichilobos, or that he had ever taken part in the conversation described by Culoa. His testimony was confined to painfully brief denial of everything that the previous witness had said. While the foregoing testimony did not directly implicate the defendant Miguel, it did document the deepening crisis over the search for Huichilobos, whose role in the drama was becoming obsessive in Zumárraga's thoughts. The prosecution remained convinced that Miguel knew more than he was telling. On September 22 Riverol had requested the services of a legal specialist, probably because of the testimony being developed by the prosecution. Now he acted with his expert counsel in requesting that the defendant be permitted to face and speak with witnesses who had been summoned in his behalf. Zumárraga agreed, stipulating that a delegate of the Holy Office be present at all such interviews. The defense was agreeable, and Bernardino de Sahagún was delegated. Zumárraga's stipulation was, of course, taken as precaution against secret exchanges in a language the Spaniards could not understand. Sahagún was one of the best linguists of his day. On November 7, after some three weeks of meetings between Miguel and his witnesses, Riverol requested recess of the trial in order to translate and transcribe testimony of rebuttal witnesses and complete preparation of the defense. The trial records indicate that his petition was granted.

With continuance of the prosecution of Miguel, the court now turned back to the case against Don Carlos. The prosecutor continued to call new witnesses and recalled some who had already testified. Riverol had difficulty in constructing a defense, since he apparently found it impossible to produce substantial witnesses who could attest to Don Carlos' claims of exemplary Christian living. Even as he accused the prosecution's witnesses of lying in hopes of gain, still others were produced who could not possibly profit from Don Carlos' conviction. By November 11 both sides had rested their cases, and it was now in Zumárraga's hands. Anyone who expected a quick verdict was to be disappointed. For a week Zumárraga pondered the evidence and implications of the case. Clearly, the charges of idolatry, maintaining sanctuaries, and sacrificing to false gods were substantially unproved and must be dropped. It was evident that he was unaware of the idols hidden in the palace to which he was linked by no more than a deed, nor was he a practicing idolater. As for his sexual vagaries, they were perhaps normal for a man of his position in the cacicazgo.

267

But it was equally clear that he did manifestly urge apostasy and therein fomented sedition. By his studied preaching of a gospel contrary to both church and state, Don Carlos was a heretical dogmatizer, and must be so convicted according to the evidence. Which meant that he should be relaxed to the secular arm and burned at the stake. But a recent decree from Spain, not yet two years old, specifically forbade relaxation of Indians to the secular arm. If the bishop let Don Carlos off with his life, would the secular arm and the society of the conquistadores countenance it? What of its effect on the vast revolutionary conspiracy that already threatened in the name of Huichilobos? Would this not be a stunning victory for Satan and his minions who so effectively opposed the evangel? Would not those who shielded Huichilobos even now be made stronger in their determination to do so? Perhaps the bishop's most poignant reflection concerned the College of Santa Cruz. Was Don Carlos truly a product of its aim and ideal? Zumárraga was now learning what experience had taught other humanists of his age: a truly free mind overleaps the highest wall that any orthodoxy can erect. After seven days of anguished reflection, Zumárraga turned to the viceroy and Audiencia for help, knowing full well that he must assume entire responsibility for resolution of the case, however it might be achieved. On November 20 the bishop sat down with the viceroy, Antonio de Mendoza, judges Ceynos, Loaysa, and Tejada, the Vicar-Provincial and Prior of the Dominican Order, and the Guardian of El Grande, the capital's Franciscan convent. In a series of meetings they studied transcripts of the entire trial, went over legal briefs prepared by experts, and discussed all aspects of the case, after which they rendered an opinion that Zumárraga accepted as a verdict.

On November 28 the court was convened for sentencing. Don Carlos, flanked by the prosecutor on one side, his defender on the other, awaited his fate. Zumárraga read his decision in slow and precise meter:

We find ourselves bound to declare, and do declare Don Carlos to be an heretical dogmatizer, and pronounce him as such; we find ourselves bound to remit, and thus do remit him to the secular arm of the Justice Ordinary of this city, whom we pray and charge to deal with him benignly.

On Saturday, the following day, criers ranged the city announcing the forthcoming auto-da-fe and sermon, which all were to see and hear under pain of excommunication.

On Sunday morning Don Carlos, clad in Sanbenito and wearing a *coroza*, the crown of infamy, on his head, and bearing a large cross before him, was taken from his cell and led to an elevated stage that had been erected in the Zócalo for the fete. The viceroy, oidores, religious and lay officials, conquerors, and caciques were all present, surrounded by a vast sea of Indians. Zumárraga preached an appropriate sermon, and was followed by the secretary of the Holy Office who read an official account of Don Carlos' crimes and judgment, all of which was then repeated in Nahuatl. At this moment Don Carlos, apparently for the first time, realized his peril. Turning to the bishop, he asked for permission to recant, which given he briefly spoke, urging others to heed his errors and accept Christianity as the superior way of life. But for him it was too late. He was turned over to the secular arm whose hand garroted him and struck a spark to the faggots on which his body was placed.[32]

During the waning weeks of Don Carlos' trial, leads continued to appear in the search for Huichilobos. Don Baltásar, the cacique of Culhuacán, was charged with hiding idols, and important evidence was unearthed in the course of investigation that deeply implicated Culoa Tlapisque and Miguel in the hiding of Huichilobos. Zumárraga sent investigators to open sealed caves around Culhuacán, but they found that others had been there before them, leaving nothing but tantalizing evidence in abundance that Huichilobos had in fact

269

been there, and possibly recently. One of the witnesses, Don Andrés, a principal of Culhuacán, admitted that he and Culoa were old friends, and that it was he who had persuaded Culoa to testify in the first place. If Culoa was holding anything back, according to Don Andrés, it was because he feared that Zumárraga would have him slain, so great was the secret he kept. Although the trail seemed warm at first, the bishop watched it cool as mounting testimony introduced unfathomable contradictions. He had to be satisfied with the consensus that Huichilobos was somewhere around Tula in a hidden cave.[33]

Subsequent cases proved to be worthless upon preliminary investigation, even as others gave more promise.[34] As Zumárraga carried his search for Huichilobos into January of 1540, he surveyed his evidence and found himself more strongly convinced that Culoa, Achicatl, and Miguel held the key to the mystery of Huichilobos' hiding place. It seemed probable that all three knew the secret, but how to get it from them? Culoa was not a Christian and therefore could not be taken into custody. Achicatl had been a Christian but one year; and since not one shred of evidence had been found to indicate wrongdoing in that time, he too was exempt from the Inquisition's jurisdiction, even though it was obvious that he was lying when he denied Culoa's testimony. Not even that could be proved against him.

On January 30, 1540, Zumárraga ordered that Miguel be put to judicial torture. Riverol offered immediate and strenuous objection, holding that evidence was much too tenuous to warrant such procedure, nor were there enough witnesses or sufficient circumstantial evidence to support it. Such procedure, he declared, was both illegal and unjust. The bishop was desperate and refused to alter his sentence, and the defense refused to accept his refusal. Appeals and rejections occupied clerks of the court until the middle of March when Riverol gave way, doubtless because in the end there was no other recourse. Zumárraga had permitted the delaying actions with the probable hope that new evidence might come to light that would make torture unnecessary. Besides which, he knew very well that he was treading on shaky legal ground, to say the least. Riverol was quite correct in his objections. But no new evidence had been found, nor did any seem likely. The court had exhausted the last lead. And Zumárraga meant to have Huichilobos at any cost. Immediately following Riverol's accession to the sentence of torture, Miguel fell ill and defense counsel thereupon requested that sentence be suspended indefinitely. If sentence should be executed now, warned Riverol, it would endanger Miguel's life, and the quality of testimony given under such circumstances would of necessity be suspect. Trial records now fall silent, indicating that Zumárraga had his physicians examine the defendant. The sentence was suspended.

By the middle of May Miguel had recovered sufficiently to undergo his torment. Taken from the cell that had become his home, he was led to a small, dark chamber that was dimly lit, there being no windows. Present were the prosecutor, chief constable, and the secretary of the Holy Office with his interpreter. The bishop's provisor was in charge. Miguel's eyes fell on a horizontal rack, a frame slightly larger than the body of a man. It was the *burro*. Marched before the provisor, he was first admonished to tell the whole truth and was then questioned. Miguel had nothing to say. Turning, the provisor ordered the constable to strip his body of clothing and tie him to the burro. Once fixed to the rack, knotted cords were wound around his limbs and head. Now bending over him, the provisor demanded that he confess the truth; in solemn formula he intoned the demand three times. Miguel repeated that he had nothing whatever to say. The provisor made a sign with his hand, and the knotted cords were twisted until they bit into flesh. At the same moment, a funnel was forced into his mouth and a jar of icy water was poured down his throat. When the funnel had emptied, the provisor again bent over the victim and thrice demanded that he confess the truth. Miguel refused. Another signal by hand. The cords twisted and bit deeper. As the pressure increased, another jar of water was introduced. When the provisor again bent over to make his demands a third time, he started in fright. Miguel was losing consciousness. Quickly, he ordered him cut loose and removed from the rack. The questioning would not be resumed unless the Inquisitor himself directed it.[35]

On the floor above, Zumárraga anxiously awaited word from the interrogation room. When it came, he was struck as if by a blow. It was finished. Technically, a confession so obtained was had in order that the accused might be reconciled with the church. Miguel's torment had been a last and desperate attempt to find Huichilobos, and there was a formidable distinction here. He dared not proceed; he had already gone too far. Retreating to his chancellery, Zumárraga dictated a sentence that closed the case against Miguel. The accused was to be incarcerated in El Grande where he would be indoctrinated in the Holy Faith; there he was to search his memory, and he was to be watched night and day so that when he did talk someone would be there to listen. He was never to leave El Grande without written order signed by the bishop. Zumárraga felt as only a man who had been bested by a stone idol could feel.

Miguel disappears from the sources, and it is not unreasonable to suppose that he died in El Grande, carrying whatever secrets he had to the grave. Just as Zumárraga was finishing with his case, the crown and the Council of the Indies heard of the relaxation of Don Carlos. There was an uproar of protest and indignation, all of which fell heavily on the bishop's already sagging shoulders.[36] He was now seventy-three years old and utterly spent under the burdens of office. The search for Huichilobos had ended with Miguel's sentence, yet the dual problem of idolatry and rebellion continued as reports from the field made plain. But never did Zumárraga feel more powerless. Don Juan, the cacique of Iguala, was denounced for apostasy and sedition, and for performance of extraordinary sexual feats: "*Item.* With scorn for the Holy Church he raped two girls in the chapel, and during Lent, too!" He also raped his wife's sisters, his aunt, and a nine-year-old girl, all apparently within hours. Zumárraga feebly warned him that if he did not behave, he would be punished.[37] The bishop was also having trouble with the riffraff who swarmed in from the Caribbean in search of easy wealth. As his hunt for Huichilobos hit stride in 1539 and 1540, the newcomers caught fire and set out upon their own search for solid gold idols they *knew* to exist. Indian cemeteries were dug up and graves were robbed; many communities and towns were literally sacked by Old Christians in search of precious idols.[38] Taking everything into account, it seemed to Zumárraga as though his entire labor had been in vain. Even the ideal behind the College of Santa Cruz had failed, or so it appeared, and he withdrew his endowments, transferring them to the Indian Hospital instead.[39] He was a grievously wounded man. Just as he had to suffer the consequences of the Don Carlos affair alone, so had he to suffer his comprehension of the colonial scene in silence and quite by himself. Certainly, neither the crown nor the Council of the Indies understood its influence upon his decisions. Currently working out the New Laws, they were not at all conscious of his level and turn of thought; his relaxation of Don Carlos could be nothing but reprehensible to them.

And so, if he had been a lesser man, Zumárraga might have gotten some satisfaction out of an ominous religious rebellion that broke out on the northwestern frontier in 1541. Known to history as the Mixton War, it threatened to engulf the central plateau and push the Spaniards into the sea. The greater part of Nueva Galicia, especially the Lerma River basin, went up in flames as determined Indians battled the Spaniards in final challenge to their seizure of sovereignty. As Spanish power emanated from the capital, those who would resist it moved beyond its reach, which is why nearly all of Zumárraga's significant Indian cases were centered in the north, as were most traces of Huichilobos. After he increased inquisitorial pressure, political and religious refugees fled northward in growing numbers, there to make a last and desperate stand. Organization was centered in the Valley of Tlaltenango, then spread to Suchipila, the Sierra of Tepic, Nochistlán, and points south. Rebellion was fomented by hispanicized Indians for the most part, those like Don Carlos who had seen the conquerors' society from inside out. Promises to all who would follow the rebellion were both lavish and instructive: eternal youth would come to all participants; all would be rich, their gardens self-tending, firewood ready-cut and stacked; there would be no further dependence upon rain. Women and wine would abound. Strategically, the leaders of the revolt planned to wipe out Jalisco and Guadalajara, then sweep over everything from Michoacán to Guatemala. As long as Vazquez de Coronado was governor, he held Nueva Galicia in check, although as Zumárraga's investigations indicated, powerful forces were building under his nose. When he left for his ill-starred conquest of the Seven Cities of Cibola in 1540, Coronado weakened the frontier by drawing off men and matériel in degree sufficient to invite rebellion. When it began in the spring of 1541, churches and monasteries became the prime targets of the rebels. Images and crosses were desecrated as robed warriors used implements of the Mass in calculated and ludicrous mockery. Spanish forces were consistently defeated until the viceroy himself led a hastily conscripted army supported by thousands of Indian allies against the rebels. It took a savagely fought war to put final end to the most dangerous revolt of the colonial period.[40]

Historians would say that the rebellion was planned and executed by disaffected mortals, like the great cacique Xuiteque, or Petacal, who was the brother of the lord of Nochistlán and a constable of the crown and baptized with the name of Don Diego Zacatecas. But Zumárraga knew better. In his mind was the idea of Huichilobos, the eternal Huichilobos who sat waiting for restoration in his secret northern cave, where he continues to wait to this very day.

NOTES

NOTES

Abbreviations Used in the Notes

AC	*Anales de Chimalpahin*
AGN	*Archivo General de la Nación,* Mexico
AT	*Anales de Tlatelolco*
BD	*Historia verdadera de la conquista de la Nueva España por Bernal Díaz del Castillo*
CD	*Colección de documentos para la historia de México,* ed. J. García Icazbalceta
CM	*Crónica mexicana, por* Hernando Alvarado Tezozomoc
CR	*Códice Ramírez*
DI	*Documentos inéditos del siglo XVI para la historia de México,* ed. Mariano Cuevas
DII	*Colección de documentos inéditos relativos al descubrimiento, conquista y organización de las antiguas posesiones españolas*
DIM	*Documentos inéditos o muy raros para la historia de México,* ed. Genaro García
DSH	*Colección de documentos para la historia de la formación social de hispanoamérica, 1493–1810,* ed. R. Konetzke

ENE   *Epistolario de Nueva España,* ed. Francisco del Paso y Troncoso

FC   *Florentine Codex,* trans. A. J. O. Anderson and C. E. Dibble

GA   *Gesammelte Abhandlungen Zur Amerikanischen Sprach-Und Alterthumskunde*

NCD   *Nueva colección de documentos para la historia de México,* ed. J. García Icazbalceta

ZUM   *Don Fray Juan de Zumárraga,* ed. J. García Icazbalceta

Chapter I

1. Mesoamerica may be considered to be that area between about 22° of latitude, or a semicircular line drawn through the Pánuco and Lerma river basins, and central Honduras, wherein the calendar and agricultural techniques provide common cultural foci.

2. For the best discussion and summary of Mesoamerican pre-history see Eric R. Wolf, *Sons of the Shaking Earth,* chaps. i–vii.

3. FC, Bk. X, chap. xxix (all quotations from the *Florentine Codex* are given as translated by Anderson and Dibble).

4. Diego Durán, *Historia de las indias de Nueva España, cap.* lxxx (all citations refer to the 1867 edition unless noted otherwise). Also see Alfredo Chavero's "Explicaciones del códice geroglífico de Mr. Aubin," *cap.* vii, appended to Durán, Vol. II (1951 ed.); Alonso de la Rea, *Crónica de . . . Michoacán, cap.* vi; *Relación de las ceremonias y ritos . . . de Mechoacán;* "Relación de Pátzcuaro," *Papeles de la Nueva España,* II, 110; *Codex Magliabecchi,* 30ʳ, 31ʳ (unless otherwise indicated, reference is made to the Nuttall facsimile). Eduard Seler, "The Animal Pictures of the Mexican and the Mayan Manuscripts," *GA,* IV, Pt. i, 38–42, finds the hummingbird as motif in fixed relationship with human sacrifice in both Mexican and Mayan areas, which probably portrays the hummingbird before it was intentionally involved with Huitzilopochtli cult.

5. *Historia, Lib.* I, *cap.* i. It is necessary to use the *Historia* in addition to Anderson and Dibble's translation of it as the *Florentine Codex* because the latter work excludes most of the prologues, appendixes, and interstitial commentaries of Sahagún.

6. FC, Bk. X, chap. xxix.

7. CR, 22 (all citations of the *Códice Romírez* refer to the 1878 ed.).

8. See, for example, Ignacio Bernal, "Huitzilopochtli vivo," *Cuadernos Americanos*, XCVI (Nov.–Dec., 1957), 127–52.

9. In 1039, according to the *Anales de Chimalpahin*, in Paul Radin, *The Sources and Authenticity of the History of the Ancient Mexicans*, p. 128 (translations by Radin). The Mexica counted the New Fire ceremony of 1455 as their eighth since leaving Aztlán. Since the ceremony was held at fifty-two year intervals, calculation is a simple matter, even though proving it is not.

10. *NCD*, III, 77. Cf. Radin, Pt. I. The same complaint was later echoed by Juan Bautista Pomar in his *Relación de Texcoco*, pp. 2–3. The loss of codices was compounded by the loss of persons who could interpret them.

11. Throughout this work I have used Nahuatl singular and plural forms of nouns, although on occasion I employ the Spanish habit of converting a Nahuatl singular into a plural by adding the Spanish "s" or "es." On the other hand, such nouns, when used adjectivally, are frequently anglicized by adding "n" or "ns." I have done so in response to custom and convention.

Chapter II

1. For general discussion of calpulli organization, see Jacques Soustelle, *Daily Life of the Aztecs*, chap. ii, which in part supersedes G. C. Vaillant, *The Aztecs of Mexico*, chap. vi.

2. Gerónimo de Mendieta, *Historia eclesiástica indiana*, Lib. II, cap. xxxiv. Cf. Durán, *cap*. vi.

3. *CR*, 34–36; Durán, *ibid*.

4. Durán, *cap*. ix; *CR*, 51–52.

5. Respectively *Tlacochcalcatl, Tlacatecatl, Ezhuahuacatl, Tlillancalqui*. Durán, *cap*. xi; *CR*, 56–58.

6. *CR*, 59. Also see *CM, cap*. xx.

7. Durán, *cap*. xiv; *AC*, 126.

8. Fernando de Alva Ixtlilxochitl, *Historia Chichimeca*, caps. xxxv–xxxvi. Also see Diego Muñoz Camargo, *Historia de Tlaxcala*, *cap*. xii, for similar development beyond the immediate realm of Mexican influence. In all cases the size of land grants was regulated by availability.

9. The land system is neatly summarized in Alfonso Caso, "La tenencia de la

tierra entre los antiguos Mexicanos," *Memoria del Colegio Nacional*, Mexico (December, 1959), pp. 29–54. On Cholula, see *AC*, 130.

10. Mendieta, *Lib.* II, *caps.* xxxvi, xxxviii–xxxix; *FC*, Bk. VIII, chap. xxi; Zorita, *Relación*, pp. 91–98; the best secondary account is Soustelle, *Daily Life*, chap. ii.

11. Mendieta, *ibid., cap.* xxxvii. For specific example of the use of females in diplomacy, see the *Codex Telleriano-Remensis*, Pt. IV, 48–49 (in Radin, *Sources and Authority*).

12. According to Chimalpahin, Montezuma and Tlacaellel were born in 1398, both being sired by Itzcoatl's brother but apparently having different mothers. They were thus thirty years of age when their group achieved political power. On Nezahualcoyotl, see Ixtlilxochitl, *Historia, caps.* xxiii–xlix.

13. Durán, *caps.* x–xii, xiv; *CR*, 57–61, 100; *FC*, Bk. IX, chap. xiv.

14. *FC*, Bk. I, chap. xix; Bk. IX, chap. v; Mendieta, *Lib.* II, *cap.* xxvi. Enemy spies captured by the Mexica were kept in a special prison, the *Macuilcalli*, close to Huitzilopochtli's temple, and there tortured with slow dismemberment. Also see Sahagún, *Historia, Lib.* I, *Appendice* ii. On the merchants, see Miguel Acosta Saignes, *Los pochteca*.

15. Mendieta, *Lib.* II, *cap.* xxvi; on temple-burning, see *Códice de Yanhuitlán*, p. 10; *FC*, Bk. VIII, chap. xvii; *Anales de Cuauhtitlán*, pp. 43–44, 76. Both Durán and *Códice Ramírez* give numerous examples. Angel María Garibay Kintana, *Historia de la literatura nahuatl*, goes further, relating that the Mexica intentionally destroyed all documented history of the past, ostensibly so that history could begin anew under their domination (I, 22–23). One is put in mind of Orwell's society of 1984.

16. *Anales de Cuauhtitlán*, pp. 26, 8–13. For varying interpretations, see Paul Kirchhoff, "Quetzalcoatl, Huemac, y el fin de Tula," *Cuadernos Americanos*, LXXXIV (Nov.–Dec., 1955), No. 6, 164–96, and Wigberto Jiménez Moreno, *Historia antigua de Mexico*. Also see Fernando Díaz Infante, *Quetzalcóatl*, and Seler, "Some Remarks Upon the Natural Bases of Mexican Myths," *GA*, III, Pt. ii, 1–29.

17. Mendieta, *Lib.* II, *cap.* xxxii; *Codex Telleriano-Remensis*, Pt. IV, 47–48. Also suggestive is Ixtlilxochitl, *Relaciones*, "Troncos de las naciones americanas." It is certain that war captives were used for sacrifice by the Tarascans of Michoacán, but it is not possible to say whether the custom was adopted before or after the Mexica began to use it. Orozco y Berra, *Historia*, I, 154 ff., begrudgingly acknowledges that the Mexica were the innovators of political sacrifice, but fails to link it to Huitzilopochtli cult.

18. Ixtlilxochitl, *Relaciones*, "Relación XI."

19. *AC*, 127.

20. Durán, *caps*. xv, xviii; *CR*, 24, 124; Ixtlilxochitl, *Historia*, *caps*. xxxiv, xlvii, xxxvii. The latter is unclear about many details. He reports the sham as real war that is won by Nezahualcoyotl, who goes on to dominate the Triple Alliance. That, of course, didn't happen, nor have I found any reasonable alternative that would explain relegation of powerful Texcoco to second place in the alliance and subordination to the rule of Huitzilopochtli.

21. *CR*, 66; *CM*, *cap*. xxxvi.

22. Sahagún, *Lib*. VIII, *cap*. xxxiv; *CR*, 63. Also see Seler, "On the Words Anáhuac and Nahuatl," *GA*, II, Pt. i, 34.

23. This was in 1462. The Chalca were not finally vanquished until 1465. *CR*, 65–66, 125–26; *AC*, 128.

24. Durán, *caps*. xviii–xix.

25. *Historia*, TR. I, *cap*. xii.

26. *CR*, 124, 133–35, 62–65; Mendieta, *Lib*. II, *cap*. vii.

27. Ample examples of which are given in Durán, *caps*. xx, xxix, lxvi, *passim*.

28. See Sahagún, *Lib*. II, *caps*. i, xxii. Seler guessed close to the truth, although he was not aware of its chronology: "At the time when the augural calendar (*Tonalamatl*) was invented, the entire aggregate of mythical and religious conceptions seems to have been brought into a kind of system by the priests of a certain school. . . ." "Mixed Forms of Mexican Divinities," *GA*, III, Pt. iii, 58–62.

29. *AC*, 128; Durán, *cap*. xx; *CR*, 131–33; *FC*, Bk. II, chap. xxi; Pomar, *Relación de Texcoco*, NCD, III, 18–21. Soustelle, *Daily Life*, p. 16, repeats the hoary myth that the Temalacatl was brought to the capital by 50,000 men with ropes and rollers.

30. Durán, *cap*. xix. Most writers follow Alfonso Caso, *La religión de los Aztecas* and *El pueblo del sol*, in his assumption that the Mexican practice of human sacrifice stemmed from philosophical and religious convictions. It is obvious, however, that human sacrifice as a political instrument preceded by far its later philosophical and symbolic adornment. Also see L. Séjourné, *Burning Water*.

31. In Chapter XXIII the editor of Durán (1951 ed.) believes the text to be in error in attributing the Sun Stone to Montezuma's reign, essentially because the Stone that was in use at the time of the Spanish conquest carried the name of Tizoc, who ruled 1481–86. But Durán clearly establishes Tlacaellel as the innovator in Chapter LXVI. What apparently happened was that a new Sun Stone was later carved, and it was this one that was in use when the empire fell.

32. *CR*, 130; Durán, *caps*. xxiii, xxxvi, *passim*; *Codex Magliabecchi*, 18^r; *FC*, Bk. IX, chap. ii.

33. Mendieta, *Lib.* II, *caps.* xxxvii–xxxix; *Codex Magliabecchi*, 58ʳ, 59ʳ.

34. *AT*, 58 ff.; *Codex Telleriano-Remensis*, Pt. IV, 48; *AC*, 127; Durán, *cap.* xxi, *passim.*

35. See Francisco Pimentel, *Lenguas indígenas de Mexico*, especially *cap.* ii, in *Obras completas*, I.

36. On disease, see Sherburne F. Cook, "The Incidence and Significance of Disease Among the Aztecs and Related Tribes," *Hispanic American Historical Review*, XXVI (1946), 320–35.

37. All are named by Durán, *cap.* xxv. I use the term "presidium" to designate the few lords who spoke and acted for the mass of the Pipiltin.

38. Durán, *cap.* xviii; *CR*, 101. The bread mentioned was the maize tortilla.

39. Francisco López de Gómara, *Historia de la Conquista de México*, *cap.* lxxvii.

40. Durán, *caps.* xviii, xliii; *AC*, 128; Gómara, *cap.* lvii; Ixtlilxochitl, *Historia*, *cap.* xli, misses the point completely.

41. Durán, *cap.* xxix; *CR*, 132; *CM*, *cap.* xlvi.

42. Durán, *cap.* xlii.

43. *FC*, Bk. II, chap. xxi, Bk. IX, chap. ii; Durán, *cap.* lviii. Cf. Sahagún, *Lib.* II, *cap.* xxi.

44. Durán, *cap.* xliii, xlii, xxxvi–xxxvii, liii–liv; *CR*, 75.

45. Most writers identify Axayacatl as Montezuma's son. The *Anales de Chimalpahin* (p. 129) insist that he was Montezuma's cousin; his sons were said to despise Axayacatl and to have opposed his election.

46. "El Marqués del Valle, sobre información de los términos donde se pobló la villa de Toluca, San Miguel Totocuitlapilco, San Bartolomé Tlaltelulco, Matalcingo. Cítase al rey Axayacatl, padre de Moctezuma, y el reparto de tierras hecho al señor de Tlaltelolco Mexico, al de Texcoco, y al de Tacuba Euytzotzin," *AGN: Archivo Hospital de Jesús, legajo 70–expediente* 4; Ixtlilxochitl, *Historia, cap.* liii; Durán, *caps.* xxxvi, xlv.

47. Durán, *caps.* xxxii–xxxiv; *CR*, 68–70; *Codex Cazcatzin* (in Radin), pp. 16–17; Sahagún, *Historia, Lib.* VIII, *cap.* ii; *AC*, 129; *AT*, 58 ff; *FC*, Bk. IX, chap. i.

Chapter III

1. Parthenogenetic birth was a common idea in Mesoamerica. Quetzalcóatl's mother was said to have conceived when she swallowed a piece of jade. Seler believed the fictitious birth of Huitzilopochtli to be based upon ancient sun myth:

the rising sun that defeats the stars becomes Huitzilopochtli who vanquishes his brothers and sisters. See "Some Remarks Upon the Natural Bases of Mexican Myths," *GA*, III, Pt. ii, 1–29.

2. The early history of the Mexica is in *Lib.* II, *caps.* xxxii–xxxiv. For data on the author see *Lib.* V, *caps.* xxxiii–xxxv.

3. *Historia, Lib.* X, *cap.* xxxix. His major research assistants were Martin Jacovita of Tlatelolco, Antonio Valeriano of Atzcapotzalco, Alonso Vegerano and Pedro de San Buenaventura of Cuauhtitlán, Diego de Grado and Bonifacio Maximiliano of Tlatelolco, and Mateo Severino of Xochimilco. See *Lib.* II, *Prologo.*

4. *Historia, cap.* x, and *Relaciones,* "Rama y descendencia de los señores de Mexico."

5. *AC*, 124; Sahagún, *Lib.* X, *cap.* xxix.

6. *FC*, Bk. X, chap. xxix.

7. *Relaciones,* "Rama y descendencia."

8. *Sources and Authority,* p. 24.

9. "Explicación del Códice geroglífico de Mr. Aubin," appended to Durán, II (1951 ed.).

10. The *Códice Ramírez* must be divided into two parts. The first, so colorfully interpreted, is patently lacking in historicity. But the second part, commencing with the fall of Atzcapotzalco, is a remarkably reliable chronicle of the empire. Both Durán and Tezozomoc used many other sources for the post-Itzcoatl period, yet the *Códice Ramírez* checks well against them for accuracy.

11. *FC*, Bk. X, chap. xxix.

12. Mythical Aztlán, the "White Place," or "Land of the White Heron," has been postulated everywhere from Michoacán to Puget Sound, although never upon physical evidence. Seler finally concluded that Aztlán was simply the city of Mexico removed to the vague past. See his essays "On the Origin of the Central American Civilizations," and "Where was Aztlán, the Home of the Aztecs?" *GA*, II, Pt. i, 11–22, 23–32.

13. *CR*, 24.

14. Tezozomoc, *Crónica mexicayotl,* p. 50.

15. *CR*, 28.

16. The mythologians are here accounting for their adoption of the goddess Toci.

17. *CR*, 28. Tlacaellel's imperial philosophy is obvious here.

18. *CR*, 29. This accounts for incorporation of Xipe cult and bears the stamp of Tlacaellel's macabre humor. The absence of religious motive is striking.

19. *Crónica Mexicayotl*, pp. 54–58; *CR*, 29–30.

20. *CR*, 30–31.

21. *CR*, 32.

22. *CR*, 32–33. The symbolism involved here was demonstrably of much later manufacture.

23. *CR*, 37–38. Huitzilopochtli is here being given credit for invention of the chinampa. Actually, the chinampa appears to be no older in origin than mid–fourteenth century, hence the official history is approximately correct in its dating of first use by the Mexica, even though the interpretation is absurd.

24. *CR*, 46–50.

25. Sahagún, *Lib*. X, *cap*. xxix; Ixtlilxochitl, *Relaciones*, "Rama y descendencia"; Mendieta, *Lib*. II, *caps*. iv, vi, xxxii.

26. Durán, *cap*. xxvii.

Chapter IV

1. Durán, *caps*. xxxi–xxxiii.

2. *CR*, 68–70; *AC*, 130.

3. Durán, *cap*. xxxvi.

4. *Ibid*., *caps*. xxxvii–xxxviii.

5. *Codex Telleriano-Remensis*, Pt. IV, 48.

6. Ixtlilxochitl, *Historia*, *cap*. lviii; Duran, *caps*. xxxix–xl; *CR*, 67. The anonymous compiler of the *Códice Ramírez* got Tizoc's reign in the wrong slot.

7. Durán, *caps*. xl–xli; *CR*, 70–72.

8. Durán, *cap*. xlii.

9. *Ibid*., *caps*. xliii–xliv.

10. Full description is given in Sahagún, *Lib*. I, *Appendice* ii.

11. Presumably, three of the staircases were temporarily installed for this fete,

since later descriptions describe but one great staircase. The eastern staircase would have to be fed by prisoners from one of the other lines, there being no eastward causeway.

12. Sherburne F. Cook, in "Human Sacrifice and Warfare as Factors in the Demography of Pre-Colonial Mexico," *Human Biology*, XVIII (May, 1946), 81–102, estimates that it took two minutes per victim at the slab, which, multiplied by four, would give 120 victims per hour, or 11,520 in the four-day period, given constant operation. However, Durán (*caps*. lviii, lxxxi, lx) describes other ceremonial slaughters in which victims appear to have been dispatched at a rate upward of 230 per hour, or fifteen seconds per victim. Obviously, they had varying speed schedules for massive sacrifice. In the case under discussion symbolism was unimportant and unobserved, the only aim being to get the job done. The slabs were engineered for speed, their convex surfaces making it possible to "cut into the victim's middle as easily as though it were a pomegranate." Besides which, "the slab was placed so close to the top of the staircase that there was no more than two feet of space between the sacrificial slab and the top step; thus with a kick they sent the body over the edge and down the steps. . . ." (*CR*, 100). There was loss of neither time nor motion. The rate of 230 per hour, multiplied by four, would give 920 per hour, or a possible 88,320 for the four-day period. Hence, the commonly given figure of 80,400, while still doubtful, may have been a lesser exaggeration than has been thought.

13. ". . . y era tanto el hedor de la sangre que no avia quien lo sufriese, del cual cuenta la historia, y dice que era un hedor acedo, abominable, que no lo podían sufrir los de la ciudad (Durán, *cap*. xliv).

14. Ixtlilxochitl, *Historia, cap*. lx; also see the *Anales de Cuauhtitlán*, p. 58.

15. Durán, *cap*. xlviii. *CR*, 67, has his death premature, evidently through error of the compiler.

16. P. 127. Juan de Torquemada, in his *Monarquía indiana, Lib*. II, *cap*. liv, found Tlacaellel too incredible a figure—and solved his problem by simply denying that there ever was such a man.

Chapter V

1. Ixtlilxochitl, *Historia, cap*. lviii.

2. Durán, *cap*. xlvii; *CR*, 124.

3. Also see Durán, *cap*. xlvii; Gómara, *cap*. ccxxxv; Motolinía, *Memoriales, cap*. xvi; and Seler, "A List of the Mexican Monthly Feasts," *GA*, I, Pt. ii, 11–16.

4. *BD, cap.* lxxvi.

5. *Codex Borbonicus,* plate xxi.

6. Ixtlilxochitl, *Historia, caps.* lxvi, lxx; Durán, *caps.* xlviii–xlix.

7. *CR,* 72–73; Durán, *cap.* lii; Ixtlilxochitl, *Historia,* lxx; *FC,* Bk. IX, chap. ii. Montezuma had been Ahuitzotl's commanding general during the early years of his reign.

8. Durán, *caps.* liii–liv; *CR,* 75. Borah and Cook, in their *Aboriginal Population,* pp. 45 ff., find that the tributes of Xoconochco were ordered paid twice yearly, instead of the older and traditional eighty days, the first payment being due in time for Tlacaxipehualiztli. This was the big fete to which the Enemies-of-the-House were invariably invited, hence this alteration of schedule may have been made for propaganda purposes.

9. Sahagún, *Lib.* VI, *cap.* x; Gómara, *cap.* lxxxiii; Durán, *caps.* liii–liv; *CR,* 76; *Codex Magliabecchi,* 23ʳ; *FC,* Bk. IV, chaps. xi–xii.

10. Ixtlilxochitl, *Historia, cap.* lxvi; Durán, *caps.* xlviii, lv; Torquemada, *Monarquía indiana, Lib.* VIII, *caps.* xx–xxi.

11. Durán, *cap.* lxxx.

12. *Ibid.* Ixtlilxochitl, *Historia, cap.* lxiv.

13. Durán, *cap.* lvii, cites the official chronicles, hence, does not reflect or report the intrigue. But Ixtlilxochitl, *Historia, cap.* lxxi, provides the missing details.

14. *CR,* 74–75, 77; Durán, *caps.* lv, liii; *Codex Magliabecchi,* 60ʳ; José de Acosta, *Historia Natural, cap.* xiv; *CM, cap.* lxxxiii; F. A. MacNutt, ed. and trans., *Letters of Cortés,* I, 264–65 (hereafter cited as *Cortés*).

15. Motolinia, *Memoriales, cap.* liii; Gómara, *caps.* lxxvi–lxxvii; *CR,* 76; Durán, *caps.* lv, lxii; *BD, cap.* lxxi.

16. For description see Sahagún, *Lib.* I, *Appendice* ii.

17. Burgoa, *Geográfica descripción,* I, 266–76; Gómara, *cap.* xxxiii; Mendieta, *Lib.* II, *caps.* ix, xix; *AT,* 58 ff. Also see Seler, "On the Words Anahuac and Nahuatl," *GA,* II, Pt. i, 33–52.

18. Ixtlilxochitl, *Historia, caps.* lxxi–lxxii. The double standard began in the days of Acamapichtli in the secrecy with which the lords screened their biological creation of the Pipiltin, and was subsequently retained to serve the myth of divine blood.

19. Durán, *cap.* lvii.

20. *Códice de Yanhuitlan,* pp. 10–11; *Codex Telleriano-Remensis,* Pt. IV, 48; Durán, *cap.* lvii; Ixtlilxochitl, *Historia, cap.* lxxiii.

21. Durán, *caps.* lvii, lix.

22. Durán, *cap.* lxii. For Toci fete, see the *Codex Magliabecchi,* 26ᵛ, 27ʳ, and Sahagún's treatment of *Ochpaniztli.* The site of Toci's temple was to become the site of the shrine of Guadalupe, and "Our Mother" was in some respects to become "Our Lady."

23. W. Borah and S. F. Cook, *Aboriginal Population,* p. 68.

24. Durán, *caps.* xlvii, xxiii–xxiv, lviii; Gómara, *caps.* lxxvii–lxxviii; Juan de Zumárraga to Emperor, Nov. 25, 1536, *ZUM,* IV, 127; Zumárraga, "Instrucciones," 1537, *ibid.,* 136; *CR,* 76, 97; Ixtlilxochitl, *Historia, caps.* xxxviii, xlvii; Mendieta, *Lib.* II, *caps.* xxix–xxx; *CM, cap.* xxxvi; Sahagún, *Lib.* VIII, *cap.* x; Camargo, *Historia, cap.* xvi; Oviedo, *Historia,* X, *Lib.* xiv, *cap.* li; Borah and Cook, chap. ii.

25. *Codex Mendoza,* Part II, in Radin, *Sources and Authenticity,* pp. 50–56; Sahagún, *Lib.* III, *cap.* iv; cf. *FC,* Bk. IV, chaps. iv–v. Also see Zorita, *Relación,* p. 115; Mendieta, *Lib.* II, *cap.* xxx; and the *Codex Magliabecchi,* 39ʳ.

26. *CR,* 74; Cortés, I, 264–65, 267; Gómara, *cap.* lxxvi.

27. Sahagún, *Lib.* II, *caps.* i–iv, xx–xxi; Ixtlilxochitl, *Relaciones,* "Relación XI"; Codex Magliabecchi, 18ᵛ, 19ʳ, 19ᵛ, 24ᵛ, 21ᵛ, 31ᵛ, 32ʳ; Cortés to Emperor, Oct. 15, 1524, *CD,* I, 470–85.

28. *FC,* Bk. VIII, chaps. xiv, xvii; Gómara, *cap.* lxxvii; Mendieta, *Lib.* II, *cap.* xxiv.

29. Mendieta, *Lib.* II, *cap.* xxxi; *FC,* Bk. IV, chaps. iv–v; Codex Magliabecchi, 33ᵛ, 34ʳ; *CM, cap.* xxx; Sahagún, *Lib.* II, *cap.* xx.

30. Ixtlilxochitl, *Historia, caps.* xlix, lvii; Oviedo, *Historia,* VIII, *Lib.* xiv, *cap.* x; Gómara, *cap.* lxxi; Camargo, *Historia,* pp. 44–47.

31. "Historia de los mexicanos por sus pinturas," *NCD,* III, *cap.* ii; Mendieta, *Lib.* II, *cap.* xiii; Gómara, *cap.* lxii.

32. Mendieta, *Lib.* II, *cap.* xl.

33. Durán, *cap.* lxv; Sahagún, *Lib.* II, *caps.* i–iv, xx–xxi; Codex Magliabecchi, 60ʳ, 61ʳ; Cortés, II, 104; *BD, cap.* lxxxiv. The taboo against eating the flesh of one's own captive was a ceremonial nicety, but was hardly more effective than Christianity's taboo against adultery.

Chapter VI

1. Ixtlilxochitl, *Historia, cap.* lxxi; Durán, *cap.* lviii; *AC,* 128.

2. *CR,* 77–79; *FC,* Bk. XII, chap. i; Cervantes de Salazar, *Crónica, Lib.* I, *cap.*

xxxii; Gómara, *cap.* cxlv. It is always necessary to recognize the Christian qualities in these reports that were read in after the conquest.

3. Duran, *cap.* lxi; CR, 77–78.

4. *Ibid.*

5. *Codex Telleriano-Remensis,* Pt. IV, 49, gives 1509. Other sources give varied dates. Ixtlilxochitl, Durán, and Sahagún agree on 1510. Whether the comet was also observed in Europe is hard to determine. Barnard's Comet was seen in Europe in 1504, as was Halley's in 1506. But until relatively late in the sixteenth century, European cometary records are incomplete.

6. Durán, *caps.* lxiii–lxv; Ixtlilxochitl, *Historia, cap.* lxxii; CR, 77–78. Durán has the soliloquy being delivered in the presence of Nezahualpilli, which Montezuma would never have done. But priests who stood within range may well have heard and "frozen" it through glyph-writing as they did so many things.

7. Durán, *ibid.; Codex Telleriano-Remensis,* Pt. IV, 49; Ixtlilxochitl, *Historia, cap.* lxxiii; Motolinía, *Historia,* Tr. I, *cap.* ii.

8. Duran, *cáp.* lxv; Ixtlilxochitl, *Historia, caps.* lxxiii–lxxiv.

9. Ixtlilxochitl, *Historia, caps.* lxxv, xlvii; also see his *Relaciones,* "Relación XII," and "Noticias de Nezahualpilli."

10. Gómara, *cap.* cxlv; Ixtlilxochitl, *Historia, cap.* lxxiii; Sahagún, *Lib.* VIII, *caps.* i, vi; CR, 79; *Codex Telleriano-Remensis,* Pt. IV, 49.

11. Durán, *cap.* lxvi.

12. Motolinía, *Memoriales, cap.* lv. The trunk was probably from the wreck of a Spanish slaving expedition plying the Honduran coast.

13. Motolinía, *Historia,* Tr. I, *cap.* xii, tells of ships' bleached sails, pyramidal in shape, being taken for seagoing temples in earliest contacts. Cervantes de Salazar, in his *Crónica, Lib.* III, *cap.* i, suggests that vanguard merchants were active in Yucatan at this time. Bernal Díaz, *cap.* xiii, gives Montezuma's version.

14. Durán, *cap.* lxvi. Unfortunately, Montezuma was wrong. The gallery was gradually destroyed by various colonial landscaping projects, and then almost entirely by viceregal administrative order in the middle of the eighteenth century.

15. Durán, *cap.* lxvii; BD, *cap.* lxxxiii.

16. Sahagún, *Lib.* VI, *cap.* x; Durán, *cap.* lxviii.

17. Durán, *ibid.,* says that like good sorcerers they simply vanished. Other documents indicate that they effected an ordinary escape. See below, p. 249.

Chapter VII

1. *BD, caps.* viii–xi, lxxxiii; Durán, *cap.* lxix; Gómara, *cap.* vi.

2. *FC,* Bk. XII, chap. ii.

3. Durán, *ibid.* Durán confuses his sources and places Doña Marina with the Grijalva expedition. This vessel was the "Trinidad" and was captained by Pedro de Alvarado. Thus did the first contact between Spaniards and Mexica take place on the Papaloapán, and not, as has previously been thought, on the Río de Banderas.

4. *FC,* Bk. XII, chap. iii; *CR,* 80–81.

5. *FC,* Bk. X, chap. xxix; Durán, *cap.* lxx.

6. *Ibid.*

7. *BD, caps.* xxxv, lxxxii–lxxxiii; *Cortés,* I, 140–41; Gómara, *cap.* xviii. This would be mid-March by the Christian calendar. The Cortés fleet left Cuba on February 18, 1519, proceeding to Yucatan.

8. Vera Cruz. Messages were carried from coast to capital in twenty-four hours or less by special runners posted for that purpose. Andrés de Tapia subsequently found it necessary to hasten to Vera Cruz from the capital to spy out Narváez' arrival. Traveling all day by foot and carried at night by tamemes, he made it in approximately eighty hours; hence, unburdened post runners could easily do it in twenty-four. See Andrés de Tapia, *Relación, CD,* II, 587.

9. *FC,* Bk. XII, chaps. iii–iv.

10. *Ibid.,* chap. vi.

11. *CR,* 81–83; *FC,* Bk. XII, chaps. v–vii. Also see *BD, cap.* xxxv, and Gómara, *cap.* xxv.

12. *FC, ibid.,* chap. viii. This apparently happened just after the Spaniards disembarked, probably on Saturday, April 22. Bernal Díaz merely says that the Indians brought food. At the time he might have been on other duty or simply forgot the details.

13. *AT,* 62; Durán, *cap.* lxxi.

14. *FC,* Bk. XII, chaps. viii–ix; *CR,* 83; *BD, caps.* xxxiv–xxxv; Ixtlilxochitl, *Historia, cap.* lxxx.

15. *FC, ibid.;* Ixtlilxochitl, *Historia, caps.* lxxx, lxxix; *BD, caps.* xxxv–xxxvi; *CR,*

83–84. Durán is less useful for the precise moment of arrival because the sources are badly confused.

16. *BD, cap.* xxxvii; Ixtlilxochitl, *Historia, caps.* lxxx–lxxxi.

17. *FC,* Bk. XII, chaps. x–xiii; *BD, caps.* lxxxvi–lxxxvii; *CR,* 84–86.

18. *FC,* Bk. XII, chap. xiv; *BD, cap.* lxxxi.

Chapter VIII

1. *BD, cap.* xxvii.

2. *Cortés,* I, 165.

3. *Ancient Law,* p. 148.

4. Quoted in George F. Willison, *Saints and Strangers* (New York, 1945), p. 392.

5. Oviedo, *Historia,* I, *Lib.* II, *cap.* viii; Ramón Menéndez Pidal, "La idea imperial de Carlos V," *Revista Cubana,* X, Nos. 28–30 (Oct.–Dec., 1937), 5–31.

6. Juan de Grijalva, *Discovery of New Spain,* pp. 44–45, 80; Gómara, *cap.* vi; Cervantes de Salazar, *Crónica, Lib.* II, *cap.* ix; *BD, cap.* xii. In editing the Grijalva documents, Henry R. Wagner mistook the Papaloapan River for the Tabasco.

7. Grijalva, p. 37.

8. Juan Díaz, "Itinerario," in Grijalva, *Discovery,* p. 73. *BD, caps.* xii–xiii; Grijalva, pp. 123, 40–43; Henry R. Wagner, *The Rise of Fernando Cortés,* p. 26.

9. *BD, cap.* xiii.

10. Gómara, *cap.* ix.

11. See Motolinía, *Historia, Tr.* I, *cap.* xii, and *Memoriales, caps.* xv, xxxiii; Mendieta, *Lib.* I, *caps.* ii, vii; *Lib.* II, *cap.* viii; José de Acosta, *Historia,* pp. 347 ff., for detailed statements on the teleology of conquest. John L. Phelan's *Millennial Kingdom of the Franciscans* contains excellent discussion. For Cortés' thoughts see *Cortés,* II, 245. Also see Oviedo, *Historia,* X, *Lib.* xiii, *cap.* xlvii, and *BD, cap.* xxvii.

12. Gómara, *cap.* xiii.

13. Aguilar was shipwrecked en route from Darien to Española in 1511. He and a few crewmen made land on the coast of Yucatan, after which nearly all perished.

Cortés ransomed him from his Indian masters, whereupon Aguilar became a vital member of the Conqueror's staff as an expert in the Mayan language.

14. Gómara, *caps.* xiii–xv.

15. *Cue* presumably being the Spanish pronunciation of the Mayan *Ku,* meaning "deity," or something akin thereto.

16. *BD, caps.* xxx–xxxii. By the greatest coincidence final victory was won on March 25, 1519, which on the religious calendar was the Day of Our Lady.

17. Gómara, *cap.* cv.

18. Wagner, *Cortés,* pp. 196–97, puts forth the fanciful theory that Sahagún invented the entire matter of Montezuma's confusion of Cortés and Quetzalcoatl at the time of arrival.

19. *BD, cap.* xxxiv; Gómara, *caps.* xxv–xxvi; Ixtlilxochitl, *Historia,* cap. lxxix.

20. The settlement was merely founded on paper and did not become a physical reality for several weeks. *BD, caps.* xxxv–xxxviii, xlvii–xlviii; Ixtlilxochitl, *Historia, cap.* lxxx. On the odor of the Spaniards, see Artemio de Valle-Arizpe, *Andanzas de Hernán Cortés* (Madrid, 1940), p. 64.

21. *BD, caps.* xli–xlii; Gómara, *cap.* xxxiii; *Cortés,* I, 188 ff.; Ixtlilxochitl, *Historia, cap.* lxxxi; Starr, *Mapa de Cuauhtlantzinco.*

22. *BD, caps.* xliii–xliv; Ixtlilxochitl, *Historia, caps.* lxxxi–lxxxii.

23. *BD, cap.* xxxvii.

24. *BD, caps.* xlvii–xlviii; Ixtlilxochitl, *Historia, cap.* lxxxiii.

25. Gómara, *cap.* xliv; *Cortés,* I, 196–97; *BD, cap.* liv.

26. *Cortés,* I, 198–212; *BD, caps.* lxx, lxv–lxvi; Gómara, *caps.* lv–lvii.

27. *BD, caps.* lxxii–lxxv; Ixtlilxochitl, *Historia, cap.* lxxxiv.

28. *Cortés,* I, 218; *BD, cap.* lxxvi; Gómara, *cap.* lx, Tapia, *Relación,* p. 576. Wagner, *Cortés,* pp. 175–76, agrees with Las Casas that the Cholulans were "poor tame sheep" and therefore finds that in his *Brevíssima relación* "Las Casas was absolutely right."

29. *Cortés,* I, 188; *BD, caps.* lxxvi–lxxviii; Gómara, *cap.* lxiii; *CR,* 85; *FC,* Bk. XII, chap. xii.

30. *BD, caps.* lxxix–lxxxi, lxxxiv; *Cortés,* I, 226–27, 232–34; Ixtlilxochitl, *Historia, cap.* lxxxv; *FC,* Bk. XII, chap. xiv; Durán, *cap.* lxxiv. Doña Marina was always called "Malintzin" by the Indians, and in the course of the march on the capital, Cortés also acquired the name, except that the Spaniards corrupted it to "Malinche."

Chapter IX

1. *Cortés*, I, 234–36; *CR*, 87; *BD, cap.* lxxxii. Bernal Díaz mistakenly places this meeting on the following day.

2. *BD, cap.* lxxxiii.

3. *BD, cap.* lxxxv. Editors of Bernal Díaz have long taken his word that he describes the view of Tenochtitlán from atop the pyramid in Tlatelolco, adjacent to the great market place. But his description of the convergence of streets and causeways could only be made from Huitzilopochtli's temple in Mexico. He also mentions the burial vaults of the Mexican kings, who would never have been interred in Tlatelolco under any circumstances. Apparently, Bernal Díaz was cribbing from Gómara, which he frequently did, and forgot that he and the party had returned to Mexico after visiting the market place at Tlatelolco; hence he wrote: "Mucho me he detenido en contar de este gran cu del Tatelulco y sus patios pues digo era el mayor templo de todo México. . . ." In borrowing from Gómara, who didn't make the same error, Bernal Díaz got his *cues* mixed.

4. The foregoing dialogue is supplied by *BD, cap.* lxxxv; Tapia, *Relación*, pp. 583–84.

5. *Cortés*, I, 237–41; *BD, caps.* lxxxvi–lxxxvii; Tapia, *ibid.*; Ixtlilxochitl, *Historia, cap.* lxxxv.

6. *BD, caps.* xcii, lxxxix.

7. *Cortés*, I, 249–52; *BD, caps.* xc–xciii.

8. *BD, caps.* xcviii–xcix; Tapia, pp. 593–94; Cervantes, *Lib.* IV, *caps.* xxx–xxxi; Oviedo, *Historia*, X, *Lib.* xiv, *cap.* xlvii.

9. The foregoing dialogue is supplied by Tapia, pp. 584–86, and Cervantes, *ibid.*, who writes from personal descriptions by Ojeda and others, all of which have long since been lost. Oviedo, *Historia*, VIII, *Lib.* xiv, *cap.* x, supposes that Cortés' daring act was permitted by God, ". . . but for me I hold the great forbearance of Montezuma and the Indian lords to be a genuine marvel, seeing their temple and idols so treated."

10. In subsequent letters Cortés claimed to have rolled the idols down and effectively forbidden human sacrifice. *Cortés*, I, 260–61; Gómara, *caps.* lxxxv–lxxxvi. Bernal Díaz forgot most of this episode and in mistrust of Gómara's account rejected it and simply telescoped his own version in Chapter XCIX. When he wrote his

Crónica, Cervantes had to make intensive researches to get the story. He did not use Andrés de Tapia, yet their versions match very well.

Chapter X

1. Cervantes, *Lib*. IV, *caps*. xxx, xxxiii; Tapia, p. 586; Ixtlilxochitl, *Historia*, *cap*. lxxxvi; *BD*, *cap*. xcix.

2. Toxcatl was composed of several layers. Originally a plea for rain in a predominantly agricultural rite, it became associated with Tezcatlipoca and was one of his major fetes. With development of the empire, it was taken over by Huitzilopochtli cult. There is currently some question about the placement of Toxcatl in the religious calendar; whether it belongs in the May slot is really not important to the issue at hand. The sources make it abundantly clear that the central figure in the ceremonial was a great amaranth seed statue of Huitzilopochtli; that it was one of his greatest feast days; that his worship was inextricably linked with the *poder estatal*.

3. Duran, *cap*. lxxx; *BD*, *caps*. c–cv; *Cortés*, I, 268–69; Tapia, p. 587. One witness in the *Procesos de residencia contra Pedro de Alvarado* fixes the garrison strength at 130 men (pp. 36–39).

4. *BD*, *caps*. cxiii–cxiv; Ixtlilxochitl, *Historia*, *cap*. lxxxviii, *Relaciones*, "Relacion XIII"; *FC*, Bk. XII, chap. xx; Wagner, *Cortés*, pp. 288–89, 291; *Procesos de residencia contra Pedro de Alvarado*, pp. 63 ff.

5. *CR*, 88–89; *FC*, Bk. XII, chaps. xx–xxii; *AT*, 62–63; *Procesos de residencia* claims that upward of three thousand were slain (pp. 3–4).

6. *FC*, *ibid.*; *CR*, *ibid.*; *AT*, 63–64; Wagner, *Cortés*, pp. 288–90. Also see Sahagún, *Lib*. XII, *caps*. xx–xxiii.

7. Ixtlilxochitl, *Historia*, *cap*. lxxxviii.

8. *Cortés*, I, 292; Gómara, *cap*. civ; *BD*, *cap*. cxv; Wagner, *Cortés*, pp. 293–94. It is said that this same image of the Virgin was subsequently worshiped in the Church of Los Remedios near Tacuba.

9. *BD*, *cap*. cxv; *CR*, 89. Bernal Díaz gives a different interpretation, holding that the attacking lords were generally loyal to Montezuma, which was not the case at all.

10. Duran, *cap*. lxxvi; *FC*, Bk. XII, chap. xxiii; *AT*, 63–64; Ixtlilxochitl, *Historia*, *cap*. lxxxviii; *CR*, 90–91; *BD*, *caps*. cxv–cxvii; *Cortés*, I, 289–90, 296 ff. Bernal Díaz' account of the manner of Montezuma's death and Spanish sentiment concerning it is unacceptable in the face of Durán's and Sahagún's sources. In my

opinion he simply concocted a fairy tale to euphemize an ugly reality. Orozco y Berra, *Historia*, IV, 436 ff., came to the same conclusion.

Chapter XI

1. *Cortés*, I, 291, pointedly identifies the swarming attackers and defenders of the temple as "notable persons." This was no plebeian uprising.

2. Gómara, *cap.* cii; Motolinía, *Memoriales, cap.* ii

3. *FC*, Bk. XII, chap. xxix.

4. *Cortés*, I, 294–95, 318–21; Gómara, *cap.* ccxi; Sahagún, *Lib.* XII, *caps.* xxi, xxviii.

5. *BD, caps.* cxvii–cxix; Gómara, *cap.* cxxxii.

6. Bernal Díaz is apparently confused in calling the king of Texcoco by the name of Coanacochtzin. He is refuted by Cortés and the *Códice Rámirez*, both of which are specific.

7. *CR*, 136–37. Ixtlilxochitl, *Relaciones*, "Relación XIII," gives the mistaken impression that the foregoing did not occur until 1524.

8. *BD, cap.* cxx; *Cortés*, II, 13–17, 21 ff.; Gómara, *cap.* cxxii.

9. *BD, caps.* cxxi–cxxv.

10. *Cortés*, II, 60 ff.; *BD, caps.* cxxvi–cxxxvi; Ixtlilxochitl, *Relaciones*, "Relación XIII"; *FC*, Bk. XII, *caps.* xxx–xxxv; *AT*, 65–73. Also see C. H. Gardiner, *Naval Power in the Conquest of Mexico*.

11. *AT*, 66. Huitzilopochtli cult had long been inextricably associated with the creation and preservation of Tlatelolco's mercantile wealth. See *FC*, Bk. IX.

12. *Cortés*, II, 77–85; *AT*, 67–70.

13. *FC*, Bk. XII, chap. xl.

14. *FC, ibid.* Bernal Díaz himself deleted several disparaging remarks concerning this event from his original manuscript, a copy of which may still be seen in Guatemala's national archives. Most editions of his work consequently lack them also.

15. *Cortés*, II, 102 ff., 120–27, appendix, 151 ff.; *BD, cap.* cxxxvi; *AT*, 70–76; *FC*, Bk. XII, chap. xl; Gómara, *cap.* cxl.

Chapter XII

1. Ixtlilxochitl, *Relaciones,* "Relación XIII;" Gómara, *cap.* cxliv.

2. *BD, cap.* cxxxvii; Zorita, *Relación,* p. 170; Gómara, *cap.* clxiii. Largely because the chroniclers refer to preconquest nobles as "caciques," we erroneously assume that they possessed the characteristics that identify the post-conquest cacicazgo. This leads us to postulate greater class continuity than actually existed before and after the conquest. The new caciques were created in a post-conquest world that was different from the old one, and although the caciques lived as they *thought* their forbears did, they were more often than not conforming to distortions that resulted from hispanicization of their culture. Also see Charles Gibson's "The Transformation of the Indian Community in New Spain," *Journal of World History,* II (1955), 581–607, and "The Aztec Aristocracy in Colonial Mexico," *Comparative Studies in Society and History,* II (1960), 169–96.

3. For creation of cacicazgo in the north, see P. W. Powell, *Soldiers, Indians, and Silver,* pp. 159–60, *passim.* Also see Gómara, *caps.* cxl–cl.

4. As soon as the crown realized what he intended, it moved to reduce his authority; but this fails to detract from his intent, which is the most significant consideration.

5. Cortés to Emperor, Oct. 15, 1524, *CD,* I, 475.

6. Comparative analysis of Castilian juridical background and Mesoamerican feudalism is too cumbersome for presentation here, but does comprise a portion of my forthcoming work on cultural mestizaje.

7. *BD, caps.* lxxxix, cxxv; Tapia, pp. 586, 593.

8. *Cortés,* I, 43–44. MacNutt here attempts to untangle the Conqueror's alliances, but without complete success. No one will ever know his box score.

9. Cedula of 1533, *DSH,* I, 147.

10. Rodrigo de Albornoz to Emperor, Dec. 15, 1525, *CD,* I, 492. Numbers are difficult to fix, but there can be little doubt that many mestizos were absorbed in the *rescate.*

11. For specific examples see Ixtlilxochitl, *Historia, cap.* ccx, and *Anales de Cuauhtitlán,* pp. 20–21, 36.

12. Seler, "The Land Register of Santiago Guevea," *GA,* III, Pt. i, 1–24; Zorita,

Relación, pp. 99–106; Mendieta, *Lib.* IV, *caps.* xxxii–xxxiii; Motolinía, *Historia,* Tr. I, *cap.* i.

13. Audiencia to Crown, Aug. 14, 1531, *DII,* XLI, 42–45, 92. For the most recent summary of tribute collection see Borah and Cook, *Aboriginal Population,* chaps. i–v.

14. King to bishops of Mexico, Guatemala, Antequera, Aug. 23, 1538, *DIM,* XV, 45–54; Zorita, *Relación,* pp. 175, 222–23. On the silk industry, see W. W. Borah, *Silk Raising in Colonial Mexico,* pp. 16–17, 44–45.

15. Sandoval to Prince Philip, Sept. 9, 1545, *ENE,* IV, 210; Mendieta, *Lib.* III, *cap.* 1; Cedula of Feb. 22, 1549, *DSH,* I, 255–56; "Capítulos de gobernadores y regidores," July 2, 1530, in Puga, *Cedulario,* I, 207, 216. Also see François Chevalier, *La Formación de los grandes latifundios en Mexico,* pp. 151 ff.

16. Cedulas of Nov. 9, 1526, and Aug. 17, 1529, *DSH,* I, 87, 129; "Ordenanzas sobre el buen tratamiento de los indios," Nov. 17, 1526, *ibid.,* 89–96; "Ordenanzas sobre el tratamiento de los indios de la Nueva España," Dec. 4, 1528, *ibid.,* 113–20.

17. Ayala de Espinosa, "Memorial" [Primero], Dec. 23, 1567, 195^r–199^v, and "Memorial" [Segundo], Feb. 3, 1568, 209^r in *Collection of original interrogatories taken for the most part on oath before Juan de Ovando, 1567–68.* British Museum, Additional MS 33,983. Escalating tribute levies are recorded for the town of Tepetlaoztoc for 1521–35, showing precise tempos of increase. "Memorial de los indios de Tepetlaoztoc," in *Códice Kingsborough.* Also see Motolinía, *Memoriales, cap.* ii; "Capítulos de la junta eclesiástica de 1539," *ZUM,* III, *art.* iv; Zorita, *Relación,* pp. 99–100; Zumárraga to Council of the Indies, Nov. 24, 1536, *ZUM,* IV, 122, and same to Emperor, Nov. 25, 1536, *ibid.,* 127.

18. Pedro de Gante to Confreres, June 27, 1529, *Cartas de Fr. Pedro de Gante,* p. 14; Motolinía, *Memoriales, caps.* xiii, xxxvii–xxxix, 1, lxii, and *Historia,* Tr. I, *caps.* ii–iv, Tr. III, *cap.* iii; Mendieta, *Lib.* III, *caps.* xxxii, xxxviii, liv, xli–xlii; "Carta al capítulo general de Tolosa," June 12, 1530, *ZUM,* II, 300–302.

19. On subservience to nobles see Gante to Confreres, *ibid.;* Fuenleal to Emperor, Nov. 3, 1532, *Ternaux,* X, 251; Audiencia to Crown, Aug. 14, 1531, *DII,* XLI, 42 ff.

Chapter XIII

1. This problem of cultural transference and religious syncretism is discussed in depth and detail in my forthcoming volume on life and religion in Mexico in the sixteenth century.

2. See Zumárraga's *Regla cristiani breve* (Mexico, 1951). On his life, see Icazbalceta, *Zumárraga*, I, and Fidel de Chauvet, *Zumárraga*.

3. Audiencia to the Crown, Aug. 14, 1531, *DII*, XLI, 88-89, 92-93; Camargo, *Historia*, pp. 242-43, 245-49; Mendieta, *Lib*. III, *caps*. xliii, xlvii-xlviii; Motolinía, *Historia*, Tr. III, *cap*. xiv, and *Memoriales*, *caps*. xxxiv, xlii.

4. "Proceso seguido por Fray Andrés de Olmos en contra del cacique de Matlatlán," *AGN: Inquisición, México, Tomo* 40, *expediente* 8.

5. Motolinía, *Historia*, Tr. I, *cap*. iv, and *Memoriales*, *caps*. xiv, xlii; Mendieta, *Lib*. III, *cap*. xxiii; Zorita, pp. 185-86.

6. "Carta al Capítulo General de Tolosa," *ZUM*, II, 300-302. For critical discussion of mendicant destruction of *antigüedades* and the bishop's role, see Icazbalceta, *Zumárraga*, II, 87 ff. In 1581 Durán stated the case in brief but precise terms: "And thus those who (in admirable zeal but without prudence) burned or destroyed all the codices they could find erred egregiously; for they left us so ignorant [of Indian religious ideas and practices] that the Indians idolatrize before our very eyes and we don't even know it . . ." (*cap*. lxxviii).

7. Audiencia to Crown, Aug. 14, 1531, *DII*, XLI, 92-93; Camargo, *Historia*, pp. 247-49.

8. Mendieta, *Lib*. III, *cap*. xviii, *Lib*. II, *caps*. viii, xii. See the *Noticias relativas al pueblo de Tepetlaoxtoc*, pp. 40 ff., for an excellent account of the struggle with the devil. Also see Motolinía, *Historia*, Tr. I, *cap*. xii, and Acosta, *Historia natural, Lib*. V.

9. The actual town cited here was Santa Ana de Chiautempan, three miles from Tlaxcala. Motolinía, *Historia*, Tr. II, *cap*. vii.

10. "Titulo de Inquisidor," Seville, June 27, 1535, *ZUM*, III, 71-73. For an outline of Zumárraga's tenure see R. E. Greenleaf, *Zumárraga and the Mexican Inquisition, 1536-1543* (Washington, 1961). King Ferdinand, after Isabella's death, in 1504, had sold *composiciones* (virtual passports) wholesale to all comers, heretics or no, and to relatives of relaxed Jews and Moors. There was no real prohibition to their entry into New Spain until midway in the reign of Charles V.

11. "Proceso contra Taclatetle y Tacuxtetl," July 26, 1536, *AGN: Inq. Mex.* 37-1. Confinement at discretion turned out to be three years for the former and one for the latter.

12. "Proceso contra Martín Ucelo," Nov. 21, 1536, *AGN: Inq. Mex.* 38-4. Also see Mendieta, *Lib*. II, *cap*. xix.

13. "Proceso contra Mixcoatl y Papalatl," July 10, 1537, *AGN: Inq. Mex.* 38-4.

14. Zumárraga, "Instrucciones," n.d. [but obviously 1537], *ZUM*, IV, 136, 240–45; Motolinía, *Historia*, *Tr*. I, *cap*. iii; Zumárraga to Suero de Aguila, Sept. 17, 1538, *ZUM*, IV, 167; Zumárraga to Council of the Indies, Nov. 24, 1536, *ibid*., 122; "Otro parecer del Fr. Zumárraga," *ZUM*, III, 148.

15. Zumárraga, "Instrucciones," *ibid*., 233–42. Also see his second order, pp. 130–41, and the "Proceso seguida por Fray Andrés de Olmos," *AGN: Inq. Mex.* 40–8.

16. Suero de Aguila was the *corregidor* of Avila, a high nobleman and intimate friend of the emperor. Zumárraga knew him when he was Guardian of the Franciscan convent at Avila. It may have been through Suero de Aguila that Charles V first learned of Zumárraga's abilities.

17. Zumárraga to Council of the Indies, Feb. 8, 1537, *ZUM*, IV, 143; Motolinía, *Historia*, *Tr*. I, *cap*. i; Carl Sauer, *Colima of New Spain in the Sixteenth Century*, p. 93.

18. "Proceso contra los indios de Atzcapotzalco," Nov. 19, 1538, *AGN: Inq. Mex.* 37–2.

19. Cervantes de Salazar, *Crónica*, *Lib*. IV, *cap*. xxxi.

20. His letters to the Crown in which he made the claim were to be widely advertised by Oviedo in his *Historia*, VIII, *Lib*. xiv, *cap*. x. For many years the great image of Coatlicue in Mexico's National Museum was confused with Huichilobos. Frances Calderón de la Barca made a visit in 1839: "We also saw the goddess of war lying in a corner of the court, beside the stone of sacrifices, which we had already been shown." (*Life in Mexico* [London, 1954], p. 127). Edward B. Tylor later made the same error (*Anahuac* [London, 1861], p. 223), and was followed in it by Prescott, who wrote that Huitzilopochtli, a huge basalt block covered with carvings, had been in the National Museum for years. Henry R. Wagner is the most recent victim of the error in his *Cortés*, p. 262.

21. See above, pp. 184 ff.

22. This succession of events is reconstructed from the voluminous "Proceso contra Miguel," June 20, 1539, *AGN: Inq. Mex.* 37–3.

23. *Cortés*, II, 260–63; Gómara, *caps*. clxxii-clxxiii, clxxix; Camargo, *Historia*, p. 243; Ixtlilxochitl, "Relación XIII;" Motolinía, *Memoriales*, *cap*. ii; Durán, *cap*. lxxviii; Rodrigo de Albornoz to Crown, Dec. 15, 1525, *CD*, I, 506; Cortés to Crown, Oct. 15, 1524, *CD*, I, 481–82; *BD*, *caps*. cxlvi, cxlix. Cortés' action here has always been debated, with Cuauhtemoc emerging the hero and Cortés the villain. The evidence turned up by Zumárraga's subsequent search for Huichilobos rather supports Cortés' contention that a dangerous and widespread plot did in fact exist.

24. Gómara, *cap.* clxxii. In his testimony Pedro gives the false impression that his father did not go to Hibueras, but later contradicts it. This probably resulted from confusion on the part of the Holy Office notary.

25. "Proceso contra Miguel."

26. *Ibid.*

27. There is some uncertainty over Don Carlos' actual status. He may have been in possession only of the *señorío* of Oztoticpac, a dependency of Texcoco. Other evidence suggests that he had recently assumed lordship of Texcoco itself from his deceased brother, Don Pedro. His precise status is not really too important, the greater significance being vested in the fact that he was a member of the ruling caste, a great lord of the new Pipiltin.

28. "Proceso criminal del Santo Oficio de la Inquisición y del fiscal en su nombre contra Don Carlos indio principal de Texcoco por idólatra," 1539, *AGN: Inq. Mex.* 2–10. This case has also been printed as the *Proceso inquisitorial del cacique de Tetzcoco* (Mexico, 1910), (Vol. I, Publicaciones del Archivo General de la Nación). Also see J. T. Medina, *La primitiva inquisición,* I, 143 ff.

29. In addition to the *Proceso,* also see Torquemada, *Lib.* VI, *cap.* xxiii. Cf. Pomar, *Relación de Texcoco,* pp. 14–15. Zumárraga subsequently tried to have a huge water goddess removed from the Temple of the Sun of Teotihuacán, but failed because it was too heavy.

30. "Proceso contra Cristóbal, Catalina, y Martín," 1539, *AGN: Inq. Mex.* 30–9. The accused could offer but slim defense, so overwhelming was the evidence against them. In addition to the usual lashes and penance before the church, Cristóbal got three years and Martín two at hard labor in the mines.

31. "Proceso contra Miguel." It is to be understood that most of the testimony given in court had already been heard by Zumárraga as soon as it came in. Therefore, he had opportunity to examine the evidence and prepare materials for cross-examination or rebuttal during the trial. In the present instance, Achicatl could be presented immediately as a witness, having already been located and summoned to give evidence. For narrative purposes, however, it is necessary to follow the official court record in its chronology of introduction.

32. "Proceso contra Don Carlos." The case records fail to specify the garrote, although this was a customary nicety for late penitents.

33. "Información en contra de Don Baltásar, indio cacique de Culoacán por ocultar ídolos," *AGN: Inq. Mex.* 42–18. This case, as some of those previously cited, is included among the *Procesos de indios idolatras y hechiceros* (Mexico, 1912), (Vol. III, Publicaciones del Archivo General de la Nación).

34. See, for example, "Proceso contra Tlilanci," Sept. 13, 1939, *AGN: Inq. Mex.* 37–4.

35. "Proceso contra Miguel."

36. The crown's official cedula of reproval is dated Nov. 22, 1540, in *ZUM,* IV, 172–73.

37. "Denuncia contra Don Juan," July 16, 1540, *AGN: Inq. Mex.* 40–7.

38. Motolinía, *Memoriales, cap.* xxxii.

39. Zumárraga to Emperor, April 17, 1540, *DI,* p. 107.

40. On the Mixton War see López-Portilla y Weber, *La rebelión de Nueva Galicia;* Bustamante, *Mendoza, cap.* vii (and appended documents), and Aiton, *Mendoza,* chap. vi.

BIBLIOGRAPHY

BIBLIOGRAPHY

Archival Sources

Archivo General de la Nación, México: Ramo de la Inquisición

Denuncia hecha contra Don Juan, indio Cacique del pueblo de Iguala por amancebado y idólatra. 1540. Tomo 40, expediente 7.

Información [y Proceso] contra el Cacique de Matlatlán, Don Juan por idólatra y amancebado. 1539, Tomo 40, expediente 8.

Proceso del Santo Oficio de la Inquisición contra Don Baltásar, Cacique de Culoacán por idólatra y ocultar ídolos. 1539. Tomo 42, expediente 18.

Proceso del Santo Oficio de la Inquisición contra Cristóbal y Catalina su muger y contra Martín, hermano de Cristóbal por idólatras y ocultar ídolos. 1539. Tomo 30, expediente 9.

Proceso criminal del Santo Oficio de la Inquisición y del fiscal en su nombre contra Don Carlos, indio principal de Texcoco por idólatra. 1539. Tomo 2, expediente 10.

Proceso del Santo Oficio de la Inquisición contra los indios de Atzcapozalco por idólatras. 1538. Tomo 37, expediente 2.

Proceso del Santo Oficio de la Inquisición contra Martín Ucelo (Ocelotl) por idólatra y hechicero. 1536. Tomo 38, expediente 4.

Proceso del Santo Oficio de la Inquisición contra Miguel, indio. 1539. Tomo 37, expediente 3.

Proceso del Santo Oficio de la Inquisición contra Mixcoatl y Papalotl, indios, por hechicerías. 1537. Tomo 38, expediente 7.

Proceso del Santo Oficio de la Inquisición contra Taclatetle y Tacuxtetle, indios idólatras. 1536. Tomo 37, expediente 1.

Proceso del Santo Oficio de la Inquisición contra Alonso Tlilanci, indio de Izúcar. 1539. Tomo 37, expediente 4 bis.

Proceso del Santo Oficio de la Inquisición contra Martín Xuchimit por amancebado. 1539. Tomo 36, expediente 6.

Archivo Hospital de Jesús

El Marqués del Valle sobre información de los términos donde se pobló la villa de Toluca, San Miguel Totocuitlapilco, San Bartolomé Tlatelulco, Matalcingo. Cítase al rey Axayacatl, padre de Moctezuma, y el reparto de tierras hecho al señor de Tlatelolco México, al señor de Texcoco, y al de Tacuba Euytzotzin. Legajo 70, expediente 4.

British Museum, London

Collection of original interrogatories taken for the most part on oath before Juan de Ovando, 1567–68. MS Additional 33 983.

Archivo del Gobierno de Guatemala

"Historia verdadera de la conquista de la Nueva España," de Bernal Díaz del Castillo. MS.

Printed Manuscripts and Sources

Document Collections

CHAUVET, FIDEL DE J. (ed.). Cartas de Fray Pedro de Gante. Mexico, 1940.

Colección de documentos inéditos relativos al descubrimiento, conquista y organización de las antiguas posesiones españolas. 42 vols. Madrid, 1864–1889.

CUEVAS, MARIANO (ed.). *Documentos inéditos del siglo XVI para la historia de México.* Mexico, 1914.

GARCÍA, GENARO (ed.). *Documentos inéditos o muy raros para la historia de México.* 36 vols. Mexico, 1867–1920.

GARCÍA ICAZBALCETA, JOAQUÍN (ed.). *Colección de documentos para la historia de México.* 2 vols. Mexico, 1858–1866.

———. *Nueva colección de documentos para la historia de México.* 5 vols. Mexico, 1886–1892.

———. *Don Fray Juan de Zumárraga, primer obispo y arzobispo de México.* 4 vols. Mexico, 1881.

KONETZKE, RICHARD (ed.). *Colección de documentos para la historia de la formación social de hispanoamérica, 1493–1810.* 3 vols. Madrid, 1953–1958.

PASO Y TRONCOSO, FRANCISCO DEL (ed.). *Epistolario de Nueva España, 1505–1818.* 16 vols. Mexico, 1939–1942.

Papeles de la Nueva España, second series. 9 vols. Mexico, 1944——

Procesos de residencia contra Pedro de Alvarado. Mexico, 1847.

PUGA, VASCO DE (ed.). *Cedulario.* 2 vols. Mexico, 1878.

TERNAUX-COMPANS, HENRI (ed.). *Voyages, relationes et mémoires originaux pour servir à l'histoire de la découverte de l'Amérique.* 20 vols. Paris, 1837–1841.

Codices, Annals, and Histories

Annales de Domingo Francisco de San Antón Muñon Chimalpahin Quauhtlehuanitzin. Edited and translated by RÉMI SIMÉON. Paris, 1889.

Anales de Tlatelolco. Mexico, 1948.

Codex Aubin. Paris, 1893.

Codex Azcatitlán. Paris, 1949.

Codex Borbonicus. New York, 1940.

Codex Magliabecchi. Rome, 1904.

[*Codex Magliabecchi,* facsimile] *The Book of the Life of the Ancient Mexicans, Part I.* Edited and translated by ZELIA NUTTALL. Berkeley, 1903.

Codex Mendoza. Mexico, 1951.

Codex Telleriano-Remensis. Mexico, 1945.

Florentine Codex: Fray Bernardino de Sahagún, General History of the Things of New Spain. Edited and translated by ARTHUR J. O. ANDERSON and CHARLES E. DIBBLE. 11 vols. Santa Fe, 1950–1959.

Códice Chimalpopoca (Anales de Cuauhtitlán y Leyenda de los Soles). Mexico, 1945.

Códice Kingsborough. Memorial de los indios de Tepetlaoztoc al monarca español. Madrid, 1912.

Códice Ramírez. Edited by MANUEL OROZCO Y BERRA. Mexico, 1944 (also bound with Tezozomoc's *Crónica mexicana*, JOSÉ M. VIGIL, ed., Mexico, 1878).

Códice de Yanhuitlán. Edited by WIGBERTO JIMÉNEZ MORENO and SALVADOR MATEOS HIGUERA. Mexico, 1940.

The Mapa de Cuauhtlantzinco, or Códice Campos. Edited by FREDERICK STARR. Chicago, 1898.

ACOSTA, JOSÉ DE. *Historia natural y moral de las indias.* Mexico, 1940.

BURGOA, FRANCISCO. *Geográfica descripción.* 2 vols. Mexico, 1934.

CAMARGO, DIEGO MUÑOZ. *Historia de Tlaxcala.* Mexico, 1892.

DÍAZ DEL CASTILLO, BERNAL. *Historia verdadera de la conquista de la Nueva España.* 4 vols.; Paris, 1834. 3 vols., ed. GENARO GARCÍA; Mexico, 1904. 3 vols., ed. JOAQUÍN RAMIREZ CABAÑAS; Mexico, 1939. 2 vols., ed. RAMÓN IGLESIA; Mexico, 1943.

DURÁN, DIEGO. *Historia de las indias de Nueva Espana y islas de Tierra Firme.* 2 vols.; Mexico, 1867–80. 3 vols.; Mexico, 1951.

GÓMARA, FRANCISCO LÓPEZ DE. *Historia de la conquista de México.* 2 vols. Mexico, 1943.

GRIJALVA, JUAN DE. *The Discovery of New Spain in 1518.* Edited and translated by HENRY RAUP WAGNER. Pasadena, 1942.

Historia Tolteca-Chichimeca: Anales de Quauhtinchán. Mexico, 1947.

ALVA IXTLILXOCHITL, FERNANDO DE. *Obras históricas.* 2 vols. Mexico, 1891–1892.

KINGSBOROUGH, EDWARD (ed.). *Antiquities of Mexico.* 9 vols. London, 1831–48.

MACNUTT, F. A. (ed. and trans.). *Letters of Cortés.* 2 vols. New York, 1908.

MENDIETA, GERÓNIMO DE. *Historia eclesiástica indiana.* 4 vols. Mexico, 1870.

MOTOLINÍA, TORIBIO DE. *Memoriales de fray Toribio de Motolinía,* ed. LUIS GARCÍA PIMENTEL. Mexico, 1903.

BIBLIOGRAPHY

Motolinía, Toribio de. *Historia de los indios de la Nueva España.* Mexico, 1941.

Oviedo y Valdes, Gonzalo Fernández de. *Historia general y natural de las indias.* 14 vols. Asunción, 1944.

Pomar, Juan Bautista. *Relación de Texcoco.* (NCD III).

Radin, Paul (ed. and trans.). *The Sources and Authenticity of the History of the Ancient Mexicans.* University of California Publications in American Archaeology and Ethnology, XVII, No. 1 (1920).

Rea, Alonso de la. *Crónica de . . . Michoacán.* Mexico, 1882.

Rea, Vargas (ed.). *Noticias relativas al pueblo de Tepetlaoxtoc.* Mexico, 1944.

Relación de las ceremonias y ritos y población y gobernación de los indios de la provincia de Mechoacán hecha al illmo señor Don Antonio de Mendoza, virrey y gobernador desta Nueva España por S. M. Madrid, 1956.

Relación hecha por el señor Andrés de Tapia sobre la conquista de México. (CD II).

Sahagún, Bernardino de. *Historia de las cosas de Neuva España,* ed. Angel María Garibay Kintana. 4 vols. Mexico, 1956.

Cervantes de Salazar, Francisco. *Crónica de Nueva España.* Madrid, 1914.

Alvarado Tezozomoc, Hernando. *Crónica mexicana,* ed. José M. Vigil. Mexico, 1878.

―――. *Crónica mexicayotl.* Mexico, 1949.

Torquemada, Juan de. *Monarquía indiana.* 3 vols. Mexico, 1945.

Tovar, Juan de. *Historia de los yndios mexicanos.* Mexico, 1860.

Zorita, Alonso de. *Relación.* (NCD III).

Secondary Works

Acosta Saignes, Miguel. *Los pochteca.* Mexico, 1945.

Aiton, Arthur Scott. *Antonio de Mendoza.* Durham, 1927.

Barlow, R. H. *The Extent of the Empire of the Culhua Mexica.* Berkeley, 1949.

Bernal, Ignacio. "Huitzilopochtli vivo," *Cuadernos Americanos,* XCVI (Nov.–Dec., 1957), 127–52.

Borah, Woodrow. *Silk Raising in Colonial Mexico.* Berkeley, 1943.

Borah, Woodrow, and Cook, Sherburne F. *The Aboriginal Population of Central Mexico on the Eve of the Spanish Conquest.* Berkeley, 1963.

BUSTAMANTE, C. PÉREZ. *Don Antonio de Mendoza*. Santiago, 1928.

CASO, ALFONSO. *La religión de los Aztecas*. Mexico, 1936.

————. *El pueblo del sol*. Mexico, 1953.

————. "La tenencia de la tierra entre los antiguos mexicanos," *Memoria del Colegio Nacional*, Mexico (December, 1959), pp. 29–54.

————. *Los barrios antiguos de Tenochtitlán y Tlatelolco*. Mexico, 1956.

CHAUVET, FIDEL DE J. *Fray Juan de Zumárraga*. Mexico, 1948.

CHEVALIER, FRANÇOIS. *La formación de los grandes latifundios en México*, trans. ANTONIO ALATORRE. Mexico, 1956.

CLAVIJERO, FRANCISCO JAVIER. *Historia antigua de México*, ed. MARIANO CUEVAS. 4 vols. Mexico, 1958–1959.

COOK, SHERBURNE F. "Human Sacrifice and Warfare as Factors in the Demography of Pre-Colonial Mexico," *Human Biology*, XVIII (May, 1946), 81–102.

————. "The Incidence and Significance of Disease Among the Aztecs and Related Tribes," *Hispanic American Historical Review*, XXVI (1946), 320–35.

DÍAZ INFANTE, FERNANDO. *Quetzalcóatl: ensayo psicoanalítico del mito nahua*. Mexico, 1963.

GARDINER, C. HARVEY. *Naval Power in the Conquest of Mexico*. Austin, 1956.

GARIBAY KINTANA, ANGEL MARÍA. *Historia de la literatura Nahuatl*. 2 vols. Mexico, 1953–54.

GIBSON, CHARLES. "The Transformation of the Indian Community in New Spain," *Journal of World History*, II (1955), 581–607.

GIBSON, CHARLES. "The Aztec Aristocracy in Colonial Mexico," *Comparative Studies in Society and History*, II (1960), 169–96.

GREENLEAF, R. E. *Zumárraga and the Mexican Inquisition, 1536–1543*. Washington, 1961.

JIMÉNEZ MORENO, WIGBERTO. *Historia antigua de México*. Mexico, 1953.

KIRCHHOFF, PAUL. "Quetzalcóatl, Huemac, y el fin de Tula," *Cuadernos Americanos*, LXXXIV (Nov.–Dec., 1955), 164–96.

————. "Land Tenure in Ancient Mexico," *Revista Mexicana de Estudios Antropológicas*, XIV (1954–55), 351–61.

KONETZKE, RICHARD. *Das spanische weltreich, grundlagen und entstehung*. Munich, 1943.

LEÓN PORTILLA, MIGUEL. *La filosofía nahuatl*. Mexico, 1956.

León Portilla, Miguel. *Ritos, sacerdotes y atavíos de los dioses.* Mexico, 1958.

López-Portilla y Weber, José. *La rebelión de Nueva Galicia.* Mexico, 1939.

López Sarrelangue, Delfina. "Los tributos de la parcialidad de Santiago Tlatelolco," *Memorias de la Academia Mexicana de la Historia,* XV (1956), 129–221.

Maine, Sir Henry. *Ancient Law.* London, 1954.

Medina, José Toribio. *La primitiva inquisición americana (1493–1569).* 2 vols. Santiago, 1914.

Menéndez Pidal, Ramón. "La idea imperial de Carlos V," *Revista Cubana,* X (Oct.–Dec., 1937), 5–31.

Phelan, John Leddy. *The Millennial Kingdom of the Franciscans in the New World.* Berkeley, 1956.

Pimentel, Francisco. *Obras completas.* 5 vols. Mexico, 1903–4.

Powell, Philip Wayne. *Soldiers, Indians, and Silver.* Berkeley, 1952.

Robertson, Donald. *Mexican Manuscript Painting of the Early Colonial Period.* New Haven, 1959.

Rodríguez Prampolini, Ida. "El arte indígena y los cronistas de Nueva España," *Anales del Instituto de Investigaciones Estéticas,* V (1949), 5–16.

Sauer, Carl. *Colima of New Spain in the Sixteenth Century.* Berkeley, 1948.

Séjourné, Laurette. *Burning Water: Thought and Religion in Ancient Mexico.* New York, 1960.

Seler, Eduard. *Gesammelte Abhandlungen Zur Amerikanischen Sprach-Und Alterthumskunde.* 5 vols. Berlin, 1902–23. [Unpublished English translation made under the supervision of Charles P. Bowditch, Cambridge, 1939.]

Soustelle, Jacques. *The Daily Life of the Aztecs,* trans. Patrick O'Brian. New York, 1962.

Toussaint, Manuel; Gómez de Orozco, Federico; and Fernández, Justino. *Planos de la ciudad de México.* Mexico, 1938.

Vaillant, G. C. *The Aztecs of Mexico.* Suffolk, 1955.

Wagner, Henry Raup. *The Rise of Fernando Cortés.* Los Angeles, 1944.

Wolf, Eric R. *Sons of the Shaking Earth.* Chicago, 1962.

INDEX

Index

73   12 11 10 9 8 7 6 5 4 3

COLOPHON BOOKS ON AMERICAN HISTORY

*In Preparation